Banking on Change

Banking on Change

THE DEVELOPMENT AND FUTURE
OF FINANCIAL SERVICES

A collection of essays commissioned by
The London Institute of Banking & Finance

Edited by
Ouida Taaffe

Library of Congress Cataloging-in-Publication Data is Available

ISBN 978-1-119-60998-8 (hardback)
ISBN 978-1-119-60999-5 (ePDF)
ISBN 978-1-119-61002-1 (epub)

Cover Design: Wiley
Cover Images: Top Image: Courtesy of HSBC Archives
Bottom Image: © ipopba/Getty Images

Set in 11/13pt NewBaskervilleStd by SPi Global, Chennai, India

Printed in Great Britain by TJ International Ltd, Padstow, Cornwall, UK

10 9 8 7 6 5 4 3 2 1

Contents

Banking – People and Skills

Banking, Technology and the Future

The Role of the Institute as a Life-Long Partner for Education

About the Editor

Dr Ouida Taaffe is the Editor of *Financial World*, the magazine of The London Institute of Banking & Finance. She has been a trade journalist for 20 years, covering first telecoms and then banking. She has a PhD in German literature.

About the Contributors

Dr Kern Alexander is Professor of Banking Regulation at the University of Zurich and is a Senior Research Fellow at the Centre for Risk Studies, University of Cambridge. He is the author of many articles and books, including *Principles of Banking Regulation* (Cambridge University Press, 2019) and *Brexit and Financial Services* (with Moloney Bloomsbury/Hart, 2018). He was a member of the European Parliament's Expert Panel on Financial Services (2009–2014) and was the Specialist Adviser to the British Parliament's Joint Select Committee on the Financial Services Act 2012. He was an adviser to the Serious Fraud Office on the Libor cases.

William Allen is a visitor at the National Institute for Economic and Social Research. He worked at the Bank of England from 1972 to 2004 and was Deputy Director for Monetary Analysis from 1994 to 1998, Deputy Director for Financial Market Operations from 1999 to 2002 and Deputy Director for Financial Stability and Director for Europe from 2002 to 2003. He was seconded to the Bank for International Settlements from 1978 to 1980 and was a member of the EU Monetary Committee from 1994 to 1998. Since 2004, he has worked in the private sector and for the International Monetary Fund. He was a specialist adviser to the House of Commons Treasury Committee from 2010 to 2017 and to the Parliamentary Commission on Banking Standards in 2012. He has written extensively on monetary subjects, including three books – *International Liquidity and the Financial Crisis* (Cambridge University Press, 2013), *Monetary Policy and Financial Repression in Britain 1951–59* (Palgrave Macmillan, 2014) and *The Bank of England and the Government Debt: Operations in the Gilt-Edged Market, 1928–1972* (Cambridge University Press, 2019) – and numerous published articles.

David G. W. Birch is a director of the secure electronic transactions consultancy Consult Hyperion, and a visiting lecturer at the University of Surrey. He is an internationally recognised thought leader in digital identity and digital money, one of *Wired* magazine's top 15 global sources of business information and a Centre for the Study of Financial Innovation (CSFI) research fellow.

Anne Boden MBE is founder and chief executive of Starling Bank. Previously she worked in senior leadership at some of the world's best-known financial companies, among them Allied Irish Bank, where she was chief operating officer, Royal Bank of Scotland, where she served as head of EMEA, Global Transaction Banking and ABN Amro, where she was Executive Vice President Europe, Transaction Banking. She is a fellow of the Royal Chartered Institute of IT and a member of the FinTech Strategy Group, created by Innovate Finance and City of London Corporation. In 2018 she was awarded an MBE for services to financial technology.

She is also a published author and fellow of the Royal Society of Arts.

Elizabeth Corley MBE was CEO of Allianz Global Investors, initially for Europe then globally, from 2005 to 2016, and continues to act as a senior advisor to the firm. She was previously at Merrill Lynch Investment Managers and Coopers & Lybrand, and she serves on three company boards as a non-executive director: Pearson plc, BAE Systems plc and Morgan Stanley Inc. Elizabeth is a member of the CFA Future of Finance Council and of the AQR Institute of Asset Management at the London Business School, and she is chair of an industry taskforce for the UK government on social impact investing. Additionally, she is a member of the 300 Club and the Committee of 200, as well as being a trustee of the British Museum.

Andy Davis is a freelance writer on investment, finance and business. He worked as a journalist at the *Financial Times* from 1995 to 2010 and was editor of *FT Weekend* from 2007 until he left the paper 3 years later. He writes on a wide range of financial services, including pensions, banking and other retail investment products, small business finance and financial technology. He is investment columnist for *Prospect*, the UK monthly current affairs magazine, and was the 2011 winner of the Wincott Award for Personal Financial Journalist of the Year.

Shelley Doorey-Williams is a member of the board of governors of The London Institute of Banking & Finance. She is Head of Wealth Planning, Europe, Middle East and Africa, at UBS. She is also Deputy Head of Investment Platforms & Solutions (IPS), UK & Jersey. Shelley's career in general management and governance has spanned various industries: oil and gas, broadcast media, fast-moving consumer goods and telecoms.

Dr Paul Fisher is a fellow at the Cambridge Institute for Sustainability Leadership. He was previously a senior official and macroeconomist at the Bank of England for 26 years, including 5 years as a member of the Monetary Policy Committee and Executive Director for Markets, and 2 years as deputy head of the Prudential Regulation Authority. He is a member of the European Commission's High Level Experts Group on Sustainable Finance and was a member of the UK Green Finance Task Force. He holds a portfolio of other roles in finance and academia.

Alex Fraser joined The London Institute of Banking & Finance (formerly ifs University College) as chief executive in March 2015 from Cass Business School, City University London, where he was chief operating officer for 6 years. His career has encompassed management roles in the private, public and voluntary sectors. He spent 10 years working for a number of investment banks in a variety of operational roles; his last such post was as head of operations at Schroders in the late 1990s. Alex was appointed logistics director at HM Customs and Excise in 2000 and subsequently worked for a number of organisations in the not-for-profit sector prior to joining Cass in 2009.

Dr Anthony Gandy is a visiting professor at The London Institute of Banking & Finance and at Ulster University. He has worked in financial IT journalism, investment banking and bank regulation, as well as in academia. He holds a PhD from the London School of Economics and has been a fellow in the history of data processing at the University of Minnesota.

Dr Peter Hahn is Dean and Henry Grunfeld Professor of Banking at The London Institute of Banking & Finance. He had senior roles in consumer to investment banking in London and New York for 24 years, including as a managing director at Citigroup. He was a senior adviser on bank supervision to the Bank of England and the Financial Services Authority (2009–2014) and an advisor to Seven Investment Management (2014–2018). He has been a PhD/academic since 2004 and lectures on strategy and management in financial institutions.

Renier Lemmens is Visiting Professor of FinTech and Innovation at The London Institute of Banking & Finance. He has held leadership roles in a variety of financial institutions in Europe and the USA, including at GE Capital, Barclays and PayPal. He has also held a number of non-executive and advisory positions in fintech start-ups. He is currently chairman of the board at Divido and TransferGo and is a non-executive director at Arion banki.

Paul Lynam is CEO at Secure Trust Bank plc. Secure Trust is one of the UK's so-called 'challenger banks' and currently serves retail banking, SME and asset finance markets. Prior to joining Secure Trust Bank, Paul spent the majority of his 22-year career with RBS and NatWest in front-line customer-facing roles in retail, commercial and corporate banking and the asset finance business, including as managing director (banking), chief executive (UK business banking) and managing director (Lombard North Central plc). Paul holds both banking (ACIB, Fifs) and corporate treasury (AMCT) qualifications and he is a board member of UK Finance.

Alexander R. Malaket (CITP, CTFP, GTP-E) is president of Canadian consultancy OPUS Advisory Services International Inc. He is the author of Financing Trade and International Supply Chains (Gower/Ashgate Publishing, 2014) and has authored numerous white papers, policy briefs and articles. He serves on several industry boards and advisory bodies, including as deputy head of the executive committee (ICC Banking Commission), chair of the international and technical advisory committee (Global Trade Professionals Alliance), member of the World Economic Forum E-15 Initiative and member of the advisory board of Tin Hill Capital, among others.

Richard Northedge was deputy City editor of the *Daily Telegraph* and is a former banking journalist of the year.

Martin Stewart is a visiting professor at The London Institute of Banking & Finance. From 2010 to 2013 he headed the supervision of UK banks, building societies and credit unions at the Financial Services Authority and from 2013 to 2018 he was a director at the Bank of England's Prudential Regulation Authority.

Mike Thompson was director for early careers at Barclays from 2009 to 2019 and developed an apprenticeship programme that supported over 3,000 long-term unemployed people into work across the business. Working with multiple third-sector organisations, Mike has developed pathways into work for job seekers from all backgrounds. His work earned him a place on the government's Apprenticeship Delivery Board and his programmes have won 24 national awards, including from CIPD, BITC and *Personnel Today*. For 3 years he chaired the financial services trailblazer group developing new apprenticeship standards for the financial services sector. Since 2017, Mike has been employer route panel chair within the Institute for Apprenticeships (IFA), which approves all new apprenticeship standards and 'T Levels' for legal, accountancy and financial services. He has his own business, SustainHR Ltd, supporting other companies to develop sustainable HR strategies.

Dr Richard Tomlinson is an international business writer and historian who has written extensively about finance. He is a former correspondent for *Fortune* magazine in Asia and Europe and the author of *Late Shift: The Death of Retirement* (Politicos Publishing, 2006).

Dr Ruth Wandhöfer is an authority on transaction banking regulation and on innovation in financial technology. In over 11 years at Citi, she drove regulatory and industry dialogue and developed product and market strategy. Her awards include Women in Banking and Finance Award for Achievement 2015 and she was named one of the Top 10 Global Fintech Influencers of 2018 (Fintech Power 50). She has published two books: *EU Payments Integration – The Tale of SEPA, PSD and Other Milestones Along the Road* (Palgrave Macmillan, 2010) and *Transaction Banking and the Impact of Regulatory Change: Basel III and Other Challenges for the Global Economy* (Palgrave Macmillan, 2014). She is a visiting professor at The London Institute of Banking & Finance and also lectures at Queen Mary London School of Law.

Foreword

Since the foundation of The London Institute of Banking & Finance in 1879 as The Institute of Bankers, over one and a half million people have studied with us. Many of them went on to become central figures in their local communities: the bank managers and front-office staff who provided expert and impartial advice, support and often patient assistance to the customers who came to their door. So, while we have helped at least 1.5m people to develop a career in the finance sector, or develop their financial knowledge, we have also been at the forefront of helping businesses and communities to thrive.

That is an astonishing achievement for an organisation that was set up by a group of bank clerks who, faced with limited career prospects, and little recognition of their skills and specialist knowledge, came together to professionalise both their own standing and that of their industry.

They set the bar high. Banking exams from the late 1800s quickly became valued by both banks and their employees. By the 1960s, qualifications from The Institute of Bankers were a prerequisite for anybody who wanted to progress in the sector. The main focus was on professional standards and – with the support of their employers – thousands of workers took our exams every year.

But then things changed. In the 1970s, 1980s and 1990s, the sector moved away from a focus on local branch banking and lending. It entered new markets, such as mortgages, developed new products and sought new customer relationships. Traditional banking exams became less popular and, responding to the falling demand for formal banking qualifications, we evolved too. We started to develop a broad range of new qualifications. These included courses for specialists – from mortgage and financial advisers to trade finance bankers – as well as broader degrees in banking and finance. You can read a summary of our history in the Introduction.

We continue to evolve, along with the industry.

The finance sector today looks and feels very different from even 20 years ago. People working in retail banking now have to be digitally literate and customer focused. They have to be able to provide expert, professional help across any of the many channels their customers might use. They no longer spend their time behind a counter in a bank, counting out cash. They are more likely to help customers via webchat and Skype than face to face, and cash is now a small element in a fast-changing payments landscape.

This book, published to mark our 140th anniversary, looks at the role of retail and commercial banking in our society, at how the sector is changing and at some of the future challenges we face. It brings together contributions from some of the most influential and experienced commentators in the sector today, ranging from experts in retail banking, payments, sustainable finance and fintech, to commentators on diversity and the skills that bankers will need in the future.

I would like to thank all of the authors for their contributions and insights. I would also like to thank Ouida Taaffe, the editor of our in-house magazine, *Financial World*, for helping us to pull these contributions together.

I hope that you find the book an interesting and enjoyable read.

— Steven Haberman
Chair of The London Institute of Banking & Finance

About the Book

This book is being published to mark the 140th anniversary of The London Institute of Banking & Finance. Our aim was to produce a publication that is of lasting value to both students and professionals – in line with the founding principles of 'The Institute of Bankers in England' in 1879.

Financial services are going through a period of profound change, so we approached experts from across the industry to tackle some of the most exciting and contentious topics.

What, for example, will the future of retail banking look like as fintech competition heats up? Will credit provision change? How should the financial services professionals of the future be selected and trained?

We also have some more personal pieces, including a look back at the changes seen during a long career in banking, and a call for more appreciation of the value that financial services bring to society.

In the Introduction, *Navigating the Centuries*, Ouida Taaffe examines how the work of The London Institute of Banking & Finance has not only informed the development of financial services over the past 140 years, but also helped to shape the wider culture and economy.

In Chapter 1, *Banking, Finance and Society: What Keeps the Motor Running?*, Professor Peter Hahn examines why society underestimates the important social roles played by retail banks and the value they provide in being trusted guarantors of privacy and data integrity.

In Chapter 2, *Standing the Test of Time*, Paul Lynam reflects on what he has learned and experienced during his 30-year career in retail banking, and on the two constants of continual industry change and the continued need for banks – in whatever form they come.

In Chapter 3, *What Happens When Nobody is Watching: Regulation, Bank Risk Culture and Achieving Environmental Sustainability*, Kern Alexander and Paul Fisher consider the importance of banks, and in particular of bank risk culture, in developing and supporting a more sustainable economy.

In Chapter 4, *It Takes an Ecosystem: The Future of Trade Financing*, Alexander Malaket examines how trade financing will be central to tackling some of the major economic and political challenges that the world faces, including sustainability, inclusion and security.

In Chapter 5, *A New Playbook for Banks*, William Allen looks at the impact that post-crisis regulation has had on banks' capital and liquidity ratios and how the current – and prospective – macro-economic environment threatens the continued sustainability of banking as we know it.

In Chapter 6, *Sustainable Investment: The Golden Moment*, Elizabeth Corley examines how increasing consumer interest in sustainable investment has created an opportunity both for investment managers and for society as a whole – one that the industry must now grasp.

In Chapter 7, *Living 'Off Income'*, Richard Tomlinson analyses how the demographic shift in the UK has left many people ill-prepared for retirement, often in denial about adequate pension provision and in need of a wide-ranging public debate on the issues.

In Chapter 8, *Power to the Customer: Disrupting Banking*, Anne Boden explains the thinking behind the launch of her fintech retail bank, why retail financial services will be disrupted and the rise of marketplace banking.

In Chapter 9, *RIP Libor*, Richard Northedge examines how Libor developed, why it became unfit for purpose and what it tells us about the evolution of financial markets.

In Chapter 10, *Boosting UK Bank Competition: Still Many Cliffs to Climb*, Martin Stewart argues that UK financial regulation should be reformed to support the growth of new banks to help boost choice and lower costs in a market that is still dominated by incumbents.

In Chapter 11, *Changing the Face of Banking and Finance*, Shelley Doorey-Williams examines why gender diversity, particularly in the senior ranks of financial services firms, is still limited, why that needs to change and what might be done.

In Chapter 12, *Getting the Right Stuff*, Mike Thompson argues that the way in which banks approach career development needs to undergo a sea change if they are to ensure that the sector continues to thrive by hiring and training diverse talent in partnership with educational providers.

In Chapter 13, *Financial Education: How to Make it Count*, Andy Davis examines what is being done to improve financial education, what needs to be done to ensure that everyone receives a meaningful financial education and what the financial services industry can do to help.

In Chapter 14, *Banking on Identity*, David Birch examines the strategic value that banks could find in becoming the guarantors of digital identities.

In Chapter 15, *Going Over the Top*, Renier Lemmens examines the challenges that incumbent banks face in avoiding becoming utilities that provide the commoditised, underlying 'plumbing' of the banking industry while higher-margin 'over the top' financial services that consumers see and love are offered by other players.

In Chapter 16, *Banking Technology: Can the Centre Hold?*, Anthony Gandy analyses how technological developments over the past 60 years have informed the business model of retail banks and asks whether the disaggregated computing made possible by the cloud and real-time processing could trigger a paradigm shift in retail banking.

In Chapter 17, *The Future of Payments*, Ruth Wandhöfer explains why payments are at the centre of financial innovation and transformation, and what this will mean for banks.

In Chapter 18, *Life Lessons*, Alex Fraser looks at what changes in banking and the wider finance sector mean for the finance sector professionals of the future and at the role the Institute is playing.

Victorian banking: The banking hall at the Henrietta Street branch of the London and County Bank, London, 1892

Victorian London: Cheapside, City of London, circa 1900

Banking of yesteryear: Two City businessmen, one wearing a bowler hat and the other wearing a top hat, on Lombard Street in London's financial district, late 1960s

Introduction

Navigating the Centuries

Ouida Taaffe

The work of The London Institute of Banking & Finance has not only informed the development of financial services over the past 140 years but also helped to shape the wider culture and economy, as Ouida Taaffe examines.

W hen students sit down in an examination hall, the test in front of them might not seem like a particularly great invention. Exams, however, and the bodies that set them, have an importance that goes far beyond the personal. Arguably, well-conceived professional training has helped define the course of British economic and political development – and will continue to do so.

Sound far-fetched? What today is often regarded as the pinnacle of educational attainment – a university education – was in the early modern period rare and far from rigorous. For example, though the first Regius professorship in the British Isles was in medicine, at the University of Aberdeen in 1497, and Aberdeen was also the first university to set up a teaching post in medicine, it was 1787 before the first examination paper was set – and then the idea was to prevent the sale of degrees for 'ready money'.[1] Oxford and

---

[1]Rix KJ (1990) 'A short history of medical degrees in the University of Aberdeen', *Scottish Medical Journal*, 35(4), 120–121.

Cambridge fared no better. It was only in 1833 that 'the University of Oxford could say with truth that [it] was able to apply an efficient test to those who desired a degree in medicine'.[2] Practical education in medicine, as in other fields, largely relied on apprenticeships,[3] until the distinction between gentlemen (who could rely on a 'moral' education and their society contacts to build a lucrative career), scientists (who might be anyone with an enquiring mind and enough leisure to inform it), and those who actually tended to the sick began to disappear in the nineteenth century.

As that suggests, in the Middle Ages and early Modern period (1500–1800), nearly all positions of influence – that is those in the church, government and the army – went to members of the aristocracy, though some men from humbler backgrounds who had both an unusual ability and a powerful patron did prosper. There was, however, one sector that formed an interesting exception to that rule: the Royal Navy.

The Royal Navy introduced examinations in 1677, one of many reforms made by Samuel Pepys while he was Secretary to the Admiralty.[4] The lieutenant exams required would-be officers to have practical experience at sea as well as to demonstrate theoretical knowledge of managing a ship. If the mast came off in a storm, the lieutenant was expected to know what to do. The exams meant that, in principle at least, professional skill counted more than social connections. Both in Britain and overseas, people soon began to associate the advancement of British naval officers with merit.[5] As a character in Jane Austen's *Persuasion* points out in the early nineteenth century, the naval profession was 'offensive' to some people: 'As being the means of bringing persons of obscure birth

---

[2]Chaplin A (1919) 'The history of medical education in the universities of Oxford and Cambridge 1500–1850', *Proceedings of the Royal Society of Medicine*, 12(suppl), 83–107, 92.

[3]Reinarz J (2008) 'The transformation of medical education in eighteenth-century England: international developments and the West Midlands', *History of Education*, 37(4), 549–566, 565.

[4]Dickinson HW (2007) *Educating the Royal Navy: 18th and 19th Century Education for Officers*, Routledge, 2.

[5]Jenks T (2006) *Naval Engagements: Patriotism, Cultural Politics, and the Royal Navy 1793–1815*, Oxford University Press, 4.

into undue distinction, and raising men to honours which their fathers and grandfathers never dreamt of.'[6]

What has all of that got to do with finance and with the wider economy? The navy's introduction of qualifying exams made the service more cost-effective, responsive and efficient,[7] which was vital for both reasons of trade and of defence – but it also changed the culture. There was still sniping about social upstarts, as Jane Austen makes clear, but by the end of the Napoleonic wars the importance of skills-based naval officer selection was largely accepted. Everyone understood that Britain had defeated France – which had only introduced formal naval examinations at the end of the eighteenth century – largely thanks to its professional navy.[8] Everyone knew that the wealth that came with empire depended on dominance at sea.2

An Examination of Commercial Undertakings

Social acceptance of examinations as a way to gain professional standing took wider and deeper root as the Industrial Revolution progressed. In the first half of the nineteenth century, banking was not a highly formalised sector. Owners of banks (i.e. all shareholders) had unlimited liability for losses, which tended to constrain scale. Businesses themselves were also often small, so their capital requirements were limited. Further, though the Industrial Revolution had already brought growth, and made the economy much more complex, there was a 'basic view of the world as largely static'.[9]

---

[6]Austen J (1818) *Persuasion*, chapter 3.

[7]Rodger NAM (2004) *The Command of the Ocean: A Naval History of Britain, 1649–1815*, Penguin.

[8]French historians argue that the way in which the Royal Navy was able to blockade the French fleet during the revolution and the Empire period also made the British better able to train their fleet at sea, further cementing their advantages over the French. See Geistdoerfer P (2005) 'La formation des officiers de marine: de Richelieu au XXIe siècle, des gardes aux "bordaches"', *Techniques & Culture: Revue semestrielle d'anthropologie des techniques* (45), 3–4.

[9]Odlyzko A (2011) 'The collapse of the Railway Mania, the development of capital markets, and Robert Lucas Nash, a forgotten pioneer of accounting and financial analysis', *SSRN*, 47. Available at: //papers.ssrn.com/sol3/papers.cfm?abstract_id=1625738 [accessed 1 March 2019].

Investors in railways, for example, expected a new line to go through a few years of 'development of traffic' and then have stable revenues and dividends and to 'close its capital account' (i.e. the business would fund itself, as well as its dividends, from a reliable revenue stream). The heavy losses that followed the Railway Mania of the 1840s shook public confidence in that cosy view of business and investment. Book-keeping began to evolve into audit and accounting, as railway companies published the great novelty of 'financial statements' – statements that showed a much more worrying world than one where 10% dividends would be paid for life.[10] There began to be widespread calls for 'quality and competence … [in] the men employed by commercial undertakings'.[11] Societies were set up to represent civil engineers, lawyers and architects, actuaries and chemists before 1850.[12] The Society of Accountants in England was set up in 1872. The societies lobbied legislators and argued for the value of their professional qualifications – not (just) as a barrier to entry, but as a source of social good.

Before 1855 many banks, particularly those in the country, were run by part-timers. Following the Limited Liability Act of 1855 and the Joint Stock Companies Act of 1856, which made it easier to both set up companies and limit shareholder losses, joint stock banks started to build out their branch networks and full-time, professional bank managers were needed.[13] They had to deal with a 'formidable range of duties' as well as 'learning or developing techniques for assessing the creditworthiness of customers (including the largest industrial customers as well as private clients)'.[14] The railway crash and wider economic shifts meant that, by the time The Institute of Bankers was founded in 1879, the time was ripe. It came when 'directors and managers of the banks were seeking reform and

---

[10]Odlyzko A (2011) 'The collapse of the Railway Mania, the development of capital markets, and Robert Lucas Nash, a forgotten pioneer of accounting and financial analysis', *SSRN*, 47 Available at: www.ssrn.com/abstract=1625738 [accessed 1 March 2019].

[11]Green E (1979).

[12]Green E (1979).

[13]Green E (1979).

[14]Green, 28 (1979).

reorganisation of the banking system' and a way to restore both the confidence of staff and of the public.[15] The expansion and increasing sophistication of financial services meant that staff training was no longer something that could be done on an ad hoc basis. For ordinary members, much of the appeal came from 'the promise of a qualifying examination in banking' that would help them further their careers.[16] Still, it was not clear at first that the banks would formally recognise the examinations and consider them a factor in career progression. It was in the mid-1880s that the banks started to offer those who were successful in the Institute's exams a bonus or a raise.[17]

Once the banks valued the Institute's exams, the growth of the Institute was swift. In 1906, it opened its first overseas examination centres in Bombay, Cape Town and Yokohama. After the First World War, women were admitted. Then, in the 1930s, the Institute began to host visits from international guest lecturers and set up courses on British banking for international students. The Second World War put a temporary stop to collaboration with institutes in Europe, but not to exams. With the help of the Red Cross, and bankers who volunteered to teach their fellow servicemen, the Institute's exams were held around the world, in prisoner of war camps and on board battleships. After the war, in 1947, the first international summer school – at Christ Church College Oxford – was held.

By the 1960s, it was hard to find space to hold exams for all the students who wanted to take them. Over 46,000 candidates sat for the diplomas in 1970 and there were over 60,000 annually after 1975.[18] These numbers, however, only tell part of the story. Banks noticed a shift in staff attitudes in the late 1960s and early 1970s. People no longer necessarily looked for a job for life and the number of graduates was increasing. Increased staff turnover meant, on the one hand, that it made less sense for banks to invest in training staff and, on the other hand, that if banks were going to attract all of the staff

---

[15]Green, 51 (1979).

[16]Green, 54 (1979).

[17]Green, 65 (1979).

[18]Green, 165 (1979).

they wanted, they would have to take a more flexible approach.[19] At the same time, banking itself was becoming more complex and more internationalised. That led the Institute to set up the Wilde Committee in 1972 to ask: 'If we were starting from scratch today, what sort of qualification would we recommend?'[20] The Wilde Committee published two reports, in 1973 and 1974. They essentially asked for five things: more levels of qualification; greater variety of course content; a 'market value' for the qualifications outside banking; more integration with public qualifications; and suitable study leave allowance.[21] As it turned out, increasing economic problems in the mid to late 1970s eased many of the recruitment difficulties that banks faced – at least in the short term.

Training and employment in banking, just as in other walks of life, is a function of the wider culture – and rapid change is generally the result of a crisis. Women entered the formal workforce in Britain in large numbers only after the Second World War, for example. Still, even in the 1960s, a recruitment advertisement for Westminster Bank, running under the tag line 'they'll both be happy at Westminster', was promising the boys 'senior management with a generous pension' while the girls could look forward to short-hand typing and 'after five years' service, a generous gratuity on marriage'.[22] That is, they were expected to be housewives once they had found themselves a husband (possibly at the bank).

In line with that, until the early 1980s, local bank managers were generalists. 'To the public and the customers, the manager is the bank', noted James Dandy in *The Branch Banker* in 1960. The manager was 'an amalgam of accountant, solicitor, tax expert, financial adviser, adviser on current economic problems, and a sort of financial father confessor. Sometimes he must be a psychologist and at times a psychiatrist'.[23] Dandy references the Radcliffe Report of 1959 (*Report of the Committee on the Working of the Monetary System*), the first 'inquiry into the working of the monetary and credit systems' the country had

---

[19]Green, 181.

[20]Green, 183.

[21]Green, 183.

[22]Lascelles D (2005) *Other People's Money*, Institute of Financial Services, 98.

[23]Dandy J (1972) *The Branch Banker: Studies in Bank Lending*, The Institute of Bankers, 1.

undertaken since 1931.[24] He notes that, following the report's analysis of liquidity, 'we may see an increasing tendency to stretch the terms of lending, but banks are not mortgage and investment institutions. They cannot lock up more than a small proportion of their funds in this way, however desirable it might be from the customer's point of view'.[25]

The shift in banking that followed was gradual at first and it came, in part, because of US regulation. In 1959, the deposit banks (that is the London clearing banks, together with the Scottish and Northern Irish banks) held 85% of the total sterling deposits of the UK banking sector. By 1968, that share was 75% and the number of banks in London had grown by 50%, mainly because of the new eurodollar market.[26] However, there had also been a major growth in so-called fringe banks – because tight credit controls and an effective bank cartel meant that deposit banks could not meet the demand for credit. Access to banking, or at least to banking services, was becoming democratised. A vastly broader range of customers started to get bank accounts and, over time, banks offered a myriad of new products, many of them requiring specialised advice. Barclaycard introduced the first credit card in 1966. The first ATM was opened, again by Barclays, in 1967. In the early 1980s, banks started to provide mortgages. Before that, most mortgage funding had come from building societies, which demanded that borrowers had a history of saving with them, as well as a sizeable deposit.[27] That, of course, is now a vanished world. However, the 'demand that [bankers] spend [their] early years in study, and the rest of [their] banking lives in adding to [their] professional resources'[28]

---

[24]Kaldorr N (1960) 'The Radcliffe Report', *Review of Economics and Statistics*, 42(1), 14–19.

[25]Dandy J (1972), 12.

[26]Bank of England (1969) 'The operation of monetary policy since the Radcliffe Report'. Available at: https://www.bankofengland.co.uk/-/media/boe/files/quarterly-bulletin/1969/the-operation-of-monetary-policy-since-the-radcliffe-report.pdf [accessed 4 March 2019].

[27]Boleat M (1994) 'The 1985–1993 housing market in the United Kingdom: an overview', *Housing Policy Debate*, 5(3), 253–274. Available at: https://www.boleat.com/materials/the_1985_93_housing_market_in_the_uk_1994.pdf [accessed 20 March 2019].

[28]Dandy J (1972), 12–13.

still holds. What has changed is what bankers need to learn, how they learn it, and the ways in which they can learn.

Those changes have all been reflected in the development of the Institute. It gained a Royal Charter in 1987 and in 1993 it merged with the Chartered Building Societies Institute. In 1996, the BSc (Hons) in financial services was launched as a dual award with the University of Manchester Institute of Science and Technology (UMIST). The Institute was renamed in 1997, as the Institute of Financial Services – to reflect how the banking sector had changed. The Institute's own degree-awarding powers came in 2010 and, as of 2013, it became a university college in its own right.

The Future – Online and Off

To serve large and diverse populations cost-efficiently, financial services need scale. The digitisation of the industry helps underpin that with capabilities in data capture, data analysis and risk management that were still a pipe dream just 10 years ago. The regulator is encouraging fintech challengers to enter the market and it requires banks to let customers share their data with other financial services providers.

What that means for bank staff is that, in the near future, routine work will be automated. In some respects, they are likely to go back to what Dandy knew in the branch banks of the 1950s and 1960s, with a focus on individual customer service that puts a premium on financial and interpersonal skills, on being: the 'financial father [and mother] confessor. Sometimes ... a psychologist and at times a psychiatrist'. The trend can already be seen. Lloyds, for example, announced in early 2019 that it would hire around 700 financial advisers by year-end to offer personalised advice to the wealthy as part of a joint venture with Schroders. Banks are closing branches, but they are also setting up hubs where customers can seek in-depth support. The bankers who provide that will need to understand what digital banking can do for consumers, which is why the Institute launched the Centre for Digital Banking and Finance in 2018.

As large tech companies enter financial services, the differentiating services that banks offer will include deep sector knowledge, professionalism, privacy and trust – all of which depend on having expert staff. Society already has a need of these, of course. Developments such as the demise of defined benefit pension schemes mean many more people will be confronted with challenging and, potentially costly, financial decisions. Learning how to manage money starts well before retirement though, which is why the Institute established qualifications for secondary school children in 2003, initially at GCSE and then A Level. Financial education became part of the national curriculum in 2014, almost a decade later, but delivery of financial education is still patchy and often part of a broader subject such as maths or economics. No-one should leave school without the capability to make sound, essential financial decisions. The Institute's qualifications remain the only specialist financial education qualifications in schools and reach around 50,000 children each year.

The Institute is also continuing to help shape the culture and standards of financial services outside the UK with, for example, internationally sought-after trade finance qualifications and courses for central bankers in developing markets including Cuba and Abu Dhabi.

Banks, the economy and the UK have all changed greatly since 1879, but people are still vulnerable around money and will always need professional help in managing it. The London Institute of Banking & Finance will continue to strive to support the development of education in financial services and to underpin the professional standards that economic well-being relies on.

Banking, Finance and Society

What Keeps the Motor Running?

Peter Hahn

Professor Peter Hahn examines why society underestimates the important social roles played by commercial banks and the value they provide in being trusted guarantors of privacy and data integrity.

'The banks are to blame' seems to be a reflex cry. There is, certainly, plenty of blame to go around – blame for a credit crunch, followed by a recession, then a number of grubby scandals. However, perhaps we should ask a few questions before we pass final judgement.

Banks lend too much to the wrong borrowers? Yes, they sometimes do, but maybe we should save a bit more and borrow less?

They don't lend enough to support the economy? Bank loans are important in boosting growth, but perhaps we could also work on how our unrealistic business plans could fit better into uncertain economic times?

Banks don't pay enough interest on deposits and savings? Yields are certainly low, but maybe our neighbours should pay more interest on their mortgages?

Banks follow political encouragement to keep greasing (or supporting) economic expansion, don't they? They sometimes do, but stoking housing booms does tend to boost a politician's chance of re-election – at least until the bubble bursts.

Well, banks were poorly overseen by understaffed regulators following 'lite touch' political agendas, but aren't they just too complex to be regulated anyway? Sure, banks *are* complex, but doesn't that mean regulators require more sophistication?

If banks are supposed to be so sophisticated, how come they're having trouble with new tech? That's a valid point – but how easy is it to operate old tech and implement new tech simultaneously?

Are you starting to wonder whether there might be a case for the defence after all? Just a little? Well, now we come to the item on the charge sheet that probably excites the largest number of people: banks pay top managers too much. Do they have to offer big bucks because the job is too complex, or are executives given too much because shareholders don't care about the money? Gosh, who are the shareholders? Hmmm – our pension funds seem to hold big stakes.

Banks have always been easy to use as a whipping boy for problems that are about public policy and the wider culture as much as they are about financial services. I believe this has led to their societal contribution being overlooked. I'm going to gloss over much of the economic logic for banking, best known as intermediation – that is connecting those with excess financial resources and those who want to use those resources. Instead, I will point out that the root of societal conflict around banking is that savers fundamentally want their money back. To be able to repay savings, the bank must limit risk, but borrowers always want the bank to give them better terms, which means increasing risk. If half of society wants the bank to minimise risk and half of society wants the bank to take more risks, how can the whole of society be satisfied? Of course, our banking system exists to balance these contradictions – to enable our economy and society to function. Yet the very act of balancing means neither side achieves all their goals. And for banks this may be even more complicated as many, if not most, customers are both borrowers and savers – sometimes simultaneously. We are like drivers who want no red lights, no speed limits and, often, no brakes – together with a guarantee that we will always get home safely. That is why we are confused when it comes to our appreciation and consideration of banking.

Trusting That the Brakes Will Work

One of the problems we have in understanding the role of banks in society is that the concepts of trust and appreciation are not always clearly separated. Trust is much more about reliability, and that should be factual, while appreciation is much more about interpretation, and that is wrapped up in emotion.

I thought of starting this chapter with a question like 'has anyone really ever loved their bank?' I'm not sure that I have ever 'loved' any business, despite how well they may have served me, but there are few, if any, businesses that attract as much ire as banks. A UK consumer advocacy magazine recently rated airlines by customer satisfaction. The airline with the lowest rating also happened to be the most profitable. It offers some of the cheapest fares – and is often accused of being misleading – but customers flock to it. Is it loved? No. Respected? Of course. If people didn't think its planes were safe and going to get them from A to B, no one would fly with it. It isn't a business model I advocate – news reports often suggest large numbers of dislocated passengers – yet travellers sign up for more of the same even when there are alternatives. Few question the social utility of the airline, probably because it provides them with what they, as individuals, want. But though the social utility of banks is much greater, banks are neither respected nor highly rated.

This resentment of banks can go to dismaying extremes. Headlines like 'criminal bankers' that followed examination of the Libor rigging and forex fixing scandals were aimed at the whole industry – an industry in which 99.999% are not employed in the establishment of a subjective interbank rate, or in foreign exchange. A senior regulator said: 'clearly it was not the case of a few bad apples, but something rotten in the entire barrel'. The barrel? There was some irony, and understandable *schadenfreude*, when the critical authority managed to find itself tainted by the same benchmark and foreign exchange manipulation scandals – and also have one of its most senior officials depart due to a serious conduct omission – all within a short period of time. We can ask perfection of our banks or their overseeing authorities, but they are staffed by people who live in the same culture and have the same flaws as other members of society.

What Have the Banks Ever Done For Us?

The development of business sectors is always unstructured, and many failings have to be continually ironed out along the way. It seems inconceivable now, for example, that cars were on UK roads for almost a century before seat belts became compulsory – and that thousands of people died before public attitudes changed. Similarly, no one set out to invent convenient, affordable passenger air transport. Planes were dropping bombs and having aerial dogfights long before they served the wealthy as a means of convenient transportation. The internet, too, was not set up to facilitate swapping pictures of kittens in hammocks, but to ensure reliable communications systems between big research centres. Sectors do not develop in a vacuum, but within specific cultures, both anticipating and responding to changes in society.

The word 'bank' comes from the Italian 'banca' – a wooden bench set up in the town square. In the early modern period in Europe, merchants who needed credit to trade were at the centre of financial intermediation, though it was not always banking in the sense that we understand it now. What is often overlooked is that those beginnings of trade finance and foreign exchange, of deposits and 'bank money' as opposed to cash, not only benefitted the merchant families involved, they also helped drive wider economic growth. And fundamental to all of these arrangements was trust.

A detailed examination of how the ingenuity that helped develop financial services led to modern-day banking would fill libraries. There is, however, one common theme: specialist providers have, over time, been amalgamated into more diverse institutions that wanted to widen their services and their customer base. In my banking career, many have predicted the survival of specialist institutions. Still, we have come to expect banking and finance firms to expand their services to society, and to everyone in society, and perhaps to offer services well beyond banking and finance.

Responsible Road-users: Society's Non-financial Needs

I opened my first bank account with pocket money and cash received from delivering newspapers. Apart from the money, to open the account I needed a government identification number. I was too young to ponder the bank's role back then in handing over my personal financial information to the government. Of course, that simple 'reporting' information eventually led to direct tax collection and the bank passing some of my interest to government.

There are differences of degree by country, but developed world banks moved permanently from only serving society's financial needs to becoming part of government tax implementation long ago. Collecting tax is necessary, of course, and what better way to gather it than 'at source'. Today, banks not only report interest but also a range of deposits and withdrawals – particularly to support anti-money-laundering (AML) measures and to counter the financing of terrorism (CFT). I have always been surprised by the limited public debate on the way in which banks have been co-opted as an arm of law enforcement. What if car makers were required to place speed recording devices in cars that would report bad behaviour directly to the authorities? The reporting requirements and roles demanded of banks truly cross boundaries. The police are not expected to identify every criminal incident, but a bank is expected to flag up all potential transgressions. This goes further than many people might suspect. In many cases, banks must continue checks down to the level of the customer's customer and perhaps beyond. The bank becomes an intelligence network as it explores these paths to meet society's policing and political needs.

Acting as global police can mean that the economic work banks should do takes a back seat. Many Western banks, for example, have terminated longstanding correspondent banking relationships with developing markets in part because those counterparts cannot meet compliance requirements. In the UK, banks have been instructed by government to report on, and not offer services to, illegal aliens. That places banks in the front line of immigration law enforcement. I am not arguing for or against any of these requirements on banks, but they exist, are unlikely to go away, and are costly efforts that are not about providing banking and finance services. Over time, a digitised financial life integrated with a digitised currency will inevitably lead to society asking for an even wider non-financial role for banks – and banks are likely to be blamed if this doesn't work out smoothly.

Whenever I consider this wider societal role for banking and finance, I inevitably come back to considering who pays for it, financially. Computer capacity, software updates, compliance and management are real costs. Is some of the cost of banking now a form of indirect taxation? After all, if government were to undertake the above tasks without banks, taxpayers would have to fund it.

Pedal to the Metal

You might guess that I've always had a keen interest in the way cars work. Perhaps this is due to growing up in suburbia where my first real job, at age 16, required a car. That car was 14 years old, when cars were expected to last 7 years, and I often felt that I was working to keep the car running so that I could get to work after school. But the experience gave me a keen understanding of mechanics, systems and problem solving, as I did most of the repairs myself. When I hear a breezy comment on how 'the car has barely changed in a century and most of us continue to drive vehicles with the same combustion engines', I can only smile. Cars are now more efficient, more reliable, safer, faster, warmer, cooler, more comfortable, much more durable and also, in particular, cheaper. In large part, this is due to the automobile industry's adoption of technological improvements. Banking is no different. In automobiles, most of that technology is out of sight under the bonnet. In banks, it is out of sight in IT. Banks have a similar long history of leveraging technological developments to serve society.

Since the founding of The London Institute of Banking & Finance as The Institute of Bankers in 1879, technology has played a consistent part in expanding the contribution of banking and finance to society. The first commercial typewriter and Edison's patent for the electric light bulb arrived on the scene within a year of our founding and, along with them, a more productive banking work day. Imagine what it must have been like before. In 1884, Lewis Waterman came to market with the fountain pen – clerks could write sentences, paragraphs and pages without having to dip a nib in ink every few characters. It is easy to smile when thinking of the fountain pen as technology, but it meant bank clerks could spend more time serving customers more efficiently.

Facilitating better service is a consistent theme in the evolution of banking technology. Now, the transition from largely human to mechanical or digital extension of credit not only serves society, but arguably is changing society – hopefully creating a fairer world where banking decisions are based more on data and less on bias.

Technology allowed banking to become a scale business that made current accounts available to all – at least in developed markets. However, building out a branch network is expensive. Mobile telecom networks, in contrast, have a cost structure appropriate for the smallest of repetitive transactions: local phone calls. Combining basic mobile phone telephony with the financial safekeeping of banks has allowed banking and finance to reach hundreds of millions of the world's poorest citizens and help them improve their lives, most notably in the shape of M-PESA in Kenya, the first mobile money service.

The stunning viral effects and economies of scale of mobile services like M-PESA are now set to be replicated in the developed world. Wait, you might say, we already have functioning banking and payment systems. What we also have, at least in Europe, is widespread use of smartphones and Open Banking. Open Banking requires banks to make customer data available to third-party firms if the customer requests it, which means that third-party providers could build out many more services. Our current payment systems were devised before the internet was fully developed. Many of my initial online purchases (around 20 years ago) required posting a cheque that had to be cleared through the banking system before goods could be shipped. 'One-click' payment, using a debit or credit card, has revolutionised online shopping – at least in terms of customer convenience. The next step, via Open Banking, could do away with credit and debit cards altogether and enable online micropayments direct from the current account.

One of the reasons why this could take off is that the internet has already made it much easier to compare the prices of products in banking and finance and to shop around. That has encouraged a more competitive, cost-effective offering to society. Consumers and clients can see in real time what a particular service might cost and choose accordingly. The advent of machine learning and artificial intelligence applications will only enhance that trend.

White Lines and Seat Belts

Seat belts were reportedly first offered, as an option, to US drivers in 1949, but it was only around 20 years later that seat belts first became mandatory – in Australia. The evidence was overwhelmingly in favour, but fragmented industry efforts and consumer interest weren't enough to make the change. Beyond early efforts to regulate banks prudentially, were government-sponsored insurance schemes for banks the seat belts of banking? For society, they offered a peace of mind in dealing with the banking system that is taken for granted today. I recall my grandfather explaining how he lost his life savings in a bank failure in the early twentieth century; he never regained trust in financial institutions and kept his savings in a drawer.

We often forget that basic banking laws, and their oversight institutions, which protect bank users and bank creditors' rights, are not at odds with what banks aim to achieve. They are critical to the role of banking in society. Beyond the basic framework, government institutions have also set standards for more efficient financial markets and have mandated advances, such as Faster Payments or the SEPA Eurozone payments initiative. There are times when individual institutions simply cannot deliver a better system on their own – but that does not mean they do not want to do better.

The need for government intervention suggests a sector that lacks entrepreneurship and banks are, indeed, often seen as monolithic institutions. However, banks were founded, and their services expanded, by entrepreneurs who often took personal risks, or made personal sacrifices, to serve society. Friedrich Wilhelm Raiffeisen, for example, started the first German cooperative bank to serve his poor local, rural community in the mid-1800s. A range of cooperative institutions or societies across German-speaking countries still bear his name.

Trusting What's Under the Bonnet

Cars come in hundreds of different colours, shapes, sizes and interiors and offer many different levels of comfort and performance. The electronic and mechanical parts that truly differentiate a vehicle aren't as easy to observe as the gleaming paintwork, but no-one is likely to have difficulty finding information on, or learning about, the difference in performance of my Toyota Prius and the BMW Z4 two-seater parked in front of it.

Contrast that with banking products. Can you differentiate between your current account and your neighbour's? Between various forms of credit, say your mortgage and your credit card? When it isn't easy to compare, it is difficult to value. It may also be hard to trust what you can't value. Some years ago I was buying white shirts for my school-age children and was quickly pointed to the cheapest vendor. The shirts looked perfect, but when I got home I took a closer look at the quality of the cloth and regretted the purchase. The store providing the better product, albeit at a higher price, went out of business soon after. Did no-one trust that the more expensive merchant had a better product or better customer care?

My parents differentiated their banks (and banking) by the people they knew at the bank branch, not by the products. They certainly trusted the bank and banking, due to its human dimension, and this trust was developed over years of weekly visits. They did not have the same relationship with their savings bank, where they made far fewer visits. Those days are long gone in many countries, yet our interactions with our banks have increased dramatically due to our changing world of payments. Has trust, or what we trust, changed?

This is Between Us

Our banks today are repositories of our financial lives and their knowledge is growing exponentially. Two decades ago, my monthly current account statement was hardly a page. Today, thanks to 'tap and go' and online payments, my bank knows when I leave my home, what I pay for what sort of transport, what time I return, how healthily I live, how much I spend on holidays, what newspapers I read, and so much more. Imagine the bank selling those data. Using the logic of some large technology businesses, the bank might pay me to have my account. Those data, after all, are very valuable. I may not have realised it, but I trust my bank not to sell my data. I trust it to keep my data private and I trust it a lot more than I trust most technology companies. This is not about the old trust in people, but trust in the institution.

I am slowly starting to think of my bank as the protector of my financial data and what I may want, or not want, my bank to do with my data. I am not sure where that will end up. Will I trust the bank to be my portal to other goods and services? Should I pay my bank to protect my data?

Economic lives and how society functions evolve. We're rapidly moving towards a more intangible and asset-usage economy compared to an 'own' economy. Businesses have long been decreasing their investment in facilities and investing more in software and technology. Few own their space but rent, and for shorter and shorter periods; we don't buy vinyl records, we rent music online; I use a bicycle sharing scheme – I could go on. The repercussions of such societal change for banking and finance are vast, and particularly for traditional bank intermediation (i.e. lending our savings or paying us interest on our savings).

Following the financial crisis, the UK established a ring-fenced banking regime that, whether by design or accident, virtually mandates that the great majority of individual savings back the provision of home mortgages – thereby supporting house prices. Society has a strong interest in the provision of housing, yet this regime appears fraught with risk concentration and seems at odds with the increased short-term usage of assets (i.e. renting houses or flats). Imagine if the UK population were to go into a period of decline, with reducing demand for housing? Banks focused entirely on housing lending would have to seriously reconsider their business model. You might say 'not before time' – and I wouldn't argue. However, I think this re-examination of the UK bank business model is inevitable and will only accelerate banks' decreasing reliance on intermediation. After all, if and when banks reduce their intermediation efforts, and particularly in housing, they will become less loved by borrowers who are getting poorer terms and savers who are getting less interest.

Banks shouldn't worry about being loved, they need to worry about, and focus on, being trusted. More than ever, that trust is about payments integrity and data protection. Being trustworthy will be one of the vital services that banks provide to society going forward.

2

Standing the Test of Time

Paul Lynam

> Paul Lynam reflects on what he has learned and experienced during his 30-year career in retail banking, and on two constants: continual industry change and the continued need for banks – in whatever form they come.

O n 22nd March 1988 I walked into a high street branch of NatWest to start my banking career. NatWest, or National Westminster Bank as it was called then, was at that point the largest bank in the world by assets. I was instructed by the personnel department (known in the twenty-first century as human resources) to report to Mr Thomas, the administration manager. After various routine matters, including advising me of my annual salary of £4,877, Mr Thomas gave me some advice that has stayed with me in the 30-plus years since: 'Lynam', he said, 'if you want to have a successful career in banking you need to do your banking exams'.

That started a long personal association with the Chartered Institute of Bankers, the forerunner of The London Institute of Banking & Finance. Since joining as a member in 1988, I have been a student, a tutor, an examiner, a trustee/governor and, latterly, the chairman of the judging panel for the Financial Innovation Awards. The training, knowledge, skills and qualifications I have acquired through the Institute have undoubtedly helped me progress from my first job of putting bank statements into envelopes (yes, there was a time when they were all paper-based and machines did not send them out) to my current position as the chief executive of Secure Trust Bank plc, which is listed on the main market of the London Stock Exchange.

As I reflect on what I have learned and experienced over the last 30 years, there are two constants: ongoing industry change and an ongoing need for banks. Banking has been updating its working methods since the days of quill pens and parchment, and it will continue to do so. Banks that adapt to evolving customer demands and expectations will survive and prosper, at the expense of the slow and inflexible. At the same time, and notwithstanding the emergence of virtual currencies like bitcoin and distributed ledgers like blockchain, it seems to me that there are always people and businesses with surplus money they want to put to work and others who need that money. As long as that remains, there will be a place for financial intermediation and, therefore, banks. Banking in the form of lending has been going on since before the calendar featured AD after the year and, despite rumours to the contrary (usually spread by fintechs), banking is unlikely to go the way of the dinosaurs any time soon.

Hold the Campari and Ice

Over the last three decades I have watched as banking has become more commoditised and more impersonal, with much less emphasis on the relationship between a bank and its individual customers. This has been particularly the case in consumer banking, where the bulk of lending is informed by computer-based, automated decisions fed by data and algorithms – not personal knowledge. However, it is also true that business banking has become more impersonal too, especially for smaller small and medium-sized enterprises (SMEs), which is another function of change.

In many respects, that change was necessary and gradual. In 1992 I was moved into one of NatWest's regional lending centres. My role there was to assess business lending applications that exceeded the branch manager's discretionary power (DP). Essentially, each manager could say yes or no to loans up to a certain amount (their DP), and beyond that applications needed to be made to 'region'. These applications took the form of a written text using the 'CAMPARI and ICE' approach. What that meant was that all the applications were required to consider: Character, Ability, Means, Purpose, Amount, Repayment, Insurance (security) and Interest, Commission, Extras. The text was accompanied by relevant financial information, including details of the company's management and its audited accounts. Back then, these applications to region were considered by highly capable lending bankers who had frontline experience and whose only role was to opine on and make decisions related to lending requests. It was an intense and specialist environment, and therefore a great place to learn. Almost every calculation was done manually and with no computing beyond a calculator. Even the response to the applications was hand written in most cases. The more complex responses were dictated into a machine and then passed to the secretarial pool to be 'word processed'.

There were clear issues here. The first is that across an estate of literally thousands of branches, the quality of the individual branch manager and their ability to structure a lending application was infinitely variable. Some were brilliant lenders, whereas others were very poor. The latter usually operated on the basis that if they wrote enough prose, 'region' would eventually say yes to the loan request. Another issue was that the quality of the information provided in support of the request was also variable. Finally, a business model that relied on multiple specialist individuals considering, agreeing and then reviewing each loan request was cumbersome, costly and not easily scaled.

I remember those days fondly. The sheer range of bank managers I interacted with was incredible, and there were some legendary characters. You don't get bank managers like those folks these days. I learned a lot from the good ones and even more from the bad ones. Invariably, the best business and corporate bank managers were those who cared most about their customers. They worked tirelessly for them, but on rare occasions could get so focused on helping that they found it difficult to accept a decision from region not to increase a loan exposure. I recall one memorable occasion when I had declined a loan on the basis that the business in question needed more equity, not more debt, as it was clearly overtrading. I conveyed my decision to the branch manager, who was aghast. He insisted on appealing my decision to my boss, who in turn also declined the request. A few hours later, and without warning, the branch manager arrived at the regional lending centre demanding to see me and my boss. A heated meeting ensued that was abruptly ended when, in the face of the branch manager losing his temper, my boss told him to 'please keep your hair on'. The branch manager stopped, stared and then stormed out of the building. What my boss had not factored in, and in fact did not know, was that the branch manager was nicknamed 'xxx the wig' because he wore a toupee.

Banks where managers feel personally responsible for the well-being of small firms have become rare, as the separation of smaller business lending from larger corporate banking activities has accelerated. That shift is the result of what are, essentially, sensible aims: a drive to reduce cognitive bias; increase standardisation; improve portfolio management dynamics; benefit from desktop computing; and, overall, reduce costs. Such an approach is feasible when it comes to small businesses because many of them are financially more like consumers than corporates – so computer-based decision making was found to work well enough.

However, it means that today most banks' so-called SME relationship managers, based in the high street branches, have upwards of a thousand customers. They have virtually no influence over lending decisions and, because of the size of their lending portfolios, very little time to foster relationships. Moreover, over time, core banking skills have been lost, in part due to centralisation. After all, when the relationship managers for smaller SME customers have little input into the lending decision, they do not develop credit assessment skills. In the past, loans that went sour would have been dealt with by the relationship manager. Now, these 'stressed' cases are routinely taken into a business turnaround unit, depriving the relationship manager of the chance to learn from that particular case. It would be interesting to chart the evolution of centralisation against the number of people taking relevant banking qualifications. My intuition is that there will be a correlation: more centralisation, less learning.

Whatever its flaws, centralisation is not a trend that will be reversed. Increased computing power, together with the sheer quantity of data available online, will see more and more routine lending decisions being made by machines and not humans. This will dilute the value of a relationship between bankers and customers. At one level, maximising the benefits of technological advancements is understandable. It would be most unwise not to. However, if banks only use machines to cut costs, the biggest of which is people, that could be short-sighted. The majority of SMEs never borrow from their bank. However, it isn't well enough understood that banks do borrow from SMEs. Their deposits are a vital source of stable funding for banks, especially in respect of non-interest-bearing balances. SMEs are, however, an increasingly neglected cohort of customers. Because they don't borrow, the overstretched relationship managers, where they still exist, don't have the time or need to talk to SMEs and forge a relationship. That means SME customers stay with their bank more because of inertia, and because of the perceived hassle of changing, than because of the relationship they have with their individual bank manager.

Until recently, this benign neglect held little danger for the banks. Now, Open Banking and the steady demise of cash have the potential to fundamentally change business banking. The legacy incumbent banks dominate UK business banking because businesses still need places where they can pay cash takings into their bank accounts. The bank that holds the business customer's current account has an excellent insight into the behaviour and financial health of the underlying business, especially when most SMEs are no longer required to produce audited accounts, and that information asymmetry gives the incumbent banks an edge – at present. Open Banking, which makes it much easier for non-current account holding banks (and non-banks) to access the same current account data, could blunt that edge. It will give competitors the ability to make much more informed lending decisions and, thereby, compete more effectively with current account providers on a broad range of financial products and services. If, at the same time, the economy becomes cashless and SMEs no longer need bank branches in which to deposit their takings, they could take their deposit accounts to the new providers, removing an important source of funding for incumbent banks.

This is a pivotal moment for UK banking. Technology means data are much more available and, potentially, much more useful. It means that cash as a medium of exchange could disappear; it means smaller banks can become direct participants in payment portals such as BACs and Faster Payments; it means online banking is increasingly the normal way to access banking services and deposits; and it allows a general increase in the number of banks in the UK – all of whom are competing for funding. Since before my career in banking began, controlling the payments infrastructure has been a huge source of strength for the biggest UK banks.

Technology is also changing that – revolutionising the way payments are made. None of this upheaval, of course, could happen without the regulator, which appears very intent on shaking up the industry by stoking competition.

As I look forward, I fully expect to see the power of the incumbent banks to come under threat. If their business banking (and consumer) customers see what they do as commoditised and transactional, they will, quite logically, look for the provider with the least hassle at the best price.

They already have the information to do that literally at their fingertips. 2017 was the tenth anniversary of the iPhone. Ubiquitous high-performance mobile computing means the pace of change in banking is accelerating. Existing and prospective customers can now be reached in many more ways via an ever-widening range of distribution channels. Consumers and SMEs have instant information that can help them be more discerning consumers of financial products. These changes represent both an opportunity and a threat. Open Banking and technology will make it easier than ever before for existing and new banks to compete for market share, and the logical place for them to look for that share is the legacy incumbent banks.

Naturally, those incumbents are not likely to give up without a fight. I therefore expect to see an increase in the number of 'strategic alliances' between big banks and smaller firms. I also foresee some of the smaller brethren with high-quality and scalable technology being acquired by the biggest players on the 'if you can't beat 'em, buy 'em' basis.

I know from my work as chairman of the Financial Innovation Awards that there is no shortage of bright people and successful organisations willing to innovate and adapt their customer offerings in order to stay ahead in banking. This bodes well for the future.

It will be interesting to see if the iPhone exists in 2027. Who can be certain? One thing is for sure – the financial services industry and banks will remain an extremely important part of the global economy, but the industry will inevitably look and feel rather different than today. We should not fear ongoing change, but rather embrace and leverage it. Doing something new or different for the first time can be a bit unsettling, but it can also be fun and ultimately it is the only way progress happens. That said, a little piece of me wishes I could have dictated this piece rather than typed it up myself – but I don't yet have the right speech recognition technology …

CHAPTER

3

What Happens When Nobody is Watching

Regulation, Bank Risk Culture and Achieving
Environmental Sustainability

Kern Alexander and Paul Fisher

This chapter considers the importance of banks, and in particular of
bank risk culture, in developing and supporting a more sustainable
economy.

Sustainable finance has become an important concern for policymakers in their efforts to combat climate change and achieve other
sustainability objectives. The main relevance to banks as businesses
is that they depend in large part on sustained economic growth to
create new assets. Sustained growth is also the objective of most governments and central banks. However, the new sustainability agenda
sets the horizon for growth objectives at decades rather than, as has
been the case over most of the past century, the short-term business
or credit cycle.

Taking a long-term approach to business development represents a challenge for any firm, because of perceived pressures to
demonstrate ongoing returns to investors. Banks, however, deserve
special attention because, in many economies, they are the dominant
providers of credit. That includes providing initial development
finance for new projects that can enable the economy to grow and

to become more resilient to sustainability challenges. But, of course, they also provide finance for existing, unsustainable activities, which generates financial risk for themselves and systemic risks for the economy as a whole. European policymakers have already made clear that they consider banking to be important for supporting the transition to a more sustainable economy.[1] Regulators have also focused on bank culture in the post-crisis environment, because of its effect on risk taking. What has yet to happen is for policymakers and regulators to examine the cultures of banks in terms of the effect they have on tackling sustainability.

Sustainable finance is a relatively new concept. It has, nonetheless, quickly been embraced as mainstream by many governments, regulators and financial markets. Most of the literature accepts the 17 United Nations Sustainable Development Goals[2] as an appropriate reference point for the policy objectives, but sustainability is a broad agenda. Here we take a climate and environmental focus, because that is already generating significant risks for the financial sector. However, many of the arguments apply equally to other sustainability issues.

As banking is central to the economy, this chapter will examine how bank risk culture can support sustainable finance practices that, in turn, can support a more sustainable economy. It goes on to discuss the relevance of recent regulatory initiatives relating to bank risk culture and concludes with some recommendations regarding how bank risk culture and business practices could be improved to support society's sustainability objectives.

Banking and Sustainability

Banks are often referred to as 'special'. This is, in part, because they create money via deposits on their own balance sheets when they

[1]European Commission (2018a) *Action Plan: Financing Sustainable Growth.* Available at: https://eur-lex.europa.eu/legal-content/EN/TXT/PDF/?uri=CELEX:52018DC0097&from=EN [accessed 24 January 2019].

European Commission (2018b) *Final Report of the High-Level Expert Group on Sustainable Finance.* Available at: https://ec.europa.eu/info/publications/180131-sustainable-finance-report_en [accessed 24 January 2019].

[2]United Nations (2015) *About the Sustainable Development Goals.* Available at: https://www.un.org/sustainabledevelopment/sustainable-development-goals [accessed 24 January 2019].

lend. That means they can use leverage to create credit in a way that non-deposit financial institutions cannot. The business model of a bank involves providing services for deposit taking (including term savings), credit creation, risk management (e.g. through derivatives) and payments. But the liquidity mismatch between taking sight deposits and term credit creation makes it ideal for some types of finance and not others. This is an important issue in considering how bank finance can support sustainable development goals. Commercial banks are particularly good at assessing credit risk, especially for large numbers of smaller borrowers. Hence, banks dominate in providing retail mortgages and credit for small and medium-sized enterprises. Non-bank specialist lenders, in contrast, without cheap funding from a deposit base, typically compete by taking on niche credit risks (e.g. large mortgages, borrowers with irregular incomes, auto finance). Investment banks, or the affiliates of deposit-taking banks, play a complementary role by, for example, arranging/syndicating very large corporate loans or helping companies to issue bonds or equities, or facilitating government debt markets.

Given their strengths, banks (and shadow banks, including those referred to above) have a central function in originating many other types of credit as well, including longer-term infrastructure lending. But the funding sources of banks – deposits and relatively short-term debt – mean they are not ideal as 'holders to maturity' of long-term assets. Having originated long-term loans, a bank would ideally transfer at least the lower-risk credits to be funded by marketable debt securities, or otherwise sell such loans to be held by other financial institutions. Where such a process is possible, it can free up a bank's balance sheet to originate more long-term credit. In contrast, if banks were to provide a lot of large-scale, long-term loans and hold on to those assets to maturity, it could quickly lock up their balance sheets and limit their contribution to sustainability. The 'originate and distribute' model for banks, and shadow banks, is a helpful process for long-term investments.

Life insurance companies, pension funds and other long-term savings institutions or asset managers are all better matched holders of long-term assets than the banks. Indeed, the very purpose of such firms is to provide future incomes and/or lump sums based on a saver's lifecycle or other longer-term considerations, and so the sustainability of their long-term investments is a prerequisite for successfully meeting those liabilities. Perhaps the most effective bank business strategy involves the use of simple and transparent securitisation and other credit risk transfer methods to pass long-term assets to longer-term investors such as pension funds and insurance companies. Such low-risk, long-term investors typically prefer bonds or other fixed-income instruments rather than equity, as bonds provide the income stream and risk profile that would match the investing firms' obligations. Suitable market securities could include collateralised loan obligations or other asset-backed securities. In contrast, the start-up phase of a new build project is typically not an ideal investment for investors who require an income stream, although they may take a limited equity position via a structured investment.

Banks originate credit on commercial terms where they think the risk justifies the returns, although not usually beyond a relatively limited risk tolerance. For higher-risk business funding, equity is widely considered to be more appropriate than debt and banks do not typically hold equity stakes in customers (unless there is a default, and then only temporarily). Some hold a portfolio of traded equities but usually only as part of other market activity (for market making or to hedge equity derivatives, for example).

A few banks are public utilities, but most are not and, like other commercial firms, banks would not normally see it as their role to choose credits based on political or social factors. But bank behaviour has positive and negative externalities for society as a whole, just as individual behaviour does. One bank's loan to an unsustainable activity may be profitable for the bank – at least for a while – but such lending by banks collectively could seriously damage the economy over the longer term. So how can society influence banks to take account of these and other externalities and to direct more credit and investment towards sustainable economic activity and not just towards assets that generate only short-term rewards?

Part of the answer is to make banks internalise the externalities. This should be possible since these same systemic risks will ultimately undermine the banks' own business models. We suggest that regulators and other stakeholders, including shareholders, can help to change bank risk culture. Sustainability should be at the heart of bank risk management practices and wider business models. That would drive the development of more lending to, and investment in, sustainable sectors of the economy.

Bank Risk Culture: The Tone From the Top

Commercial banking organisations are complex institutions. They can only achieve their economic objective of maximising shareholder returns through the collective efforts of many individuals – individuals who share the same objectives and beliefs and who can coordinate their activities effectively. However, the size and complex structure of large, systemically important banks gives rise to a wide range of potential agency problems. These involve different major stakeholder groups, including but not limited to shareholders, creditors, depositors and other customers, employees, management and supervisory bodies. Agency problems can develop when stakeholders have differing objectives, decision making must be delegated and complete information that would allow stakeholders to control decisions made on their behalf is not readily available. The most studied agency problems in the case of banks involve (i) depositors and shareholders and (ii) supervisors and shareholders, and these problems have underpinned major design features of regulatory structures (e.g. deposit insurance and capital adequacy). However, incentive conflicts based on different understandings of ethics and norms of behaviour can also undermine the firm's pursuit of its strategic objectives, and they have become the focus of a growing literature on risk culture.

Human agency theory supplements traditional corporate governance agency theory by postulating that – as is the case in other complex organisations – bank workers do not pursue their objectives in a vacuum, based on the design of a contract. Instead, they are subject to societal norms and institutional values that influence how they coordinate their activities to achieve both their own individual objectives and the collective objectives of the institution. Successful institutional outcomes are the product of a particular business or risk culture that drives an effective coordination model. This type of human agency outcome – driven by the collective pursuits of individuals throughout an organisation – is influenced substantially by the norms and standards fostered by the institution's leaders in the pursuit of the formal objective of shareholder wealth maximisation.

It is generally accepted that the culture within banking institutions during the period prior to the crisis of 2007–2009 emphasised (excessive) risk taking to pursue short-term profits at the expense of longer-term firm performance and sustainable shareholder value. Moreover, the risk culture within institutions was driven by compensation arrangements that relied heavily on variable pay determined by short-term performance metrics. A focus on short-term revenue and profits can place a firm's long-term viability at risk and disadvantage customers. To give an example, it was (and still is) commonplace that one bad quarter's earnings in an investment bank could result in a senior business manager, with a long and successful career, being summarily dismissed or moved aside. Under such a regime, the rational response of all staff as individuals is to focus on meeting short-term goals.[3]

One of the lessons of the crisis, therefore, was that regulators should play a greater role in judging how culture drives firm behaviour, and especially risk taking, and how this impacts society as a whole. Indeed, former chief executive of the UK Financial Services Authority, Hector Sants, observed that: '[T]he end goal should be that firms understand their own culture and the potential risks posed by the wrong culture.'[4]

Although risk culture has no single definition,[5] it is viewed as a subset of broader company organisational culture and thus defined as: 'the norms and traditions of behaviour of individuals and of groups within an organization that determine the way in which they identify, understand, discuss, and act on the risks the organization confronts and the risks it takes'.[6] Significantly, firms converge on defining risk culture as everyone's responsibility – from management to employees. In other words, they understand it as

---

[3]It would be wrong to give individual examples, but some of the pressures and cultural responses in investment banks are discussed in Alvesson M and Robertson M (2016) 'Money matters: teflonic identity manoeuvring in the investment banking sector', *Organization Studies*, 37(1), 7–34.

[4]Sants HWH (2010) 'Do regulators have a role to play in judging culture and ethics?' Speech at the Chartered Institute of Securities and Investments Conference. Available at: https://webarchive.nationalarchives.gov.uk/20120303060944/http://www.fsa.gov.uk/pages/library/communication/speeches/2010/0617_hs.shtml

[5]Ashby S, Palermo T and Power M (2014) 'Risk culture: definitions, change practices and challenge for chief risk officers'. In Jackson P (ed.), *Risk Culture and Effective Risk Governance*, Risk Books, 25–46.

[6]Institute of International Finance (2009) *Reform in the Financial Services Industry: Strengthening Practices for a More Stable System*, IIF.

a system of values and behavioural norms that helps foster risk management processes and ensure an adequate level of risk control. In this context, risk culture is seen as an effective tool for reducing a firm's excessive risk taking.[7]

But a firm's culture is not just fostered internally. Importantly, regulators and policymakers provide incentives for how practitioners define risk culture. In 2009, the Basel Committee on Banking Supervision (BCBS) encouraged regulators to strengthen risk management within banks and highlighted the importance of risk culture (as a 'critical focus') in banks' business strategies.[8] This was then transposed into some of the main EU post-crisis banking legislation to 'promote a sound risk culture at all levels of credit institutions and investment firms'.[9] In this respect, in 2013 the Group of 30 (G30) declared that 'boards should identify and deal seriously with risky culture, ensure their compensation system supports the desired culture, discuss culture at the board level and with supervisors, and periodically use a variety of formal and informal techniques to monitor risk culture'.[10] The BCBS defined risk culture as 'a bank's norms, attitudes and behaviours related to risk awareness, risk taking and risk management and controls that shape decisions on risks'.[11]

Risk culture influences the decisions on risk that management and employees take during day-to-day activities. Accordingly, it is the board's task to set a 'tone at the top' to promote an effective risk culture. Supervisors are not called on to act as shadow managers

---

[7]EY (2014) *Shifting Focus: Risk culture at the forefront of banking*. Available at: https://www.ey.com/Publication/vwLUAssets/ey-shifting-focus-risk-culture-at-the-forefront-of-banking/$File/ey-shifting-focus-risk-culture-at-the-forefront-of-banking.pdf [accessed 19 January 2019].

[8]Basel Committee on Banking Supervision (2009) *Enhancements to the Basel II Framework*. Available at: https://www.bis.org/publ/bcbs157.htm [accessed 19 April 2017].

[9]European Commission (2013) Directive 2013/36/EU of the European Parliament and of the Council of 26 June 2013 on access to the activity of credit institutions and the prudential supervision of credit institutions and investment firms, amending Directive 2002/87/EC and repealing Directives 2006/48/EC and 2006/49/EC, OJEU L 176/338, Recital 54.

[10]G30 (2013) *A New Paradigm: Financial institution boards and supervisors*. Available at: http://group30.org/images/uploads/publications/G30_NewParadigm.pdf [accessed 19 April 2017].

[11]Basel Committee on Banking Supervision (2014) *Consultative Document: Corporate governance principles for banks*. Available at: https://www.bis.org/publ/bcbs294.pdf [accessed 10 January 2019].

of banks, but they should liaise with the board, its risk and audit committees, to verify whether or not the institution has adequate risk governance mechanisms and effective risk culture.[12] Furthermore, the Financial Stability Board (FSB) sets out clear guidance to help regulators and supervisors assess risk culture in financial institutions. In its 2014 'Guidance on supervisory interaction with financial institutions on risk culture', the FSB stated that 'a sound risk culture bolsters effective risk management, promotes sound risk-taking, and ensures that emerging risks or risk-taking activities beyond the institution's risk appetite are recognised, assessed, escalated and addressed in a timely manner'.[13]

The G30, in its 2015 *Banking Conduct and Culture* study, also drew a line between the roles of the board/management of firms and the supervisory authorities in relation to culture and risk culture. The former has responsibility for a firm's cultural focus and the latter cannot determine culture. Supervisors should, instead, monitor the effectiveness of a firm's own culture to deter, among other things, inappropriate behaviour in violation of regulatory norms and standards.[14] It is worth noting that the issue of risk culture from the regulatory perspective has a broader scope than a typical firm's vision. In essence, while firms address risk culture from an internal perspective, supervisors should address risk culture in the context of potential systemic implications for markets and the financial system. This is particularly so when addressing issues of sustainability.

The link between firm culture and prudential regulation was not strong before the financial crisis, but recent financial scandals have changed that. Proven misconduct – such as the rigging of the London Interbank Offered Rate (Libor) and the mis-selling of payment protection insurance (PPI) in the UK – prompted regulators to discuss risk culture in the context of so-called 'misconduct

---

[12]Basel Committee on Banking Supervision (2014) *Consultative Document: Corporate governance principles for banks.* Available at: https://www.bis.org/publ/bcbs294.pdf [accessed 10 January 2019].

[13]Financial Stability Board (2014) *Guidance on Supervisory Interaction with Financial Institutions on Risk Culture: A framework for assessing risk culture.* Available at: https://www.fsb.org/wp-content/uploads/140407.pdf [accessed 10 January 2019].

[14]G30 (2015) *Banking Conduct and Culture: A call for sustained and comprehensive reform.* Available at: https://group30.org/images/uploads/publications/G30_BankingConductandCulture.pdf [accessed 10 January 2019].

risk'. For instance, the European Systemic Risk Board (ESRB) recently analysed misconduct risk in the banking sector from a macro-prudential perspective. As part of their recommendations, the ESRB required banks to adopt adequate behaviours, practices and governance mechanisms to reduce the potential for misconduct.[15] Significantly, having an appropriate risk culture includes ensuring adequate risk management and assumes that bank misconduct has systemic implications.

This means that understanding culture – what one does 'when nobody is watching' – and ethics – the line between acceptable and unacceptable decisions – can help us to recognise, and even predict, some behaviour.[16] To illustrate this, the following section discusses the UK's regulatory initiatives in supervising bank risk culture.

Getting Personal: Recent Developments in the UK

The UK has adopted a number of regulatory and legal approaches to enhance financial institution risk culture. The UK Prudential Regulation Authority (PRA), the supervisory body now within the Bank of England, declared that even though it does not have any 'right culture' in mind, it will act 'to tackle serious failings in culture through its normal activity, through use of its supervisory powers, and through enforcement action'.[17] Similarly, the UK Financial Conduct Authority (FCA) has stressed the importance of focusing on financial institutions' culture and risk culture to prevent behaviour in violation of regulatory rules and standards.[18]

---

[15]European Systemic Risk Board (2015) *Report on Misconduct Risk in the Banking Sector.* Available at: https://www.esrb.europa.eu/pub/pdf/other/150625_report_misconduct_risk.en.pdf [accessed 10 January 2019].

[16]European Systemic Risk Board (2015) *Report on Misconduct Risk in the Banking Sector.* Available at: https://www.esrb.europa.eu/pub/pdf/other/150625_report_misconduct_risk.en.pdf [accessed 10 January 2019].

[17]Prudential Regulation Authority (2014) *The Use of PRA Powers to Address Serious Failings in the Culture of Firms.* Available at: https://www.bankofengland.co.uk/pra/documents/publications/policy/2014/powersculture.pdf [accessed 10 January 2019].

[18]The FCA's former director of enforcement, and subsequently acting CEO, stated: 'we believe that a firm's culture is a key driver of staff behaviour and, in many cases, where things have gone wrong in a firm, a cultural issue was a key part of

The strategic objective of the UK regulators – the PRA and the FCA – is to 'protect and enhance confidence in the UK financial system'. For the FCA, this primary objective is complemented by three operational objectives: (1) securing an appropriate degree of protection for consumers; (2) protecting and enhancing the integrity of the UK financial system; and (3) promoting efficiency and choice in the market for certain types of services. The UK parliament recognised that to achieve its strategic objective, the FCA should aim to promote fair, efficient and transparent financial services markets that work well for the users of these markets, including not only the banks but also the banks' customers, consumers and investors. This would better reflect the Treasury's intended purpose in the legislation, which is that the FCA should ensure that business across financial services and markets is conducted in a way that advances the interests of all users and participants.

The main regulatory change applicable to risk culture was driven by the Financial Services (Banking Reform) Act 2013. That authorised the UK Treasury to adopt a senior managers regime (SMR). Originally designed slightly differently for banks and insurance companies, the regime has been simplified, made consistent across banks and insurers, and is being extended in December 2019 to apply to *all* financial sector firms authorised by either the PRA or the FCA.

One of the aims of the SMR is: 'to make sure there is a senior manager accountable for … key conduct and prudential risks'.[19] The SMR draws up lists of necessary roles and responsibilities (proportionately for smaller firms), which a firm must publicly allocate to its most senior managers. The precise mapping of responsibilities to roles is for the firm to decide, but they must be clear, must seek regulatory pre-approval and the firm must publish its map. The nominated senior managers are then responsible for ensuring that the particular responsibilities allocated to them are fulfilled by the firm or else they will be held individually accountable. The list of responsibilities includes risk culture. In October 2018, the

the problem' [McDermott T (2015) 'Culture in banking'. Speech to the British Bankers Association. Available at: https://www.fca.org.uk/static/documents/foi/foi4350-information-provided.pdf].

[19]Financial Conduct Authority (2018) Website update. Available at https://www.fca.org.uk/firms/senior-managers-certification-regime/banking [accessed 15 February 2019].

PRA proposed extending this to make it explicit that sustainability risks are included. It issued a consultation paper with the specific proposal that:

> The PRA expects firms to have clear roles and responsibilities for the board and its relevant sub-committees in managing the financial risks from climate change. In particular, the board and the highest level of executive management should identify and allocate responsibility for identifying and managing financial risks from climate change to the relevant existing Senior Management Function(s) (SMF(s)) most appropriate within the firm's organisational structure and risk profile, and ensure that these responsibilities are included in the SMF(s)'s Statement of Responsibilities.[20]

As far as we are aware, and at the time of writing, this is the first example in the developed world of proposed regulation that would hold individual bankers (and senior managers in other financial firms) to account for managing a sustainability risk.

Bank Culture and Sustainability – *Where Should the Focus Be?*

As financial regulators start to treat sustainability as a mainstream financial risk, so banks in both developed and developing countries are doing more to address the economic and financial risks associated with sustainability challenges by incorporating, or mainstreaming, sustainability factors and guidelines into their risk management models and business strategies. And bank risk culture is responding by also beginning to incorporate sustainability into the overall cultural ethos.

Nevertheless, market structures must evolve to meet environmental sustainability needs and banks face steep challenges in managing the risks associated with that transition. Potentially, these could include price volatility and increased credit risk in assets

---

[20] Prudential Regulation Authority (2018) 12: *Enhancing Banks' and Insurers' Approaches to Managing the Financial Risks from Climate Change.* Consultation paper 23/18. https://www.bankofengland.co.uk/-/media/boe/files/prudential-regulation/con sultation-paper/2018/cp2318.pdf?la=en&hash=8663D2D47A725C395F71FD5688E 5667399C48E08.

and sectors considered environmentally unsustainable. Where such transition risks are material, they may pose systemic risks to the banking sector – and this is the source of increasing regulatory attention. To adequately address these risks, bank risk culture should fully incorporate sustainability criteria and values into risk management, remuneration incentives and strategic business objectives. Where there are institutional or market barriers, policy intervention may be necessary.

Despite progress in these areas, this chapter argues that inculcating sustainability values into mainstream bank business practices demands a more concerted focus on bank risk culture. In particular, that means a longer-term, and wider, appreciation of risks to the firm, not just of the narrow risks to a particular transaction or portfolio. Bank risk culture should address the following factors that relate to environmental sustainability.

- **Taking account of the importance of reputation.** As the financial crisis and countless other episodes have shown (e.g. the collapse of audit firm Arthur Anderson), reputation is essential for any successful business to be sustained: lose it and one's business model can follow very quickly. Pressure to maintain a good reputation can be exerted by investors – bank debt or equity holders – or by clients. However, in the past, the way in which banks offered very substantial remuneration for short-term performance could lead to staff ignoring long-term reputational risks to their firms – and that needs permanent change.

  Sustainability is quickly becoming a reputational issue, thanks to pressure from governments and the public alike. As appreciation of sustainability issues rises, what was defensible at one point in time can become indefensible. We have seen this in Australia, for example, in relation to financing a new, controversial coal project.[21] Public attitudes can also change rapidly: for example, the introduction in 2015 of a minimal charge on single-use plastic shopping bags led to a rapid collapse in their use in the UK. Then, during 2018,

---

[21]Robertson J (2017) 'Big four banks distance themselves from Adani coalmine as Westpac rules out loan', *The Guardian*, 28 April.

Western Europe experienced a sudden consumer/retailer shift away from single-use plastics on account of concerns about pollution of the oceans, a movement which has since gone global.[22] Obviously, any company specialising in such products has had their business model severely challenged.

- **Taking account of longer-term and broader risks.** In the past, banks viewed sustainability risks as a social/political/ethical issue to be managed by their corporate social responsibility departments. This has led to some good work being done, at the margin, but it has not been transformative.

  The cultural change required is twofold. First, large banks in particular need to appreciate that sustainability risks are existential and systemic. If economic growth is not sustainable, then banks' business models are likely to come under pressure and quite possibly collapse. That means the risk culture needs to be much longer-term and to be focused on broader macroeconomic factors. For example, banks must examine not just the short-term risks of an individual loan, but the future risks underlying the whole portfolio and their potential impact on the banking sector.

  Second, the sustainability agenda should be recognised as a great business opportunity as well as a financial risk. Picking up on sustainability trends could be highly profitable by going with the grain of economic transformation and political direction.

  Both changes could be classed as the internalisation of risks that have hitherto been regarded as externalities.

- **The demand for credit.** Banks are intermediaries and in a narrow sense cannot lend if no one wants to borrow. But the demand for credit is not wholly exogenous. Like most goods and services, demand can be influenced through identifying an unmet need, designing new products and advertising. Banks that can do this successfully will win market share. This is, of course, a normal approach to building profits – as well as an opportunity for mis-selling (e.g. the PPI scandal in the UK), which can cause severe reputational damage.

---

[22]Buranyi S (2018) 'The plastic backlash: what's behind our sudden rage – and will it make a difference?', *The Guardian*, 13 November.

- **The role of regulation.** In the past few years, regulators have started to identify the material financial risks represented by the potential for stranded assets and, in particular, market volatility related to climate risk. However, such risks are still seen by many as being long-term and therefore beyond the scope of risk management processes. They are, though, not just long-term:
  - Climate events can be precipitous – there is a significant financial stability risk arising from London flooding for example, which could happen at any time.
  - Technical developments are on the brink of potentially causing huge and sudden disruptions to sectors such as energy, transport (e.g. electric vehicles) and construction. That could result in very significant risks to banks exposed to those sectors crystallising within, say, the next 3–5 years.
  - On top of that, government policies globally are starting to implement the Paris 2015 agreement, which could result in a lot of unanticipated policy and regulatory risks emerging.

Given these challenges, bank risk managers need to ensure that they are not blind-sided by the sudden materialisation of sustainability risks. Such risks are not all so-called 'black swans'. A lot of sustainability risks are predictable in nature – just not in timing or scale. As the regulators turn up the volume and tighten the rules, banks need to understand the systemic risks to financial services that come with tackling sustainability if they are to avoid being continually caught out by new regulations.

There is an ongoing debate about whether capital requirements should be adjusted to reflect sustainability risks. Alexander and Fisher look at this question and conclude that changing mandatory capital weights under pillar 1 minimum capital charges (of the Basel III regulations) is not the right approach.[23] Rather, using pillar 2 of the banking supervisory approach – supervisors intervening to ensure appropriate risk management is taking place, subject to discretionary capital charges – is almost certainly the more effective method of regulatory intervention.

---

[23] Alexander K and Fisher P (2018) 'Banking regulation and sustainability'. SSRN Working Paper. Available at: https://papers.ssrn.com/sol3/papers.cfm?abstract_id=3299351 [accessed 11 February 2019].

Capital requirements need to remain risk-based to support sustainable lending. There are normal risks associated with sustainable activities, and that degree of risk is already covered by the current Basel capital calculations. If there were to be a change in capital weights, it is the newly appreciated, *increased* risk from unsustainable activities that needs to be reflected – but that would be extremely difficult to incorporate in pillar 1 capital charges. The Bank of England and other regulators seem to agree with the pillar 2 approach.[24]

Summary and Conclusion

This chapter has discussed bank risk culture – why it is important to the firm and why it is important in managing sustainability challenges (especially environmental). It suggests that bank risk culture – that is, the standards, incentives and values within institutions – is vital in determining whether banks and other financial institutions will be able to support the economy's transition to a sustainable economic path, and maintain the value of their individual franchises. The post-crisis regulatory environment has brought bank culture to the fore of improving bank governance and risk management practices. Regulators now treat culture as a part of bank governance, and it is embodied in the UK's SMR.

This chapter has also addressed some of the major challenges that banks face in incorporating sustainability criteria into their risk management and governance practices. The scope of regulation in shaping and developing risk culture with the specific aim of a more sustainable outcome remains uncertain. However, the direction of travel in many countries is clear, as the proposed inclusion of responsibility for managing a firm's risks from climate change in the SMR makes clear. Banking regulation reform and other financial sector initiatives, whose impetus was provided by the financial crisis of 2007/2008, are beginning to change significantly the risk culture within financial institutions. That change not only bears down on how they manage and control financial sector risks, but increasingly

---

[24]Prudential Regulation Authority (2018) 12: *Enhancing Banks' and Insurers' Approaches to Managing the Financial Risks from Climate Change.* Consultation paper 23/18. https://www.bankofengland.co.uk/-/media/boe/files/prudential-regulation/con sultation-paper/2018/cp2318.pdf?la=en&hash=8663D2D47A725C395F71FD5688E 5667399C48E08.

includes the risks associated with an environmentally unsustainable economy. The chapter sheds light on some areas where banks can adjust their risk culture so that the banking business can be more directly aligned with the goals and values of a sustainable economy.

The financial system has a big role to play in delivering a more sustainable economy, and banks have a special part within that. But there needs to be raised awareness: improving risk culture is crucial if banks are to both manage their own financial risks and realise business opportunities while supporting the development of the sustainable economy that is an existential necessity for their business model.

It Takes an Ecosystem

The Future of Trade Financing

Alexander Malaket

Financing is the oil in the engine of global commerce: the critical enabler of trillions of dollars annually that flow through the arteries and corridors of trade. Alexander Malaket examines how trade financing will be central to tackling some of the major economic and political challenges that the world faces, including sustainability, inclusion and security.

The financial crisis of 2008 saw steep falls in the value of global trade.[1] Ten years later, international trade is finally regaining its familiar place as a driver of global economic growth, even as geopolitical developments, trade wars and local political imperatives combine to create headwinds. Before the crisis, trade financing – often seen as an arcane specialism – was rarely part of mainstream economic discussion. Now the role of financing – specifically trade finance and supply chain finance – in enabling global commerce is more widely appreciated, with estimates from various sources, such as the World Trade Organization (WTO), suggesting that 80% of merchandise trade flows worth US$16tn–20tn annually depend on some form of

---

[1] Bank of International Settlements (2014) 'Trade finance: developments and issues'. CGFS Papers No. 50. Available at: https://www.bis.org/publ/cgfs50.pdf [accessed 28 February 2019].

trade-related financing. US$5tn or more in services trade also relies on adequate levels of financing.

This is as true for large corporates as it is for small and medium-sized enterprises, and is a feature of international business in Organisation for Economic Co-operation and Development (OECD) economies as well as in developing markets. However, analysis by the Asian Development Bank (ADB) has identified a persistent global 'trade finance gap' of around US$1.5tn a year (discussed in more detail below), with the WTO reckoning that '60 per cent of trade finance requests from small businesses [are] refused by banks'.[2] And that is not the only shift seen in the markets post-crisis.

Historically, traditional trade financing (largely documentary credits, documentary collections and various forms of guarantees) was provided by regional or international banks, and accounted for the majority of financial resources underpinning international commerce. More recently, however, there has been a near global shift toward the conduct of trade without using these traditional instruments. Importers and exporters have opted to pursue trade on 'open account' terms – that is, goods are shipped on the understanding that payment will be made once an agreed event (loading of the cargo aboard the ship, for example) takes place. Open account allows trading partners to avoid the complexity, extended transaction cycle and paper flow of traditional mechanisms, but they lose the benefits of well-established international practice, proven risk mitigation and the engagement of financial institutions with extensive domain expertise.

The trade-off in favour of faster, simpler and less cumbersome processing of open account transactions appears to be irreversible, as these transactions now account for about 80% of trade flows, according to data collected by industry bodies like the ICC Banking Commission.

This shift, which picked up momentum prior to the crisis, threatened to disintermediate banks from the business of trade financing. Seeking to remain relevant to international trade, banks have devised propositions linked to international supply chains and to the key players in those ecosystems, all under the banner of supply chain finance (SCF).[3] SCF covers a range of financing techniques and is

---

[2]WTO (2018). Available at: https://www.wto.org/english/thewto_e/coher_e/tr_finance_e.htm [accessed 28 February 2019].

[3]BIS (2014), 1.

notable in its applicability to open account trade flows, the shift from a buyer/seller view of trade to a holistic, supply chain approach, as well as the nascent character of numerous techniques, products and services.

Like traditional trade finance mechanisms, SCF techniques can offer financing solutions for buyers and sellers (suppliers), but may also extend out into supply chains, to reach beyond the parties selling directly to a large buyer, to the sub-suppliers at the farthest end of complex global supply chains: the so-called 'last mile' of international supply chains.

An 'Ecosystem' View of Trade

Over the past few years, some politicians have taken an 'exports good, imports bad' view of trade.[4] This simplistic, zero-sum-game approach does not, of course, reflect the economic reality. Even in the pre-industrial age, when production and consumption were rarely separated, societies benefitted from, and valued, what trade could bring. Modern free trade facilitates specialisation and innovation,[5] and one of the principal benefits of that specialisation is increased productivity.[6] US factories are now nearly seven times more productive than they were 60 years ago, because US firms have made use of increased freedoms in global trade, together with improved transport and communications, to draw on the best processes at the lowest cost. They built an 'integrative trade model', which has improved living standards around the world even as painful adjustments have been required of some workforces in developed markets.[7] 'The result was an explosion of specialization as markets became global and companies became more efficient.'[8]

---

[4]ICC (2018) *Global Trade: Securing future growth*. Available at: https://iccwbo .org/publication/global-survey-2018-securing-future-growth/ [accessed 28 February 2019].

[5]Poloz S (2016) 'A new balance point – global trade, productivity and economic growth'. Remarks to the Investment Industry Association of Canada and Securities Industry and Financial Markets Association, New York City, 26 April. Available at: https://www.bis.org/review/r160426g.pdf [accessed 28 February 2019].

[6]Poloz S (2016), 3.

[7]Poloz S (2016), 4.

[8]Poloz S (2016), 3.

This more holistic, ecosystem view of trade has implications for trade finance. It, too, will become more specialised and 'integrative'. There will be a shift from the product view of financing and risk mitigation, to a solution view of this critical enabler of global commerce. Financing trade will be less about products and techniques, and more about solutions rooted in a deeper understanding of global supply chains – from the physical flow of goods and services, to the parallel flow of data – the 'information supply chain'. All solutions will be related to the various aspects of trade activity that can cross multiple borders, and may involve an ecosystem anchored by a global buyer, supported by dozens of service providers and engaging with many thousands of suppliers around the world.

This ecosystem view changes the character of trade financing from transactional and product-based to solution-focused, depending on a more holistic understanding of the business of trade. This shift is likely to encourage greater consolidation among trade finance banks, even as the focus on SCF enables alternative, non-bank providers of financing to enter the business of trade financing. At the same time, the ecosystem focus encourages providers to bring adequate risk mitigation to bear – an area that has always been central to traditional trade finance but was less central to open account trade.

The blurring of lines between traditional trade finance and SCF is a natural and useful development, reflecting the convergence of propositions into a comprehensive global trade financing discipline, targeting the ecosystem view of trade. In addition to driving a convergence of trade financing capabilities and practice, the supply chain view of trade has arguably underpinned or facilitated other developments that will define the future of trade financing.

Physical, Financial and Informational: Three Elements, One Supply Chain

The industry has aspired to align the physical and financial supply chain for the last two decades or more. Now, however, evolutions in technology, market acceptance of evolving practices and the aforementioned ecosystem view of trade have come together to make this a reality. In fact, the importance of technology and data today is such that we now speak of an 'information' or data-related supply chain that mirrors the physical and financial supply chains.

Looking forward, the importance of this holistic view of trade and of the related supply chain will be that developments at one level of the supply chain which impact another aspect of it will be adequately taken into account. Advances in the physical supply chain, such as accelerated shipping and logistics, will directly affect the context in which financing requirements will be determined. Similarly, the ability to capture more and richer supply chain data, such as the location, temperature and security related to a particular container, may be equally relevant to financing from a risk mitigation perspective.

At one extreme, extended delivery timeframes due to logistical issues, lack of transportation infrastructure or even delays in customs clearance will tend to create cash flow and working capital challenges for suppliers who are waiting to be paid for the goods they have produced and shipped. This may lead to the need to secure financing to cover the extended timeframes or transaction lifecycles.

At the other extreme, recent technological developments – like additive manufacturing (3D, and also 4D printing, in which the physical product is itself programmable and can change in response to, for example, temperature),[9] as well as drone-based delivery – will significantly reduce delivery timeframes. That will shorten transaction lifecycles, accelerate payment timeframes and, all else being equal, reduce the need to use financing to ensure access to working capital.

When 3D printers become ubiquitous and are integrated into an increasing range of production activity, it may be that exports do not send goods but, instead, the algorithm that codes for them – and suppliers will be able to send a design or an algorithm directly to a buyer anywhere on the planet. That buyer will then produce the component or product locally, reducing delivery timeframes and eliminating significant portions of the shipping activity related to the physical supply chain.

The shift from traditional trade finance, particularly documentary credits, to SCF has already allowed financing to be offered earlier in a transaction lifecycle. Perhaps in a similar fashion, the advent

---

[9]Pontin J (2018) '3-D printing is the future of factories (for real this time)', *Wired*, 7 November. Available at: https://www.wired.com/story/ideas-jason-pontin-3d-printing/ [accessed 12 February 2019].

of 3D printing and the compression of the physical supply chain will motivate the development of a form of trade financing that will support the transfer of intellectual property to the buyer, or that will provide pre-production or design-stage financing for a business developing a product for export.

The same advances in transaction visibility and detailed transaction-level data that allow financiers to better track the shipment (frequently an asset against which financing is provided) over the course of its travels could redefine the scope of financing. Technology such as radio frequency identification (RFID) tracking, or the application of artificial intelligence, could allow enhanced visibility of parts of the design and pre-production processes that are typically not areas of focus today. In such an eventuality, one can envision the scope of financing activity being extended much earlier in the export and trade lifecycle, just as current evolutions are proposing financing deeper into international supply chains.

Digitisation of Trade and Trade Financing

The long-anticipated promise of digital trade is getting increasingly close, though most market observers believe that full digital trade is some years away. One reason for this muted optimism is that much of the documentation in trade finance is still paper-based. Being able to do away with paper and document flows in cross-border trade extends far beyond the current focus of extracting subsets of data from purchase orders and shipping documents, or working to secure legal and market acceptance of electronic bills of lading. It requires digitising certificates of origin, health and phytosanitary certificates and other government documents from around the world. The future of trade financing will, however, evolve with the ability to handle fully digitised documentation and – by extension – the ability to be responsive to the needs of those trading through online platforms like Alibaba, Amazon and eBay.

In this context, the important enabling elements of trade financing, such as industry practice and guiding rules like the Uniform Customs and Practice (UCP) for Documentary Credits, will need to evolve quickly, or they will be supplanted by other agreed practices, industry standards and principles. The legal framework that grew up with, and enabled, traditional trade finance holds valuable lessons to help in that evolution, but there is no doubt that new processes will eventually be woven into legal discourse. Past incremental attempts, like e-enabling UCP, will be insufficient to meet the transformational requirements of evolutions in trade.

All Together Now: Financing Gaps and Alternative Financiers

As mentioned in the introduction to this chapter, research suggests a significant level of unmet demand for trade finance. Estimates suggest that importers and exporters require additional trade finance in the range of US$1.5tn annually.

It is widely acknowledged that banks are unable to meet this demand, partly because of limits on capital and credit capacity, and partly because banks may have limited desire to service the needs of small and medium-sized enterprises (SMEs) – those most commonly affected by the trade finance gap. The evolution of trade financing to extend to SCF is happening today, in parallel with the entry of non-bank financiers to the market. Not only is there a clear requirement for additional trade financing, but new techniques aimed at expanding financing options across the supply chain will create further demand.

The future of trade financing will involve greater engagement from non-banks as providers of trade finance and SCF. The initial foray of fintech firms into the arena of trade financing is a precursor to what will evolve over the coming years, with agile, innovative entities complementing the capabilities of financial institutions as they learn the intricacies of international commerce. New entrants have contributed and will continue to contribute to the evolution of lending and financing practice.

Collateral or asset-based lending, and financing based on traditional credit adjudication, will be complemented by other modes of lending, including those more responsive to the needs of micro-enterprises and SMEs that have limited collateral and face challenges today related to the bankability of their business. Evidence of evolving financing frameworks can be seen in the attention being focused today on the financing of services trade flows – intangible flows that cannot be used as security in the traditional sense.

Additionally, traditional credit-granting practices are being up-ended to some degree by e-invoicing and the use of predictive analytics that mine rich datasets of past payment behaviour to underpin lending decisions. Even further out on the 'leading edge' today are financing programmes that are inclusion-focused, and allow for capital to be provided to micro, small and medium-sized enterprises (MSMEs) on the basis of collective community responsibility for the repayment of the loan. Inclusion and trade-based international development will increasingly be a focus for trade financiers as the importance of robust, healthy and sustainable supply chains comes to the fore. The role of working capital and access to finance in sustainability will be brought sharply into focus by market evolution and a maturing view of the ecosystem around complex global supply chains.

Multilateral institutions, export credit agencies and other policy and public good-driven entities will continue to be an important part of the trade financing landscape, both in terms of adding financing capacity and in terms of bringing vital risk mitigation to bear. They allow financing and trade flows to develop that would be non-existent if left entirely to profit-driven private sector financiers. Similarly, credit and risk insurers will remain central to the ecosystem, but will find themselves facing evolving market expectations around the risks to be assessed, mitigated and – when necessary – compensated for. As buyers become increasingly and directly responsible (and liable) for the conduct of their suppliers, the same supply chain and ecosystem view of trade that is shaping up among financiers will develop among risk insurers.

Because trade financing has shifted from relative obscurity in the last decade to being a central part of the policy and commercial dialogue around international commerce, it will attract the attention of the wider capital market, perhaps to the point where corporates and their supply-chain partners pursue direct access to capital markets to meet trade financing needs. This development has been observed in corporate finance and could become an important element of attempts to address the global gap for trade finance.

Regulation and Compliance

Trade and trade-related financing have attracted – understandably – the attention of a variety of regulatory authorities concerned about a range of issues. These issues include capital adequacy and reserve levels, anti-money-laundering (AML) measures, countering the financing of terrorism (CFT) and preventing the use of trade as a conduit for illicit activity. However, increased regulation brings increased costs, which lowers both supply and demand. Heightened awareness of the trade finance gap post-crisis has led to calls for capital requirements in trade finance that reflect the actual risk and loss rates of the instruments. The International Chamber of Commerce (ICC) Banking Commission, for example, has been collecting data on credit-related trade finance risk for over a decade, following initiation of this activity by the ADB. The ICC's annual report on the subject has shown that the risk profile of these long-established instruments is negligible even when compared with financing activity often perceived to be lower-risk.

Advocacy efforts over the last decade have been helpful in highlighting the very high credit quality of traditional trade finance mechanisms, the consequent negligible default and loss rates. But there is still work to be done, whether in terms of education and awareness-raising, or in terms of efforts to achieve and maintain risk-aligned capital treatment for trade finance. Market attention to, and understanding of, trade finance is still in its relative infancy.

Similar challenges exist today around compliance and regulatory considerations such as AML/CFT. Banks, regulators and businesses are united in wanting effective regulation and a secure financial sector protected from criminal and terrorist abuse, while ensuring adequate levels of financing and risk mitigation across the architecture of global trade. Consequently, the ADB has devised a trade finance scorecard.[10] The scorecard focuses on identifying priority issues through consultation with international bodies, regulators and industry, and was at the outset framed as an assessment of issues – not of programmes, regulatory entities or industry participants. Follow-on activities related to this ADB initiative may help boost both regulatory efficacy and access to trade finance by bringing a new engagement channel for stakeholders involved in AML, CFT and related compliance matters.

International business, including trade and investment, will continue to appear to be attractive channels (given mechanisms like invoices, letters of credit and others) through which to funnel illicit funds. Accordingly, the regulatory and compliance regime must and will continue to increase its robustness. The evolution is likely to

---

[10]Asian Development Bank (2018) *Trade Finance Scorecard: Regulation and Market feedback*. Available at: https://www.adb.org/publications/trade-finance-scorecard [accessed 13 February 2019].

be around enhanced global coordination and alignment; increased domain expertise across stakeholder groups; and enhanced data collection and analytics aimed at driving regulatory efficacy, impactful investigation and prosecution, and risk-aligned deployment of resources against AML/CFT and other compliance objectives.

Fintech and regtech (regulatory technology) will have a major role to play in this. Market leaders are having success with the application of artificial intelligence in areas like sanctions screening and other core aspects of compliance. This will continue and will run across the spectrum of intelligence, investigation, regulation, compliance and prosecution.

Non-bank Capital and the Trade Finance Asset Class

Non-banks already increasingly participate in the financing of international commerce. Similarly, the global unmet demand for trade finance will be addressed in part through the proactive, systematic attraction of non-bank capital to the business of trade financing. Historically, banks have shared risk by distributing trade finance assets (loans) primarily among themselves. Even until recently this was done on the basis of personal relationships, rolodexes and spreadsheet-based tracking. This model worked because some banks possess sufficient balance sheet capacity to maintain the business on their own books while pursuing new deals, whereas others have opted (or been compelled by balance sheet limitations) to sell portions of their trade finance portfolios to create capacity to underwrite new business. This approach of shuffling assets and capacity between banks has limitations, and is certainly not conducive to the closure of a US$1.5tn global gap in trade financing. That gap represents lost economic development and poverty reduction potential, as well as a significant loss of multiplier-based growth and prosperity.

How can non-bank capital be brought into trade finance? One option that has seen some traction, and will grow over the coming years, is to have asset managers and private equity investors pour capital into funds that are underpinned by portfolios of trade finance (and SCF) transactions. Though theoretically sound – there is significant liquidity in the market today for relatively secure assets that generate adequate returns, as well as a need for new capital in support of trade – practical execution has proved more challenging than the theoretical formulation of the concept.

In part, this is down to a couple of straightforward challenges: there is limited reciprocal awareness between capital markets players and trade financiers, and the awareness is not sufficiently informed. Trade finance assets are not visible to investment managers through key channels like Bloomberg terminals. They must be comparable with other investment options so that investors can make the choices best aligned to their objectives.

Over time, trade financing will see a significant uptick in non-bank activity at the transactional level. Perhaps more materially, it will also see the engagement of non-bank capital in both traditional trade financing and SCF. This injection of net new liquidity will extend globally and will energise cross-border supply chains and new trade corridors, further linking finance to 'real' economic activity.

What is New Under the Sun …

It is tempting to attribute transformative progress in international trade and trade financing to the innovative application of technology, to 3D printing, artificial intelligence, distributed ledger technology and a host of other such developments. However, sometimes the innovations that have the most impact are strikingly simple. Arguably, one of the most impactful innovations in global trade was the invention of a large steel box: the standardised shipping container, now ubiquitous on ships, trucks and railway tracks around the globe.

Containers remain important, but, as local, additive, manufacturing grows, and physical shipments decrease, the future of trade financing may be in understanding how to finance intellectual property and design, or it may be in shaping commercial behaviour. The Banking Environment Initiative and organisations like the International Chamber of Commerce Banking Commission have, for example, looked at the potential for rewarding desirable business practice, such as sustainable sourcing, with better access to financing. Similar initiatives could be designed to support fair trade flows, or trade activity that brings an isolationist state into the global community, increasing international security.

This is not as far-fetched as it may at first appear: a combination of pressure from civil society organisations and public sector stakeholders advanced the development of the Equator Principles. These are a framework for managing environmental and social risks in project finance and have, to date, been adopted by 94 financial institutions in 37 countries. The principles were initially linked to various forms of project finance undertaken by export credit agencies and others in the market.

Once we get past the current shallow dialogue around trade that views international commerce as a zero-sum game, to one that reverts to a more holistic view of trade in an interconnected world, we will be able to shape the next chapter of global commerce. Just as financing periodically shifts from a 'nice-to-have' to being a differentiating competitive proposition, so the political and commercial discourse on trade will realign to a more thoughtful, informed view of international commerce as being rooted in an ecosystem.

Trade financing is likely to become an element of international security. This will naturally be the case once the importance of equitable trade to global security is recognised and it becomes part of the public policy dialogue while also remaining central to the commercial discourse in international commerce.

Financing is the oil in the engine of global commerce: the critical enabler of trillions of dollars annually that flow through the arteries and corridors of trade. Just as 'Aid for Trade' and other linkages between trade and international development have evolved, so shall we see 'Trade for Security' become part of a more thoughtful dialogue on both subjects. Trade financing will be at the centre of such an evolution, not as an esoteric specialism, but as a widely recognised enabler of growth, prosperity and global inclusion within the ever-changing ecosystem of global commerce.

CHAPTER 5

A New Playbook for Banks

William A. Allen

William A. Allen looks at the impact that post-crisis regulation has had on banks' capital and liquidity ratios and how the current – and prospective – macro-economic environment threatens the continued sustainability of banking as we now know it.

In its essence, banking is an information business. Bank deposits are evidence of a certain right to command goods or services. Such evidence is the essence of a market economy, and bankers are the people who keep the records that are necessary to ensure that people know how much they can spend; that they don't spend more than they are entitled to; that their entitlements aren't stolen; and that they can make payments securely to other people.

Banks also perform maturity transformation, which is one of the reasons why the current – and prospective – macro-economic environment threatens the continued sustainability of banking as we now know it. This is an issue not just for the shareholders and staff of the incumbent banks, but also for the government, which has been able to use the banks to promote its own objectives in the past. Further, one of the main casualties of the transition to a more competitive banking industry, heavier on technology and lighter on human contact, is likely to be financial inclusion.

Bank Performance

The stock market is currently (early 2019) taking a dim view of the outlook for UK banks, as it has done for several years. The banks' market valuations are well below the equity recorded in their audited balance sheets. This suggests either that market participants think the assets are overvalued, or that they believe the prospects for earnings growth are poor.

The banks' return on equity has certainly been meagre in the last decade: it averaged 1.9% between 2010 and 2017. To a considerable extent, this reflects the cost of the extensive restructurings that the banks have had to undertake since the financial crisis of 2007/2008, and which are still in progress, alongside the heavy penalties that have been exacted from them as retribution for past misconduct. But even if you exclude these costs, the banks' return on equity averaged only 6.6% between 2010 and 2017 and has not exceeded 10% in any year since 2007.[1]

The Macro-economic Backdrop

Statistics of gross domestic product show a sharp fall during the financial crisis, followed by a gradual recovery, during which the rate of growth has been slower than before the crisis (see Figure 5.1 for the UK).

Economists have debated the possible reasons for the productivity slowdown, and whether we have entered an era of 'secular stagnation', without reaching a consensus. However, a debate does not mean that the problem exists as it is posed. There are serious questions about the measurement of output, and in particular whether the available statistics can properly capture the impact of new products and improvements in quality, and whether they can adequately gauge the impact of the revolution in information technology.[2] For example, particularly since the financial crisis,

---

[1] Bank of England (2018) *Financial Stability Report*, June, chart B.7. Available at: https://www.bankofengland.co.uk/-/media/boe/files/financial-stability-report/2018/june-2018.pdf [accessed 18 February 2019].

[2] The IMF held a 2018 conference on the subject: 'Measuring economic welfare in the digital age: what and how?,' 19–20 November. Available at: https://www.imf.org/en/News/Seminars/Conferences/2018/04/06/6th-statistics-forum.

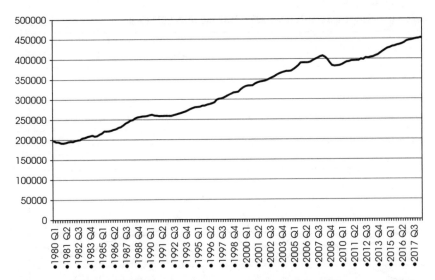

Figure 5.1   UK GDP, chained volume measure, quarterly, 1980–2018 (£m, reference year 2016).

Source: Office for National Statistics.

banks and other providers of goods and services have been obliged to devote increased resources to compliance and quality assurance. The fruits of these efforts are largely not measured, so they show up as a decrease in productivity. Nevertheless, they should properly be regarded as producing something that the public values.

For banks making loans, what matters is the borrower's ability to service the loan. It is not real income but nominal income that counts, since loans are for fixed money amounts. The sustainability of debts depends on the relationship between the rate of interest and the borrower's income, and on the borrower's debt/income ratio. The faster net income before interest payments is growing, the better, and the lower the debt/income ratio, the better.

Comparing the past 5 years with the 5 years leading up to 2007, interest rates have fallen more than income growth (Table 5.1).

Debt burdens – both the outstanding amounts and the annual servicing costs – have decreased relative to income for both households and corporates in aggregate (see Figure 5.2). They look less threatening than in 2007 – much less so in the case of corporates – though that is not completely reassuring, bearing in mind that they proved to be unsustainable in 2007.

Two points stand out. First, debt servicing costs, having fallen as a result of the collapse of interest rates since before the crisis,

Table 5.1   Interest and growth rates, 2003–2007 and 2013–2017 (% p.a.)

	2003–2007 average	2013–2017 average	Difference
Growth rate of nominal gross value added	5.4	3.7	−1.7
Bank of England base rate	4.6	0.4	−4.1
2-year fixed mortgage rate (75% loan-to-value)	5.0	1.9	−3.1

Sources: Office for National Statistics; Bank of England.

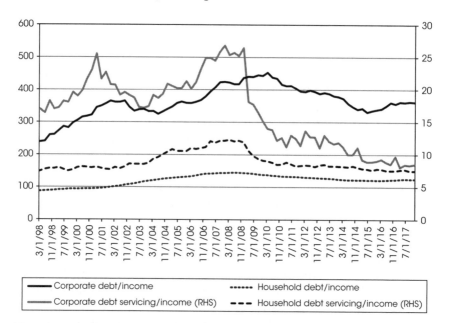

Figure 5.2   Corporate and household debt burdens, 1998–2017 (%).
Source: Adapted from Bank of England Financial Stability Report, June 2018, charts A2, A4, A5.

are now vulnerable to a rise in interest rates. The Bank of England estimates that a 100 basis point (bp) increase in interest rates (presumably it means in its own base rate) would cause the household and corporate debt/income ratios to rise by 1.3 and 1.8 percentage points, respectively, taking households back to their 1997–2006 average. However, with the Bank of England base rate at 0.75% and Consumer Price Index (CPI) inflation currently (as at December 2018) at 2% (on target), there are reasons for thinking that 100 bp might not be enough to keep inflation on target. (Though the uncertainties around Brexit policy make all forecasting challenging.) Second, debt ratios seem to have been more or less stable over the past 5 years or so: there has been no resumption of pre-crisis growth, but nor has deleveraging been prolonged. Tightening of monetary policy, when it happens, is likely to lead to an increase in borrower distress cases and bad debts.

How Banks Make Money

The banks' income growth has been sluggish since the crisis (Table 5.2). On the expenditure side, 'other items', including penalties for past misconduct, have had a serious impact on profits.

Taking deposits and making loans are among the banks' core activities. The Bank of England base rate has been very low since 2008, but banks cannot in practice impose negative interest rates on depositors. The flat yield curve further reduces banks' ability to increase the spread between what they pay for short-term funds and what they can charge for longer-term loans.

For some years after the financial crisis and the credit crunch, banks were under intense pressure to build up their liquid assets. The liquidity squeeze was unnecessarily prolonged as the Special Liquidity Scheme (SLS), introduced in 2008, was terminated prematurely

Table 5.2 UK banks' income, expenditure and profits, 2006–2017 (£bn)

	Income (+)				Expenditure (−)					
	Net interest and dividends	Fees and commissions	Trading income	Other income	Operating expenses	Net new provisions	Other items	Pre-tax profit	Tax	Post-tax profit
2006	54	25	15	17	−67	−9	2	36	−5	31
2007	64	25	3	18	−71	−11	3	32	−4	28
2008	73	23	−32	20	−76	−31	2	−21	5	−16
2009	79	21	3	17	−76	−48	−6	−11	2	−9
2010	71	22	16	18	−80	−26	−20	3	−5	−2
2011	74	21	10	23	−85	−19	−13	11	−2	9
2012	68	21	13	22	−84	−17	−19	4	−2	2
2013	67	20	11	23	−84	−11	−8	18	−4	15
2014	**73**	20	5	22	−85	−1	−9	24	−5	19
2015	84	19	3	22	−86	−1	−16	25	−5	20
2016	79	20	7	29	−93	−6	−10	25	−9	16
2017	85	20	3	28	−94	−5	−11	27	−11	15

Note: Components may not add to totals because of rounding.
Source: Based on data from Bank of England, Bankstats, table B3.2.

in 2012 and banks had to restrain their commercial lending until they had repaid their SLS debts. Further, they had to prepare their balance sheets for the liquidity coverage ratio, an aspect of Basel 3 whose significance is often underestimated. In the circumstances, they were inhibited in increasing commercial lending, so lending spreads widened.

Once the pressures put on the banks by the withdrawal of official assistance and the new liquidity regulation had eased, competition to lend re-emerged, particularly for mortgages, which carry low capital risk weights despite their long maturities. Since 2013, spreads have narrowed again (Figure 5.3), especially for higher-risk mortgages. The narrowing has progressively constrained the scope for profit. Competition is fairly intense: the 'major banks' identified by the Bank of England accounted for only 41% of net lending to households in the year to April 2018.[3]

The banking system as a whole has become more concentrated on personal lending, and mortgages in particular. The share of mortgages in total sterling assets has risen from a quarter to a third since 2010, and the share of unsecured personal lending from 4.7% to 5.7%. Meanwhile, the share of sterling assets in total assets has been little changed at just under a half.[4]

It is hard to see any scope for a new expansion of lending into previously unexplored markets. The amount of bank debt outstanding is already high by historical standards, if not as high as a decade ago. The banks exploited the liberalisation of credit in the 1970s and 1980s energetically, by greatly expanding personal, domestic corporate and overseas lending. They did not leave many opportunities unexamined, and in all these markets they encountered problems before and during the financial crisis. And, in any case, the banks would not necessarily find it easy to finance a new surge of lending.

Moreover, it is perhaps becoming more difficult for the banks to serve some segments of their customary lending clientele. For one

---

[3]Bank of England (2018) *Financial Stability Report,* June, chart B.8. 'Major banks' are Bank of Ireland, Barclays, Co-operative Banking Group, HSBC, Lloyds Banking Group, Nationwide, Royal Bank of Scotland, Santander and Virgin Money (which has since been acquired by CYBG).

[4]Bank of England statistical database; author's calculations.

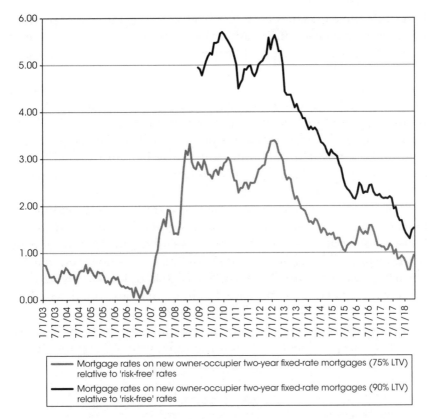

Figure 5.3   Bank lending spreads for 2-year fixed-rate mortgages.
Source: Adapted from Bank of England Financial Stability Report, June 2018, chart A8.

thing, their own funding has become relatively costlier, and their ability to provide services to borrowing customers, such as committed credit lines, is constrained by regulation. For another thing, current economic growth depends to a large extent on the application of information technology. As such, it exploits IT applications that are by nature intellectual property, rather than physical assets. Banks need marketable collateral if they are to finance investment. Intellectual property does not, however, provide good collateral for a bank. It can be stolen, and it may suddenly lose all its value if a piece of superior intellectual property is discovered by a competitor of the borrower.

Another important component of economic growth is infrastructure investment. Its financing is highly contentious, but it is clear that while the banks may earn fees from offering advice and perhaps underwriting services, the resulting assets do not and should not end up on bank balance sheets: they are much better suited to pension and other funds seeking a steady flow of income over the long term.

What other primary sources of income do banks have? Banks were required to implement ring-fencing of their retail operations by the beginning of 2019. It will cost them between £1.7bn and £4.4bn a year.[5] The government's purpose in requiring ring-fencing is to make it possible to confine any future bailout to retail banks, and thereby limit its scope. Ring-fenced banks (RFBs) can take deposits and lend to households and corporates. However, they cannot trade in or underwrite securities, trade in commodities or derivatives, lend to financial companies other than other RFBs and building societies, or buy their securitisations, or operate outside the European Economic Area. It should be noted, however, that the UK banks that got into distress in 2007/2008 did so largely because of activities, such as real-estate lending, that are open to RFBs. Ring-fencing is likely to have many unintended consequences (e.g. by denying RFBs access to upstreamed retail deposits from banks in the Crown Dependencies), and it would be wise to keep the details of the regulations under review.

Risk and Reputation

Banks, like the rest of us, just love a steady stream of income. Fee income has always been attractive for them, because it typically absorbs little or no capital. The banks' main sources of fees are provision of payment services, fees arising from the use of credit and debit cards, and the provision of credit facilities. However, the first two of these are now highly competitive, while the third now carries higher capital and liquidity requirements.

Fee income is so attractive to banks that they have been tempted to mistreat their customers in order to get their hands on it. Cross-selling is fine, but only as long as you are selling something of real value. Payment protection insurance secured fee income for

---

[5] HM Treasury (2013) *Financial Services (Banking Reform) Bill: impact assessment HMT1302*, 1 July. Available at: https://www.parliament.uk/documents/impact-assessments/IA13-21.pdf [accessed 18 February 2019].

the banks, but at an unaffordable cost. They have so far had to pay £32.6bn as redress for mis-selling; but even more seriously, their reputations – which are a different kind of capital – have been very badly damaged. It is too early to assess the total cost.

The big UK banks have for many years been active traders in foreign exchange. Some of them have been active traders in other markets at times, while others have not. The Big Bang of 1986 offered them, and others, the opportunity to become traders in UK securities markets – but none of them has found it an easy ride.

Market makers can earn profits either in a boring way, by taking a dealing spread on customer turnover, or in an exciting way, by taking positions – buying cheap and selling dear. The trouble is that the boring turnover-based profits are modest in scale, and exciting trading can easily make losses.

The big banks have a large domestic customer base which routinely requires foreign exchange for holidays, etc. Unwisely, they long ago alienated these retail customers by charging too much for foreign exchange transactions, and left room for specialist retail foreign exchange trading companies, like World First and HIFX, to take the business away from them. Larger customers are naturally price sensitive and are unlikely to provide a large income from dealing spreads.

Some banks are active market makers in gilts, and some in corporate bonds and other securities. This kind of activity is now much more heavily constrained by the Basel 3 leverage ratio, which bears especially heavily on high-volume/low-risk assets like government securities, and by the higher risk weights now applied by the regulators to market risks. Bankers complain that market making is unprofitable and seem to be devoting fewer capital resources to it. That leaves a gap, and although principal trading firms are ready and willing to trade opportunistically, there is a risk that securities markets will no longer be able to provide the assurance of continuous liquidity.

The Challenges

The big banks, which once employed armies of clerks, were fairly early adopters of information technology. Over the ensuing half a century, their businesses have developed: they have taken on new functions, they have been through mergers and acquisitions, and they have had to meet repeated waves of new reporting and regulatory requirements. Moreover, they have been pressed by governments to extend banking services to customers from whom their chances of earning a profit are negligible, in the interests of financial inclusion and, perhaps, reducing the costs that the government incurs in disbursing transfer payments.

Their IT systems have had to accommodate all these changes, and of course the systems have changed as technology has developed. The changes have had to be incremental, because the business has had to keep going through each change. The result is that the systems that the big banks have today have not been designed holistically, and are much more complicated, messy, prone to breakdown and expensive to manage than a new system designed from scratch would be. The banks have probably made their situation worse by outsourcing the provision of IT services, which are the heart of their businesses.

So, the big incumbent banks are vulnerable to competition from newcomers who are not burdened with this difficult legacy. And the regulatory apparatus in the UK, which a few years ago constituted a severe deterrent to new entrants to banking and a powerful protector of incumbents, is now accommodating and even promoting competition, for example through 'Open Banking', which forces incumbent banks to allow competitors access to customers' accounts, with the customer's permission. The threat is serious.

The banks have also been driven out of a different kind of money transmission – the facilitation of private payments to certain foreign countries, including remittances from immigrants to their families. Here the problem has been regulatory rather than, or as well as, technological. The penalties for violating anti-money-laundering regulations, even if clearly unintentionally, are so severe that some of the risks have become too much for the big banks, and other, smaller, companies have taken their place.

The Banks' Own Plans

The banks' baseline projections, as revealed to the Bank of England, are based on the assumption that current headwinds to profitability will abate. Interest rates, and net interest income, are assumed to increase, the costs of past misconduct will decrease, and the banks plan to cut their running costs. On these assumptions, they project that the return on equity will recover to 17.4% by 2023.[6]

The Bank of England's stress testing in 2017 included a special test in which the banks were required to consider and describe their 'long-term strategic responses to an extended low growth, low interest rate environment with increasing competitive pressures in retail banking enabled in part by an increase in the use of financial technology (fintech). To capture these long-term trends, the Bank calibrated a ten-year scenario, with banks submitting projections for seven years out to 2023'.[7]

The scenario envisages a fall of 40% in the spread between retail lending and deposit rates, and a reduction in the share of household savings held as retail deposits. Economic growth and interest rates are low, and asset price growth is slow; in particular, house prices increase only moderately, though they do not fall. Lending to businesses contracts. Costs of redress for past misconduct continue.

The banks' own projections in this low-growth scenario envisage a return on equity of 8.3% by 2023. That would be well below the baseline, but still much higher than the rates of return they have achieved since 2010. In this low-growth scenario, the increase in profits (from 2016) is attributable, in order of importance, to lower misconduct costs, other cost reductions, increases in non-interest income and lending growth (despite the competition), partly offset by the effect of lower net interest margins. The banks did not envisage taking more risks to counter the effect of lower profitability.

The Bank of England identified the following three main risks to the banks' projections.

(i) Competitive pressures arising from technological and regulatory changes might be more powerful than the banks assume. For example, it is likely to become easier for customers to avoid overdrafts, and the accompanying fees; and the fees that banks are paid when customers

---

[6]Bank of England (2017) 'Stress testing the UK banking system: 2017 results', 13.

[7]Bank of England (2017) 'Stress testing the UK banking system: 2017 results', 13.

use their infrastructure to make debit card payments to merchants are threatened by regulatory changes that will allow non-bank payment providers to initiate payments from customer bank accounts. Cross-selling of products to customers might get harder because customers will be able to ask for their transaction and activity data to be shared with third parties.

(ii) Banks might find it harder than they expect to cut costs. Misconduct charges might not decrease as hoped. Some customers might be more resistant than they expect to switching to digital services. And although cyber risk is of overriding importance to banks, they have not projected any increase in the costs of cyber risk protection, despite their desire to use digital techniques more. Effective protection might be more expensive than they expect.

(iii) The cost of equity might be higher than the banks expect. The banks, in aggregate, project that the cost of equity will settle at around 8% in the stressed scenario. If, however, investors required a higher rate of return, banks would need to restructure or adjust their business models. Their sustainability would be threatened.

All of these reservations seem warranted. Nobody can predict the ferocity of the gale of creative destruction. Cost-cutting is fine if it goes well, but it is risky. The recent experience of TSB's customers is a dire warning of what can go wrong in introducing new IT. Nobody can be sure that more conduct scandals or pseudo-scandals will not emerge from the woodwork. And while advocates of narrow banking predicted that the banks' cost of equity would fall if they took fewer risks and behaved more like public utilities, investors don't seem to have read the script – or perhaps they are not yet convinced that the risks really have decreased.

The challengers have a lot going for them, especially those who communicate with their customers exclusively by electronic means. But the outcome isn't certain: they could make expensive mistakes (e.g. by not realising that credit judgements cannot be wholly automated). Further, without a branch presence, they run the risk of being just another online app.

Brexit

On top of all this is Brexit. The biggest threat to financial stability is a disorderly Brexit, with no agreement and no transition period. At the time of writing, disorderly Brexit remains a possibility. The Bank of England's stress tests suggest that the large banks would be able to withstand the accompanying economic and financial shocks. However, on the Bank's assumptions, some of the contingent capital instruments that the banks have issued would automatically convert to equity, so that the availability of contingent capital resources to the banks in the longer-term future might be threatened.[8]

Brexit will not prevent the banks from continuing their purely domestic operations. It is likely to cause international financial companies and infrastructure to move away from the UK, and UK banks will probably lose some associated business. Compliance costs are likely to rise further. The UK banks' ability to exploit any new opportunities that arise as a result of Brexit is likely to be constrained by regulation and perhaps inability to raise capital.

Conclusion: The Outlook For Banks

The Bank of England has been at pains to stress that banks' capital and liquidity ratios have improved greatly since 2007, so that they are much better equipped to face bad debt problems than they were then. The question remains whether banks can earn enough to remunerate the capital they now have.

In the last prolonged period of low interest rates, which began in the 1930s, the big banks protected themselves from the surrounding financial stress by acting as a cartel and fixing prices: for example, they charged a minimum interest rate for commercial loans of 5%, even though the Bank rate was 2% from 1932 onwards and money market rates were much lower. They did little to promote economic growth, preferring to accumulate government securities. However, they managed to remain financially stable, and the UK avoided

---

[8]Bank of England (2018) *Financial Stability Report*, 3 November. Available at: https://www.bankofengland.co.uk/financial-stability-report/2018/november-2018 [accessed 18 February 2019].

a general banking crisis in the early 1930s, unlike many other countries. Building societies, by contrast, expanded their lending very rapidly in the 1930s, in a way that might have been considered financially irresponsible, but in doing so they financed the housing boom that did so much to promote economic recovery.[9]

The cartel option is not open to the banks now. The threat of a banking crisis is supposed to be contained to acceptable levels by more stringent regulation of capital and liquidity. The banking industry is not going to be a spearhead of economic growth.

---

[9]Samy A (2016) *The Building Society Promise: Access, Risk and Efficiency, 1880–1939*, Oxford University Press, chapter 3.

CHAPTER

Sustainable Investment

The Golden Moment

Elizabeth Corley

Elizabeth Corley examines how increasing consumer interest in sustainable investment has created an opportunity both for investment managers and for society as a whole – one that the industry must now grasp.

Sustainability, *noun definition:* The ability to be maintained at a certain rate or level; the avoidance of the depletion of natural resources in order to maintain an ecological balance.

There is strong and growing interest among individuals in ensuring that their savings, investments and other financial products are 'sustainable'. Barely a week goes by without the publication of a survey showing this growing trend. In April 2019, for example, the Global Sustainable Investment Alliance estimated that global sustainable investment had reached US\$30.7tn at the start of 2018, up 34% in two years. In Europe, the number had reached US\$14tn, a more than 16% increase in 2 years.[1]

---

[1]GSIA (2018) *Global Sustainable Investment Review*. Available at: http://www.gsi-alliance.org/wp-content/uploads/2019/03/GSIR_Review2018.3.28.pdf [accessed 3 April 2019].

But what is sustainable investing? There are almost as many definitions as there are surveys and the rapid development of the market is adding to, not diminishing, the variations in terminology used. As a result, even though customers are interested, they are also confused. So too are their financial advisers, and research has revealed that having a financial adviser makes people less likely to invest sustainably.[2] When UK independent financial advisers (IFAs) were asked why they were reluctant to offer such products, the main reason was lack of understanding combined with concern about the risks of mis-selling in an area where they were not confident of their competence. Fifty-eight percent of advisers believed that training and continuing professional development would help them expand the range of products they offer their clients.

Whenever there is growing demand, innovation of supply and underdeveloped intermediary capability, one of two things can typically happen in a market: either the market matures rapidly so that the depth of professionalism and breadth of infrastructure expands; or the pull of 'easy money' leads to mis-labelling, inadvertent mis-selling or downright mis-representation, such that risks grow to the extent that they tarnish the reputations of those involved.

With sustainable investment, we could be on the cusp of that dilemma. However, I am cautiously optimistic that, far from being a reputational challenge that the finance industry might fumble, this time there is a serious opportunity for us to 'get it right'.

One Decade On

In the years since the global financial crisis, the pace of technological innovation has accelerated beyond measure. A simple Google

---

[2]Davies GB (2018) *Social Impact Investing: Attitudinal and behavioural research.* Centapse. Available at: https://assets.publishing.service.gov.uk/government/uploads/system/uploads/attachment_data/file/659060/Social_Impact_Investment_Attitudinal_and_Behavioural_Research__Centapse.pdf [accessed 3 April 2019].
See also Department for Digital, Culture, Media and Sport (2017) *Growing a culture of social impact investing in the UK.* Available at: https://assets.publishing.service.gov.uk/government/uploads/system/uploads/attachment_data/file/664321/Full_Report_Growing_a_Culture_of_Social_Impact_Investing_in_the_UK.pdf [accessed 3 April 2019].

search of inventions throws up pages of results: the iPhone in 2007; widespread use of touchscreens shortly afterwards; and in 2010 Google launched its Nexus handset running the Android operating system.

Put in the same search question for *financial innovations* and, apart from ATMs (which at over 50 years old are hardly leading edge),[3] virtually all the recognised innovations are in wholesale financial markets: increasingly sophisticated derivatives; block chain applications; electronic trading... This is not to suggest that consumer products and services have not evolved, for example with online banking, crowd-funding and the application of digital technology to the delivery of personal financial services. However, in terms of *products*, nothing stands out that has changed people's lives in a way that they would recognise if unprompted.

Sustainable investment has the power to be noticeable because it can make saving relevant and personal. More than that, it is a vital opportunity for financial services companies to build deeper customer relationships and contribute to restoring trust in the system and its institutions. However, for that to work, we need to agree on how to proceed.

Sustainable Investing: Environmental, Social and Governance (ESG) and Impact Investing – Name Your Terms

In 2005 a ground-breaking study used the term ESG for the first time.[4] It built on a well-established investment concept of socially responsible investing (SRI), which typically allowed savers and investors to exclude certain types of companies from their portfolios for ethical or faith reasons.

ESG went beyond that: it was based on the assumption that ESG factors can be relevant financially. In other words, just as, for example, cash flow, balance sheet and margin are all relevant factors in looking at an investment, so too are ESG data. This was

---

[3]Batiz-Lazo B (2009) 'Emergence and evolution of ATM networks in the UK, 1967–2000', *Business History*, 51(1), 1–27.

[4]Knoepfel I (2005) *Who Cares Wins: Investing for long-term value.* Conference report from the International Finance Corporation. Available at: https://www.ifc.org [accessed 3 April 2019].

backed up by the 'Freshfields Report'[5] and together they formed the foundation for the launch of the UN Principles for Responsible Investing (UNPRI) in 2006. The subsequent growth in signatories has been impressive. The UNPRI has over 1,900 members, as of 2018, representing more than US$90tn of assets.

'Job done', you might say? Sadly not. Despite this extraordinary progress, the investment industry's commitment to responsible and sustainable investing is not generally recognised or understood – and the principles are subject to widely varying application. The lack of recognition is because, in addition to the challenge of proliferation of terms for sustainable investment, many customers also have a more basic concern that investing is too complicated and isn't for them.

For sustainable investment to flourish in a healthy market, consistent definitions are vital, and this will require a clear framework, a taxonomy of terms, translation into straightforward language and a presentation that consumers can relate to. Fortunately, considerable ground work has been done already – at least in the first two areas – and examples of good practice are emerging in the third.

A Clear Framework – The Spectrum of Capital

For more than 2 years, a global group of financial services market participants has been developing a toolkit for financial professionals to use when considering sustainable finance.[6]

The Impact Management Project engaged and consulted widely to produce a 'Spectrum of Capital' that considers the investment approach being used, what the financial goals are (including risk, return and duration) and what the impact goals might be. It is frequently argued that all investment decisions have an impact because they shape capital flows directly. However, these impacts are not always intentional, measured or reported on.

---

[5]Freshfields Bruckhaus Deringer (2005) *A legal framework for the integration of the environmental, social and governance issues into institutional investment.* Available at: www .unepfi.org/fileadmin/documents/freshfields_legal_resp_20051123.pdf [accessed 3 April 2019].

[6]See: https://impactmanagementproject.com/

Choices and strategies for investors on the 'spectrum of capital'

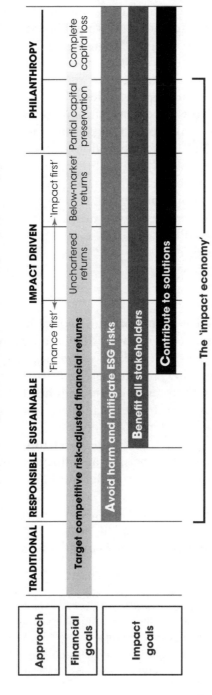

Source: Bridges Impact+ and the Impact Management Project

With the rise of sustainable investing, the attention being given to impact goals and outcomes is growing. For example, the Financial Stability Board's Task Force on Climate-Related Financial Disclosures highlighted the need for consistent information to allow investors, lenders and insurance underwriters to assess and price appropriately climate-related risks and opportunities.[7]

In March 2019, the European Parliament adopted its report on Sustainable Finance Taxonomy, for consideration by the Council in due course. The UNPRI has a methodology that allows an investor to determine the impact of ESG integration on their fund's returns, and to assess the importance of ESG factors on performance through sensitivity analysis. Of course, many investment managers also employ their own proprietary methods to do this, but the extensive resources developed by the UNPRI mean that even small firms can consider ESG with confidence.

What Good is It?

Asset owners, as well as regulators and central banks, now routinely ask investment managers what steps they are taking to avoid harm and/or mitigate environmental risks. Beyond risk mitigation and avoidance, however, there is the potential to consider the impact goals of an investment in terms of the benefits that will flow from it to all stakeholders and/or to seek actively to contribute to solutions that will benefit the planet and/or people.

At the 'impact-driven' end of the spectrum, further analysis of more data is required pre-decision and throughout the life of the investment. This is a more narrow definition of 'sustainability', but the assets under management are still substantial (US$502bn according to 2019 estimates from the Global Impact Investing Network).[8]

The deployment of this capital, with a focus on returns that go beyond financial, allows asset managers to answer their clients

---

[7]TCFD (2017) *Final Report: Recommendations of the Task Force on Climate-Related Financial Disclosures*. The Financial Stability Board. Available at: https://www.fsb-tcfd.org/ publications/final-recommendations-report/ [accessed 3 April 2019].

[8]Mudaliar A and Dithrich H (2019) *Sizing the Impact Investing Market*. Global Impact Investing Network. Available at: https://thegiin.org/research/publication/impinv-market-size [accessed 3 April 2019].

when they ask about the full impact of their savings or investments. Outcomes and benefits, for people or planet, can resonate more with savers and investors than financial returns alone. Developments in digital technology, combined with better-quality data, mean that, for some investment funds, savers already receive updates on impact directly on their mobile devices. Such information on how their money is doing good while it grows makes investment and pensions more personal, less abstract and, when it is delivered well and consistently, contributes to stronger customer relationships and satisfaction.

Sustainable Investment and Consumer Trust

Interest in one's savings and pensions is important for many reasons, not least because from interest grows curiosity, enquiry and contact. Regular contact is one of the ways in which trust can be established and maintained. There are significant variations in levels of trust across the financial services sector, with insurers and investment firms among industries with lower levels.[9] Differentiation between financial services brands is significantly less than in many other industries. This is despite the fact that, on average, 8% of budgets are allocated to marketing in financial services.[10]

To break through and break out from undifferentiated products and perceptions takes a significant, authentic and sustained approach and there is some emerging proof in the UK that this is starting to happen, at least in retail banking. Despite continuing mixed headlines, brand-tracking data from YouGov suggest that in the retail banking sector consumer perception is gradually improving, which is not the case in insurance and investment management.

The Purposeful Business

One of the reasons is that retail banks are paying serious attention to improving the customer experience, with innovations in service

---

[9]Mintel Reports (2018) *The Role of Trust in Financial Services*. Available at: https://reports.mintel.com/display/923664/?__cc=1 [accessed 3 April 2019].

[10]Deloitte (2019) *The CMO Survey*. Available at: https://cmo.deloitte.com [accessed 3 April 2019].

delivery, personalisation and attention to addressing real needs (as opposed to product features). Another reason is that the branding and positioning of banks has been changing, to become more purposeful and more human.

A sense of purpose in an organisation matters. Behaving purposefully matters even more. Governments and the public that businesses serve place particular value on this. Delivering great products and value could be considered a purpose. Doing so in a way that intentionally contributes to sustainability, for example in the achievement of the UN sustainable development goals, is purposeful.

A purposeful business sees the provision of products or services in the context of tackling wider problems, by managing or reducing/eliminating the negative effects of business practices, and/or contributing in a measurable way to improvements that will benefit people and planet.

Customers and employees alike are smart. A product that is badged sustainable but is produced and sold in a way that does nothing to contribute to measurable and intentional improvement in sustainability will ultimately disappoint those who buy, and those who produce it. The challenge for investment business leaders and heads of product strategy is how to test their ideas and delivery of product against the benchmark of a contribution to a purposeful strategy. Without clarity on what 'good' looks like, even well-intentioned product innovations can miss the mark and add to, rather than reduce, scepticism and lack of trust.[11]

The need for business strategy to go beyond profit is increasing in all sectors, not just investment and finance. In July 2018, the UK's Revised Corporate Governance Code was published. The new code places emphasis on businesses building trust by forging strong relationships with all key stakeholders. It also introduces the idea of alignment of company purpose with business strategy.[12] Initiatives at

---

[11]Keaney M (2016) 'What do we really mean by "purposeful" business?', *Marketing Week*, 6 June. Available at: https://www.marketingweek.com/2016/06/06/what-do-we-really-mean-by-purposeful-business/ [accessed 3 April 2019].

[12]Financial Reporting Council (2018) *The UK Corporate Governance Code*. Available at: https://www.frc.org.uk [accessed 3 April 2019].

a European and member state level are also increasing the focus on sustainable finance.[13]

Expectations are growing for corporates, asset owners and asset managers to evidence purpose and a sustainable approach in how they conduct their businesses. Within the investment management industry, there are growing examples of companies stepping up to meet this expectation. The Investment Association of the UK has launched an industry-wide consultation on sustainable and responsible investing; the FRC is consulting on revisions to the UK Stewardship Code, with a wider definition of stewardship in mind. A Green Finance and an Impact Investing Institute are to be established. Hence my cautious optimism.

There is a real focus across the investment management industry on taking sustainable investment seriously, not only as a business opportunity but also as a stewardship responsibility. Naturally there will be firms that excel in their approach – and some that do not. However, we have the opportunity to set the level of expectations for the industry's behaviours and adoption of good practice, to applaud those that aspire to contribute to genuine sustainability, and to work with intermediaries, advisers, pension fund trustees, personal finance commentators and regulators to be explicit about what 'good' looks like.

If we do this well, we will also have the chance to engage transparently with our customers to explain how their money is being put to work to do some good while it grows. As Samuel Johnson said: 'To improve the golden moment of opportunity, and catch the good that is within our reach, is the great art of life.' Never has there been a more important and appropriate time for finance and investment to hone that art.

---

[13]See: European Commission (2018) *Commission Action Plan on Financing Sustainable Growth*. Available at: https://ec.europa.eu/info/publications/180308-action-plan-sustainable-growth_en. Also: De Nederlandsche Bank (2018) *Sustainable Finance Platform*. Available at: https://www.dnb.nl/en/about-dnb/co-operation/platform-voor-duurzame-financiering/ [accessed 3 April 2019].

CHAPTER 7

Living 'Off Income'

Richard Tomlinson

Richard Tomlinson analyses how the demographic shift in the UK has left many people ill-prepared for retirement, often in denial about adequate pension provision and in need of a wide-ranging public debate on the issues.

In his 1983 memoir *Still Life*, the historian Richard Cobb recalled growing up in Tunbridge Wells between the wars. He remembered with particular affection his cousins the Limbury-Buses, a family of four who lived near his parents' home 'in a big Victorian house with a dank, dripping overgrown garden'.[1] What most impressed the young Cobb about the Limbury-Buses was their inertia.

The family had an 'income', allowing Mr Limbury-Buse, born in the 1860s, never to do a day's work in his life, despite originally planning to become a solicitor. Most days, his wife stayed in bed till 3 pm, when she rose to help their elderly maid prepare a lavish afternoon tea. There the couple was joined by Geoff, their bachelor son, who had retired to live with his parents after a nebulous few years in the film industry, and Geoff's unmarried sister Olive, who earned a little pocket money each winter as a skiing instructress in Switzerland.

---

[1] Cobb R (1983) *Still Life: A Tunbridge Wells Childhood*, Chatto & Windus, 84.

With his historian's eye, Cobb grasped what had made the Limbury-Buses' settled routine possible: an economy where a well-invested, index-linked annuity (or preferably several) allowed countless middle-class families to live wholly or partially 'off income', as people put it, before switching the topic of conversation over tea to something less vulgar than money.

Cobb, born in 1917, went on to become a distinguished historian of the French Revolution and Professor of Modern History at Oxford University. As such, he would have been eligible on his retirement in 1984 to a defined benefit pension from the well-endowed Universities Superannuation Scheme (USS), pegged to his final professorial salary. He enjoyed 12 years of productive retirement, writing several more volumes of memoirs until he died at his home in Abingdon in 1996.

The reason to follow Cobb to his own death is not to suggest that he was as financially well off in retirement as the Limbury-Buses had been in the 1920s and 1930s. The thrice-married Cobb appalled his mother by not gaining salaried employment as a university lecturer until he was 38, having spent almost a decade after the Second World War living hand-to-mouth as a student in France. Yet in his later guise as a historian of bourgeois England, Cobb would have appreciated the coincidence that he died just as the universal post-war promise of a secure retirement began to disintegrate, even for the professional middleclass.

Today, the promise has been replaced by a threat: that we will all have to work ''til we drop', as the tabloid press puts it, because none of us will be able to afford to retire. At the core of this doom-laden prophecy is the inescapable fact that the British, like people in most developed countries, are living longer, but not becoming healthier, placing an insupportable strain on the pension system. Public Health England notes that the number of years lived in poor health in England from 2013 to 2015 was 16.1 for men and 19 for women.[2] This naturally raises the question of whether anyone can advise us about how we can avoid the terrible fate of armies of frail elderly people who need to work but cannot, at a price we might be able to afford.

---

[2]Public Health England (2017) *Health Profile for England: 2017*. Available at: https://www.gov.uk/government/publications/health-profile-for-england/chapter-1-life-expectancy-and-healthy-life-expectancy [accessed 12 February 2019].

In actuarial terms, the statistics are stark. In 1948, when the modern state pension was introduced, the average 65-year-old man could expect to live a further 13.5 years, or less than one-quarter of his adult life. Today, average male life expectancy at 65 has stretched to almost 23 years and is slightly higher for a 65-year-old woman.[3] Looking forward, the Office for National Statistics projects that the number of people over the state pension age in the UK will rise from 12.4m in 2017 to 16.9m in 2042.[4]

That increased longevity has gone hand in hand with declining birth rates. In 1964, the height of the post-war baby boom, there were 875,972 live births and the total rate of fertility (the average number of live children per woman) was 2.93, according to the Office for National Statistics (ONS). In 2017, the figures were 679,106 live births and a total fertility rate of 1.76, well below the population replacement rate of just over two children per woman. The result is an increasingly inverted demographic pyramid. The dependency ratio, that is the number of people of state pension age per 1,000 people of working age, was 299.1 in 1982 (when the children born in 1964 turned 18). In 2039, when they are 75, the dependency ratio is projected to be 361, according to the ONS. A smaller cohort of working age adults required to support a larger number of older people, together with an ongoing struggle to boost national productivity, does not bode well for the state pension system.

However, increasing longevity is not only eroding the financial foundations of the state pension system. Over the past quarter of a century, Britain's ageing population has also propelled the wholesale switch by public and private sector employers from defined benefit (DB) workplace pension schemes to much less expensive (and therefore less well endowed) defined contribution (DC) schemes. The sense of grievance felt by employees who believe they are being robbed of a comfortable retirement is unlikely to dissipate after they quit work.

'I can see retirees placing ever greater pressure on the government of the day to raise state benefits to complement a very inadequate private pension top-up,' says Ian Neale, a director

---

[3]Department for Work and Pensions (2017) *Proposed New Timetable for Pension age Increases*. Available at: https://www.gov.uk/government/news/proposed-new-timetable-for-state-pension-age-increases [accessed 12 February 2019].

[4]Department for Work and Pensions (2017).

of Aries Insight, a London-based pension legislation and policy research company. 'People are not going to be willing to accept the huge drop in their income when their salary is no longer available.'

Looming in the background is Britain's seemingly endless, inconclusive debate about how to fund the rising cost of long-term care for older people. All the projections are alarming. For example, in 2015 the parliamentary Select Committee on Public Service and Demographic Change predicted that annual public expenditure on social and health care for older people would increase by 37% between 2010 and 2022, to £12.7bn.[5]

Yet politicians remain paralysed by the challenge of how to meet these costs. In 1999, the Royal Commission on Long-Term Care recommended free nursing and personal care for all older people, funded by general taxation.[6] There is a question mark, of course, over whether that is affordable. One of the problems that besets an ageing population, after all, is that it is less productive. Worker productivity reaches its peak around age 50. In the UK, productivity growth has slowed and is projected to go into reverse around 2030.[7] To prevent this, the country will need to invest in its physical and human capital,[8] rather, perhaps, than in pensions and care homes. The full economic effects of an ageing population are also not captured by analysis of the increased dependency ratio and the likely falls in productivity. As the proportions of people in the over 40 and over 50 age brackets increase, for example, so do private savings, which pushes down real interest rates. As the number of people aged 80+ goes up, care costs rise – as does the need for care workers who may be taken out of other, more productive, sectors.

---

[5]Institute and Faculty of Actuaries (2015) *Pensions and the Funding of Long Term Care*. Available at: https://www.actuaries.org.uk/news-and-insights/public-affairs-and-policy/ageing-population/social-care [accessed 12 February 2019].

[6]The Royal Commission on Long Term Care (1999) *With Respect to Old Age: Long term care – rights and responsibilities*, Stationery Office.

[7]Lisack N, Sajedi R and Thwaites G (2017) 'Demographic trends and the real interest rate'. Bank of England Staff Working Paper No. 701. Available at: https://www.bankofengland.co.uk/-/media/boe/files/working-paper/2017/demographic-trends-and-the-real-interest-rate [accessed 7 March 2019].

[8]Saunders M (2018) 'Some effects of demographic change on the UK economy'. Speech given at the Bank of England, 22 November 2018, 2. Available at: https://www.bankofengland.co.uk/-/media/boe/files/speech/2018/some-effects-of-demographic-change-on-the-uk-economy.pdf [accessed 7 March 2019].

The complexity of addressing the challenges raised by an ageing population helps explain why no political party has so far had an honest debate with voters about the subject. In particular, no party has managed to persuade the same electorate that perhaps older people with sufficient means should pay a greater proportion of their care bill.

The latest retreat came during the 2017 general election, when the Conservative Party backed away from a pledge to make older people with property assets worth more than £100,000 pay for some or all of the cost of their residential and nursing care, on a means-tested basis. This aborted measure was immediately dubbed a 'dementia tax', which at least highlighted a major reason why the cost of care for older people is bound to spiral over the next few decades. There are already about 850,000 people with dementia in the UK, with the Alzheimer's Society forecasting that numbers will double from 1m to 2m between 2025 and 2051.

Dementia in all its terrible forms is not simply an inevitable consequence of an ageing population. In the cruellest clinical sense, the disease can deny a person the ability to plan rationally for their retirement. 'People are afraid of deteriorating mental capacity but don't quite know what to do about it,' says Gillian Dalley, a visiting research fellow at Brunel University who is an expert on the financial abuse of older people. 'The risk is that they leave it too late to make decisions, especially as people can get very stubborn in the first stages of dementia.'

Wealth Protection

Set in this bleak context, the concept of 'wealth management' for the majority of older people seems a misnomer. A better description would be 'wealth protection' in an insecure world where, rationally, most of us will have to work for longer before we retire and then be content with a steep drop in income, not least to pay for all the care we will need in our 80s and even 90s.

At which point, one truth collides with another indisputable fact: overwhelmingly, the baby-boom generation, born in the 1950s and 1960s, is not willing to accept this reality. 'Most people believe they have a right to more than twenty years in retirement, but that's not how the world will work in future', says Alistair McQueen, head of savings and retirement at Aviva. 'Current pension provision is financially unsustainable.'

It is not that baby boomers are too obtuse to understand in a general sense that there may be trouble ahead. In a survey of over 50s in 2018, The London Institute of Banking & Finance found that, when asked what they would do differently if they had their time again, 60% of over 50s would start investing earlier and 58% would save for retirement earlier. Just over a third (34%) said they will have to work longer than planned so they can afford to retire – on average more than 7 years longer than they expected when they set out on their careers. But despite not feeling well prepared for retirement, respondents said it would take a windfall of over half a million pounds before most would call in a financial adviser.[9]

As that suggests, it is easier to postpone a reckoning with reality, an attitude that for many people approaching, or in, retirement is not quite as unreasonable as it sounds. In 2017, as part of a project on 'financial resilience in retirement', the charity Age UK commissioned a survey of retired older people aged between 60 and 89.[10] While most respondents acknowledged the benefits of 'being prepared' for retirement, they agreed that it was also important 'not to worry too much about the future'. Living for today appeared a better option than fretting about incapacity, illness and death.

'There is a balancing act between enjoying one's time now and planning for a future of indeterminate length,' says Lucy Malenczuk, senior policy manager at Age UK. 'You can't ask people to keep putting off their life, especially when they may be watching their own friends and family suffering and dying around them.'

The Advice Gap

The question of how best to provide affordable 'wealth management' services to an ageing population therefore raises a more

---

[9]Tilston H (2018) 'Over-50s think they need a £500K windfall to make financial advice worthwhile', *Insights*, 26 November. Available at: https://www.libf.ac.uk/news-and-insights/news/detail/2018/11/26/over-50s-think-they-need-a-500k-windfall-to-make-financial-advice-worthwhile [accessed 20 March 2019].

[10]Age UK (2018) *Financial Resilience During Retirement: Who is well placed to cope with life events? Summary and implications.* Available at: https://www.ageuk.org.uk/globalassets/age-uk/documents/reports-and-publications/reports-and-briefings/money-matters/rb_apr18_financial_resilience_summary.pdf [accessed 12 February 2019].

specific issue: Will the customer be willing to buy it? Viewed from the seller's perspective, the need for financial advice when planning for old age appears self-evident. Four in 10 British adults do not know how to manage their money, according to the government's 'Financial Capability Strategy for the UK'. This assertion is backed up by figures showing that 16m working-age people have less than £300 in savings, while 8m are in 'serious debt'.[11] In October 2017, the Financial Conduct Authority (FCA) added its voice to the chorus of official alarm, warning that around 15m people, or a third of all workers, were not saving into a personal or workplace retirement scheme to complement their state pension.[12]

Official exasperation is heightened by the knowledge that all the considerable efforts to dispense 'free', taxpayer-funded pension advice since the 1980s have failed to shift British saving habits – or rather, the lack of them. The Pensions Advisory Service, set up in 1983, was joined in 2011 by the Money Advice Service and in 2015 by Pension Wise. These bodies have now been merged into the Single Financial Guidance Body (SFGB), whose remit covers everything from pensions and money guidance to helping 'develop a national strategy to improve people's financial capability'.

Still, the public plods on incapably, with few people bothering to take advantage of all this free advice. 'We have to bridge this gap somehow,' says Neale, 'because otherwise people will continue to make their retirement planning decisions based on what knowledge they can accumulate and their own personal prejudices'. In particular, Neale advocates a public financial and retirement planning service that properly 'advises people rather than simply signposting towards guidance, a solution akin perhaps to the NHS for our health'.

Such a service would need in the first place to overcome the passive attitude towards saving for retirement that has afflicted the British since the Second World War. The roots of this mentality go all the way back to the 1946 National Insurance Act. Once the immediate post-war austerity years were behind them, it was easy for many working-class people to believe – during the 'never had it so good'

---

[11]Financial Capability (2018) *Key Statistics on Financial Capability*. Available at: https://www.fincap.org.uk/en/articles/key-statistics-on-uk-financial-capability [accessed 12 February 2019].

[12]Phillips T (2017) 'Millions forced to work until they drop', *The Mirror*, 17 October.

1950s and 1960s – that the state would always provide them with a comfortable pension.

For a start, the comparison with the immediate past of mass unemployment, followed by war, was so stark. In addition, few people grasped that their National Insurance contributions were paying for their parents' state pensions, not their own (a common misunderstanding that still endures). Besides, there was no need to think about the contribution, since it was generally deducted 'at source' from an employee's pay cheque and therefore did not feel as if it had been paid out of wages. A parallel situation existed with defined benefit (DB) employee pension schemes, whose members ranged from chief executives and civil service mandarins to postmen and coal miners. The only advice anyone required about a DB scheme was to enrol as quickly as possible, since the employer was typically undertaking to pay an agreed, index-linked pension, pegged to a final salary, until the retiree died.

An Englishman's Home and His Pension

The post-war British infatuation with home ownership added another layer of false security when people thought about their retirement; for what could be more agreeable than the thought of doing nothing while you occupied a rapidly inflating financial asset. Since 1980, the average price of a residential UK property has increased approximately 10-fold to about £230,000 (a figure admittedly skewed by the housing boom in London and the south-east). By contrast, average French house prices have less than doubled in the same period.[13]

It is small wonder that so many older property owners see their home as the ultimate insurance against penury in old age. In 2018, research by the Institute for Fiscal Studies found that around 40% of working-age people in their 50s expected to use their primary housing or other property to finance their retirement.[14] Cumulatively

---

[13]CGEDD (2019) Available at: https://www.cgedd.developpement-durable.gouv.fr/house-prices-in-france-property-price-index-french-a1117.html [accessed 12 February 2019].

[14]Crawford R (2018) *Retired People Look Set to Bequeath Rather than Use Most of their Wealth*. Available at: https://www.ifs.org.uk/publications/13041 [accessed 12 February 2019].

this is big money, since around 80% of home owners are over the age of 50. Age Partnership, a financial consultancy for older people, estimated in 2016 that the total housing wealth of the over-55s in England alone amounted to £1.5tn, more than Italy's national GDP.[15]

The social injustice caused by house price inflation and the hoarding of property assets by older people is plain. 'We're reaching the stage where many children and grandchildren are never going to be able to save enough for a deposit for a house unless they can get some assistance,' says Vince Smith-Hughes, head of business development at Prudential. 'We see a lot of clients where money is being gifted to them by their parents, as the only way to get them on the property ladder.'

It does not appear to matter that most financial advisers would argue strongly against investing too much money and hope in property as a potential nest egg, for several reasons. They include the illiquid nature of bricks-and-mortar, the need to pay for another roof over one's head and the crippling level of stamp duty. Yet, time and again, older people place their faith in the nominal value put on their house by an estate agent rather than the sober warnings of pension and financial advisers. 'There is no trust,' says Neale despairingly. 'Many people think property investment is the way to go. The regulators could help rebuild trust in the great majority of advisers and providers who are trying to do the right thing, instead of behaving all the time like a police force focused on criminal activity.'

Here perhaps is the toughest historical lesson of all for the personal wealth management sector. Past mis-selling scandals, such as endowment mortgages in the 1970s and payment protection insurance (PPI) in the early 2000s, would be impossible today precisely because of belated regulatory action. Yet the reputational damage persists, bolstering the resistance of older people to seeking expert advice about their finances rather than relying on their own instincts and judgement.

'I won't see any financial advisers,' one respondent said in Age UK's 2018 report on building financial resilience. 'They're a waste of

---

[15] Age Partnership (2016) *Over 55s Hold more Wealth in their Homes than the GDP of Italy.* Available at: https://careers.agepartnership.co.uk/over-55s-hold-more-wealth-in-their-homes-than-the-gdp-of-italy/ [accessed 12 February 2019].

time … It seems they want to put money in their pockets rather than help you.'[16]

Time to Talk

In sum, the basis for a sensible, reasoned debate about personal 'wealth management' in a rapidly ageing society does not exist. The only certainty is that the debate has to happen soon, before it is too late – not least because the 'pensions freedoms' introduced in 2014 have transferred a daunting load of financial responsibility onto a generation that grew up in an era when their parents and grandparents were mostly passive recipients of state and workplace pensions.

'More and more people are reaching retirement and having to make huge financial decisions about what to do with their pension pot,' says Vince Smith-Hughes of Prudential. 'With a DB scheme, you knew it would pay a certain amount per year, topped up by the state pension. Now, many savers are looking at an accumulated sum of, say, £250,000 and wondering what on earth they should do with it.'

Options include cash drawdowns, equity releases and a range of other measures that are not easily explained in everyday English. One solution is simply to stuff the money in a low-interest savings account and ignore all the dire warnings issued by pension advisers about multiple risks, from inflation to the onset of dementia. This is self-evidently unwise, as Professor David Blake, director of the Pensions Institute at Cass Business School cautioned in the 2016 *Independent Review of Retirement Income*: 'For anyone who understands the risks involved in retirement income provision, it is clear that many […] people will find themselves in the same kind of control as a yachtsman in the middle of the Atlantic in a force nine gale.'[17]

Yet it is also clear that the kind of advice required to navigate these waters will not be cheap, even if more people in future will be disposed to seek help with their bafflingly complex pension 'freedoms'. One fashionable quick fix is so-called 'robo-advice', where

---

[16]Age UK (2018), 14.

[17]Blake D (2016) *We Need a National Narrative: Building a consensus around retirement income*. Available at: http://www.pensions-institute.org/IRRIReport.pdf [accessed 12 February 2019].

computerised questionnaires supposedly guide the clueless individual to a safe retirement harbour, based on their personal financial and actuarial profile. At Prudential, Vince Hughes-Smith says that the notion of 'robo-advice' is misleading, because almost everyone will still need some kind of human interaction with an expert, whether in person or on the telephone. 'People talk about robo-advice as if you go through the whole financial planning process by only liaising with a computer screen,' he says.

As Hughes-Smith argues, it is more realistic to see technology as a way to drive down the cost of advice, which for many people is bound to come as an unwelcome shock.

Consider, for instance, the evolution of workplace pensions, superficially one of the more positive developments in recent years. Between 2012 (when auto-enrolment was introduced) and 2017, the proportion of UK employees paying into a workplace pension scheme has risen from 47% to 73%, according to the ONS.[18] This sounds like good news, reinforced by the fact that the UK's network of DC workplace schemes rests on more solid foundations than continental company-based pensions, because of the UK's National Employment Savings Trust (NEST), which offers access to a pension at institutional pricing 'regardless of the broader market's appetite to supply'.[19]

However, even the best-structured workplace pension system depends on the willingness of its members to contribute at a sufficient level to fund a decent retirement income. Here, there is a double problem. On the one hand, as Neale observes, 'there has been a gradual movement of the pendulum towards employers providing the minimum contribution that they can get away with, as prescribed by auto enrolment'. On the other hand, employees are declining to pay in enough money to shoulder their share of the burden. In 2017, for example, average member contribution rates

---

[18]ONS (2018) Data available at: https://www.ons.gov.uk/employmentandlabour market/peopleinwork/workplacepensions/articles/pensionparticipationatrecord highbutcontributionsclusteratminimumlevels/2018-05-04 [accessed 12 February 2019].

[19]Hurman N (2018) 'Charges, returns and transparency in DC: what can we learn from other countries?' Data available at: https://www.pensionspolicyinstitute.org .uk/media/2903/20181204-ppi-charges-returns-and-transparency-report-final.pdf [accessed 12 February 2019].

in private sector 'career average' schemes was about 8% of their salary, according to official statistics.[20]

'At present rates, many members of workplace schemes will not receive much more than the national minimum wage,' says McQueen, who believes the minimum mandatory savings rate should rise from 8% of salary to 12%. However, what that may leave out of the equation is what people feel they can afford, especially when housing costs are high. The median household disposable income for the non-retired in the UK in 2017/2018 was £30,846.[21] (For retired households it was £23,239.)

Now consider a separate challenge involving 'wealth management' in retirement that cannot be reduced to dry statistical projections. Between 2010 and 2018, the gradual raising of the state pension age (SPA) for women from 60 to 65 'led to a modest increase in employment among women at older ages', according to an analysis by Neil Amin-Smith and Rowena Crawford of the IFS in *The Dynamics of Ageing*.[22]

Yet the same analysis observed neutrally that many women still retire at 60. Frequently, of course, they are not 'retiring' at all, says Hilary Cooper, co-founder and director of the consultancy Caring4Elders and an associate director at The Finance Foundation: 'Nobody ever asked what women in their fifties actually did when they retired at 60 or thought about the fact that in the past a lot of them were looking after their grandchildren when their daughters or sons were out at work, or were taking care of their elderly parents.'

By increasing the state pension age, the government has in practice given too many women a choice of evils, both for themselves and

---

[20]ONS (2018) *Occupational Pensions Schemes Survey, UK*. Data available at: https://www.ons.gov.uk/peoplepopulationandcommunity/personalandhousehold finances/pensionssavingsandinvestments/bulletins/occupationalpensionschemes survey/uk2017 [accessed 12 February 2019].

[21]ONS (2019) Data available at: https://www.ons.gov.uk/peoplepopulationand community/personalandhouseholdfinances/incomeandwealth [accessed 12 February 2019].

[22]Amin-Smith N and Crawford R (2018) 'State pension age increases and the circumstances of older women', in Bank J, Batty GD, Nazroo J and Steptoe A (eds), *The Dynamics of Ageing: Evidence from the English Longitudinal Study of Ageing 2002–2016 (Wave 8)*, 9–39. Also available at: https://www.elsa-project.ac.uk/ publicationDetails/id/13512 https://www.ifs.org.uk/publications/13664

the rest of society. They can either carry on working, thus removing a whole segment of informal care from the teetering welfare system, or they can 'retire' before they are 65 without their full state pension, unless they continue voluntarily to pay NI contributions. Quite simply, it is not fair.

Conclusion

This chapter is not the place to prescribe policy solutions to any of these challenges. What a long-term historical perspective can bring, however, is a keener awareness of how past mistakes can be avoided in the future, as Britain ages and the pension system potentially buckles. Three in particular stand out.

First, it is wrong to see retirement planning and 'wealth management' for older people as a purely financial matter. 'It's never just about money', Age UK concluded in its report on building financial resilience. 'Older people think of their finances in the context of their life as a whole. To engage older people, financial matters should be approached as part of other aspects of retirement, like relationships and health.'

Second, politicians of all parties need to find the courage to tackle the consequences of increased longevity and inadequately funded state, workplace and corporate pension schemes. This is easier said than done when votes are at stake, as shown by the dismal trail of postponed and then quietly shelved pension and social care reforms over the past 25 years. 'Politicians have to encourage people to cut back on spending and save more money,' says McQueen. 'But that is not politically popular with voters and there is a big risk that the can will get kicked further down the road.'

Third, the public needs its own dose of sober realism. Contrary to popular belief, the British are not naturally a nation of savers. Too many of us spend too much, too soon, while nursing delusory dreams about 'sorting out' our retirement once the mortgage is paid off. 'We have to put our hand in our pocket and salt it away and that requires significant self-discipline,' says Neale.

An instructive example of self-discipline in action can be found in the UK's network of credit unions. These admirable institutions, with their emphasis on thrift, honesty and reliability, are also substantial lenders. In June 2017, the UK's approximately 300 credit unions had total outstanding loans of £803m, against deposits of around

£1.25bn. A significant number of the 1.3bn people who borrow from credit unions lead lives that are right on the edge of harsh poverty. Yet the 'wealth management' advice given by credit unions to their neediest members is applicable to anyone who takes responsibility for their finances. 'Credit unions are trying to get people to start saving as a habit,' says Matt Bland, head of policy at the Association of British Credit Unions. 'If you join a savings union you have to save a certain amount every month, even if it is only a few pounds.'

Bland explains that a diligent credit union member who makes regular contributions over a long period of time is still unlikely to build up enough 'wealth' to finance a pension. Nonetheless, if they stick to the task, they should avoid piling up debt as they enter retirement. 'They might not have enough to sun themselves by the Mediterranean, but they will be a lot better off in later life than if they had borrowed more and saved less.'

It is hard to disagree with this sound advice and, as Britain's lamentable personal wealth management history since the Second World War demonstrates, even harder for most people to follow it.

CHAPTER

Power to the Customer

Disrupting Banking

Anne Boden

> Anne Boden explains the thinking behind the launch of her fintech retail bank, why retail financial services will be disrupted and the rise of marketplace banking.

After witnessing Amazon transform the way we shop, Airbnb remodel our holiday aspirations and Uber shift our travel plans up a gear, it was only a matter of time before consumer attention turned to banking.

It took a while for banks to embrace this change in expectations, despite a long-held, uneasy sense that improvements needed to be made to retail banking. Most early efforts to explore the zeitgeist were clumsy too. In fact, it was an initiative to 'talk to' digital natives that first prompted me to think about starting a new bank that did meet the needs of modern, connected consumers. As chief operating officer of Allied Irish Banks I was involved in the opening of a high-tech branch in Dundrum, Ireland in 2013. The branch was given the enticing modern moniker of The Lab. Yet, as I looked along the row of PCs being made available to customers so they could log in and talk to our advisers elsewhere, I realised that this was not very different from what most people could already do with a laptop from the comfort of their own homes. It was a very long way indeed from the disruptive business model that had already irrevocably changed other industries.

I thought long and hard about what customers expected from a retail bank as I started to plan Starling, the mobile-first bank, which launched in 2016. We all have complicated relationships with money. It doesn't matter what background you come from, rich or poor, emotions around what we spend and save are hard to control because they are so closely entwined with our sense of self-worth and shaped by our social circumstances. While, for example, those raised in thrifty households are more likely to be diligent savers, if our close friends have nice cars, or top-of-the-range electronics all over their homes, it is highly likely we'll follow their lead, even if it stretches our finances to the limit. While it is up to each individual to take responsibility for their own finances, the big question is this: Is there anything that banks could do to make this process easier?

Disruptive online models such as Amazon, Airbnb and Uber have already paved the way in showing that customers readily respond to products and services that make things simpler. People want to feel appreciated and valued and that the businesses they patronise are putting them first. They also want to know exactly what they are paying for at all times.

Looking at it from the customer viewpoint, it was easy to see where retail banking had been getting it wrong. The banking model was characterised by a lack of transparency, perhaps more so than any other industry. The fee structure was complicated and opaque, frequently leaving customers frustrated and confused by unexpected payment penalties that sent them plunging into the red (which can then set off further fees, pushing an account into a downward spiral).

There has also been an apparent one-size-fits-all strategy, where banks would frequently aggressively push add-on products, regardless of whether or not they actually suited an individual. Account holders could be forgiven for thinking that too little attention was being paid to getting to know them as an individual, much less respect them as a valuable customer. As for when something went wrong, even the growing power of social media didn't always seem to encourage many large banking groups to listen to, and resolve, what often turned out to be significant complaints.

While high street banks have offered apps for a while, they can be limited in functionality. Certainly, when apps are not user-friendly, it is easier to, well, not use them. This makes it easier for anyone who perhaps prefers not to think about money day-to-day to ignore any potential problems.

The global credit crisis of 2008 didn't help either when it came to one of the biggest issues with banks: trust. And, arguably, not a great deal has been done since to correct this view. Plus, there is the ever-present, somewhat thorny issue of data. While banks have long insisted that they have been doing their utmost to protect customer data, there's a niggling feeling that this may not always be the case. Once again, lack of transparency is the issue.

As I imagined my mobile-only bank back in 2014, I had a clear starting point. In my view, banking was broken. Without a doubt, it was time for banking to be disrupted, just as retailing, travel, health and leisure industries had been before it. We needed to approach things in an entirely different way. What made that possible was a number of technological developments, in particular smartphones, high-speed mobile networks and the very widespread use of application programming interfaces (APIs).

At their simplest, APIs represent a kind of language that lets one product or service exchange data with another. The underlying theme of this kind of disruption is the unbundling of supply and service. Banking has come late to the unbundling revolution. But now, the sector is ripe for it and for the kind of transformation that will allow customers to pick and choose and pay for applications as they use them.

As a starting point, I thought about how banking services should be 'always on', offering an immediate and meaningful response at any time of the day or night. The service I pictured should not just restrict itself to doing its job and working 'OK' either. It needed to be something that was enjoyable to use. Stressful operations, such as account opening or setting up payments, needed to be super-fast and incredibly straightforward. It was important too to give customers all the tools they wanted, so they felt in full control of their finances, rather than always experiencing that somewhat helpless feeling that their bank is keeping them at arm's length.

Most of all, the entire banking process needed to be seamless. The reason the disruptors have been successful is that they have perfected the delivery of products and services in an accessible and visible way. Customers are accustomed to seeing at a glance what they owe on utility bills and how simple changes in behaviour will save money. They know that when they log on to a comparison site for insurance, they will find all their details there, stored and ready to go. Buying a new mobile phone? You'll find it activated and ready to use, straight from the box. It doesn't matter what it is: the emphasis is that the product or service is there for the convenience of the customer, not the business delivering it. For my new banking service this meant looking at the customer journey and finding out how to give them the best possible experience through digital means.

At that time, with fintech in its infancy, my wish list did seem rather ambitious. I also knew how challenging technology could be in this sector, thanks to a lifetime working in so-called traditional banking. In fact, technology has always been one of the sector's biggest bugbears since many large banking groups still rely on outdated, legacy technology. Some systems have origins going back decades, with each new iteration of IT having to be bolted precariously onto the last. Any big leaps forward are virtually impossible because even small tweaks risk bringing the whole lot crashing down. There have been plenty of well-documented banking IT disasters, with one of the most notable recent ones being TSB's attempt to migrate customers to the platform belonging to its new owner Banco Sabadell. The subsequent IT failure cost the bank £178m and in Q3 2018 over 16,000 people switched out of TSB.

One of the greatest benefits of building a bank from scratch is that you can get rid of all the things that don't work and would hold it back. For example, you are not stuck with separate data silos that stop you offering the customer a single view of their finances. My previous experiences also showed me how outdated and detrimental many of the accepted working practices were in the hugely corporate world of banking. In this very hierarchical environment, any new product or service can take months of planning. Dozens of different people from dozens of different departments will be involved and, even then, there is no guarantee that the end result will see the light of day. In any technology-based project, for every US$100m spent, it was not unusual for US$99m of that to be disbursed on everything from committees, to governance, to contingency. Plus, don't forget, I was envisaging something that meant introducing a large range of new products. In fact, I was creating an entirely new product altogether: a current account fully embedded in the user's life.

Eradicating bureaucracy was high on my list of priorities. I knew that once we had put in layers of committees, project managers and processes (or checkers to check the checkers), we'd have lost. By ignoring the accepted hierarchical, or physical, structure, it became easier to use up-to-date working practices such as agile working, automated testing and continuous delivery. Most importantly, though, I wanted to completely eradicate the concept of an IT department. If technology is in everything you do, then you don't need to have a department for it: it *is* everything you do.

If we had followed the usual accepted practice, where each new part of the service was months in the planning, followed by further months of building and testing, the next logical step would have been the 'big launch'. Generally, this is done in the early hours of the weekend, so that if it all blows up there is minimal disruption. Instead, once we'd built and launched the beta of the app, we embarked on a programme of constant, incremental innovation. Rather than working on a few huge developments, our teams worked on dozens and dozens of small continual improvements. Once something has been developed, the goal at Starling Bank is to get updates released in under an hour. Compare this to a large bank which would typically take three months or more to release a product following extensive testing and sign-off. Starling Bank aims to run around 15 fully compliant updates to its core banking platform each week. I don't remember a single day since the bank was launched when we have not released at least something, but if that day did come I think the entire team would be pretty gutted.

Of course, all this requires a considerable tolerance for mistakes. While we never ever want to see our customers harmed, I'll put my hand up and admit it: we do occasionally release something that doesn't work as we'd hoped. That's fine, we roll it back and change it and I am pretty sure we do it fast enough that most people don't even notice. Even if they do, the magnitude of the impact will always be tiny because the improvements to the service are consistently small and incremental. Also, we have programmed each part of the application to react independently, so if something does break, the whole lot doesn't go down.

We don't just sit back and wait for mistakes to happen either. We regularly break things on purpose, just to see what happens. We use a piece of technology based on one pioneered by Netflix called Chaos Monkey, which will randomly disable parts of the system to see how everything else responds to the outage. The scale of failure is at a far greater rate than anything that might happen in real life, so we are constantly fully prepared for pretty much any surprise.

The crucial thing is, we are constantly innovating. Our culture is one where we readily accept mistakes. What we won't ever accept is lack of innovation and delivery. No one on the Starling team is ever scared to put their hand up and say 'we got that wrong'. Besides, the way our internal communications systems are set up, there is nowhere to hide. We use a cloud-based team collaboration tool called Slack, which everyone monitors all the time. Someone will pop up and ask for X, and elsewhere someone will invariably respond: 'granted'. This is great for a number of reasons: it makes our office a friendly, informal place to work, but at the same time there is a built-in audit trail. Everyone knows what is happening and everything is kept open to encourage a constant exchange of ideas.

Our objectives have been helped considerably by the European Union's introduction of Revised Payment Service Directive (PSD2) and by the UK's equivalent, Open Banking. The fact that developers can now freely use a bank's data via APIs to create new financial products and services is to everyone's advantage and has ultimately offered more choice to customers. It promotes greater transparency too, since customers can actively compare products, which can only ever be a good thing. Competition is nothing to be feared: it just means we all need to up our game. All the time.

One of the most positive developments to come out of PSD2 and Open Banking has been marketplace banking, which is where we provide our customers with direct access to various third-party apps, from mortgage companies, to insurance brokers. These carefully chosen partners are integrated with the bank app, so, say, if a customer was seeking a mortgage, they could opt to share their data with the mortgage brokers we work with in order to simplify the whole process. The mortgage broker will have real-time access to the customer's financial situation, and will therefore be able to quickly recommend the best possible deal without the customer having to go through a mound of paperwork and checks beforehand. Once again, transparency is key. Data are owned and controlled by customers and nothing can be shared with third parties unless it is authorised by a customer. This is a world away from previous banking culture, which seemed more geared to 'owning' the customer and where account holders were warned they were breaching their terms and conditions if they shared their data.

We've not kept all our developments to ourselves either. We know first-hand that all the best improvements come through cooperation, so we have opened up our marketplace to outside developers to see what they can come up with. We've run a hackathon event, inviting some of the brightest fintech minds to meet and build their own products using the Starling API. A number of inspiring new payments and banking apps came out of this, again which are all positive developments for the customer and retail banking as a whole.

So, have these improvements met the original brief? Has fintech truly managed to disrupt banking and offered an entirely new, more accessible and, dare I say it, enjoyable service? I like to think so. Right from the beginning, the process of opening a Starling account takes just minutes and checking in after that is easy, thanks to facial recognition which identifies account holders. Ditto setting up direct debits and standing orders, or even one-off payments to friends. One of the most powerful aspects of our mobile accounts is instant insights into what individual customers are spending, and where, with alerts on any activity on the account, whether it is card payments, ATM withdrawals, or standing orders.

Our accessible approach goes a long way towards shaping a better attitude to money. When it's easier to see what is going where, and that everything is properly accounted for, there is less chance of surprises.

We don't have all the answers. We know that. Collaboration is the way forward and constant incremental improvements are key. Open Banking should help foster that. I am sure I am not the only one who is excited to see just how much further banking can change in the months and years ahead. Each new development is another step towards making sure customers are in complete control of their own financial destiny, which is just the way it should be.

C H A P T E R

RIP Libor

Richard Northedge

Richard Northedge examines how Libor developed, why it became unfit for purpose and what it tells us about the evolution of financial markets.

The London Interbank Offered Rate was created in the late 1960s as a way to buffer the exposure of banks, which were lending long term, to fluctuations in their short-term funding costs.[1] When Libor was conceived, financial markets were very different. Capital and banking markets were domestic, with little cross-border activity, and most corporates had a 'house bank' that handled all of their business. Market participants tended to know each other personally and corporate governance was not necessarily codified. Market misbehaviour could often be tackled with social sanctions. The Governor of the Bank of England, for example, was supposedly able to stem bad behaviour by raising his eyebrows, something that might not be particularly effective today.[2]

---

[1]Zombanakis M (2012) 'The life and good times of Libor', *Financial World*, June, 27–28.

[2]House of Commons Treasury Committee (2012) 'Fixing Libor: some preliminary findings', 99. Available at: https://publications.parliament.uk/pa/cm201213/cmselect/cmtreasy/481/481.pdf.

Despite the relative cosiness, it was a time of change. In particular, the so-called 'eurobond' market had just started, with its home in London. As the associated 'euromarkets' grew, so did the need for interbank funding. Then, as City banks increased in size, complexity and global reach, the importance of Libor increased with them and it was adopted as an international benchmark for short-term interbank loans in the mid-1980s. Libor not only allowed the banks to compare their short-term funding costs with the market rate, it was itself treated as a risk-free rate and used to determine rates for bonds, commercial paper and interest rate derivatives. Andrew Bailey, chief executive of the Financial Conduct Authority (FCA) recently cited the latter use as 'an important reason for reform', noting that 'it is striking with the benefit of hindsight to think how long and to what an extent this has gone on'.[3]

From the mid-1980s, the portfolio of Libor benchmarks expanded, as did the panel of banks providing data, apparently adding to the prestige and accuracy of the daily yardstick. Initially, Libor was calculated for sterling, dollar and yen borrowing, but the range of currencies reached 16 before the euro amalgamated European foreign-exchange rates. The number of borrowing periods swelled too, to cover tenors from overnight to 12 months. Other countries launched their own versions of the successful interest-rate measure – Tibor in Tokyo, for instance, or Euribor in the eurozone – but London retained ownership of Libor. Not only does Britain's timezone sit centrally between America and Asia, but sterling dominated finance in a divided Europe.

Libor's reputation grew as it gained usage, and it gained usage as its reputation grew. It became the global benchmark of choice for corporate treasurers, life companies, pension funds and investors. The booming bond markets and the growth of syndicated loans added to the appetite for Libor. The number of basis points above Libor that had to be paid served as a proxy for a credit rating. And Libor effectively moved from wholesale to retail markets when applied to student loans or mortgage lending: the interest on most US variable-rate home loans is linked directly to the London rate.

---

[3]Bailey A (2018) 'Interest rate benchmark reform: transition to a world without Libor'. Speech given in London, 12 July. Available at: https://www.fca.org.uk/news/speeches/interest-rate-benchmark-reform-transition-world-without-libor [accessed 20 February 2019].

Estimates of the value of financial instruments priced on Libor comfortably top US$300tn, with 3 month dollar-denominated rates by far the most popular.[4] Yet the pricing of all these enormous and intertwined financial commitments was (and still is) dependent on a small panel of bankers reporting rates on what could be thin trading volumes: the tail wagging the dog. The value of bonds being issued, or of mortgage loans being made, massively outweighed the amount of funds passing between the banks that reported interbank prices. Pension funds and others were valuing huge investments without much – or sometimes any – market data to underpin the prices. However, to put this into context, Libor was not the only London market mechanism that lacked initial rigour. The FTSE 100 share index, for example, was not launched until 1984. Before that the FT 30 share index was calculated once an hour using prices collected by young staff visiting jobbers on the Stock Exchange floor and bringing back paper lists to the newspaper's office to be crunched by men with slide rules.

The Evolution of a Gentlemen's Hypothesis

Administration of Libor was taken over by the British Bankers' Association (BBA) in 1986, with computation handed to what became Thomson Reuters. The methodology remained much the same: the panel for each currency/tenor reported on the price it could borrow at just before 11 am each working day and the top and bottom submissions were disregarded to exclude outliers. Then, after verification and calculation, the average was published between 11.30 am and noon. Even in 2012 there were still 15 currencies, each with 10 borrowing durations, which meant 150 calculations every morning.

The question posed to the panels, however, did change in 1998. Instead of being asked 'At what rate do you think interbank term deposits will be offered by one prime bank to another prime bank for a reasonable market size today at 11 am?', the wording became: 'At what price could you borrow funds, were you to do so, by asking

---

[4]HM Treasury (2012) 'The Wheatley review of LIBOR: final report', 76. Available at: https://assets.publishing.service.gov.uk/government/uploads/system/uploads/attachment_data/file/191762/wheatley_review_libor_finalreport_280912.pdf [accessed 20 February 2019].

for and then accepting interbank offers in a reasonable market size just prior to 11 am?' As the current administrators of Libor point out, that meant Libor went from 'being a hypothetically offered rate to a hypothetically transacted rate'.[5] It also meant that the assumptions about market behaviour that had held sway in the late 1960s, before Big Bang and globalisation – in which banks would 'offer' short-term funding to their partner banks in a market that could still be overseen by a small number of institutions – no longer held. It is hard to know whether 'gentlemen's agreements' and 'governor's eyebrows' ever really functioned as well as has been suggested, but when the City still had large numbers of small firms and many deals involved personal relationships, exposures were managed differently. The problem with Libor, when large sums in far-away places are at stake and bankers' primary loyalty is often to their bonus, is that hypothetical questions can have subjective answers. Banks could report a price even when there had been no transaction. That did have benefits. It enabled expert wholesale market participants to price a market even when market liquidity was low. However, it also unintentionally paved the way for the less meticulous, the mischievous, the malevolent or the immoral to make up responses.

Libor's potential weaknesses were, however, largely overlooked – particularly as money markets prospered. But there were many flaws. Governance was one: the rate was being set by bankers, for the same bankers. There was an oversight committee, but it too comprised those bankers and lacked transparency or sanctions. That presented scope for conflicts of interest. Further, despite increasingly formal regulatory regimes covering finance, Libor remained an unregulated activity and the rate-setters did not need to be approved persons. Within the reporting banks, compliance and risk management could be weak. And the whole system relied on trust rather than regulation when, elsewhere in the City, rulebooks were replacing such relaxed behaviour.

Ironically, some measures aimed at strengthening Libor were actually potential weaknesses too. Increasing the size of the reporting panels should have made them more robust, but in fact brought more marginal borrowers into the calculation. The Libor concept

---

[5]ICE Benchmark Administration Ltd (2015) 'Second position paper on the evolution of ICE LIBOR', 28. Available at: https://www.theice.com/publicdocs/ICE_LIBOR_Second_Position_Paper.pdf [accessed 20 February 2019].

assumed that all banks are equally creditworthy and that lending between them is risk-free. In practice, however, banks are not homogenous and have different credit risks. So, while a small panel of prime banks might be borrowing on roughly equal terms, adding less-prime lenders would mean their respective rates were no longer comparable. Further, publishing each bank's submissions each day might have seemed a welcome display of transparency, but it revealed which banks were forced by the market to pay premium rates to secure funds. When the credit crunch came, banks having trouble borrowing that had submitted the real rate would have been forced to advertise their difficulty worldwide – potentially cutting them out of the markets and tipping them into insolvency. Submitting a fictionally low figure avoided compounding existing problems.

The (Credit) Crunch

The scene was thus set for the scandals that have brought Libor close to its end. In the run-up to the financial crisis of 2007/2008, many banks had a model far removed from the longer-term and relationship-driven approach familiar in the late 1960s. They were highly leveraged and relied on being able to roll short-term, whole-sale funding. That funding did not necessarily come from other banks, or even from the same jurisdiction. Indeed, when US-based money market funds 'broke the buck' in September 2008, after the collapse of Lehman Bros, dollar funding to non-US banks dried up.[6] This was a significant problem, because European banks had foreign assets (in all currencies) of over US$30tn in early 2008 – and no foreign currency deposit base to back them. Libor – which had closely tracked the bank rate in previous years – jumped sharply. The Fed stepped in to ease access to dollars. Later, central bank measures such as the Bank of England's funding-for-lending scheme provided finance without the need to use the interbank market.

The credit crunch was a challenge for Libor in a number of ways. With fewer actual deals on which to base the information being

[6]Baba N, McCauley RN and Ramaswamy S (2009) 'US dollar money market funds and non-US banks', *BIS Quarterly Review*, March, 65–81. Available at: https://www.bis.org/publ/qtrpdf/r_qt0903g.pdf [accessed 20 February 2019].

passed to the Libor collators, panel banks increasingly had to resort to subjective submissions. Some put forward figures that deliberately flattered their own institution by pretending it could borrow more cheaply than it could; some took the opportunity to make a turn for their desk when low volumes and volatile markets threatened profits (and bonuses). The practice of ignoring submissions in the top and bottom quartiles – usually the highest and lowest four – should have excluded the extreme outliers, but it meant that a bank which deliberately depressed its high figure could move from the top band into the middle quartile where its inaccurate submission would be included in the Libor reckoning. At times during the crisis, though, so many banks were submitting false figures that rejecting the upper and lower quartiles might not have been enough to exclude all fictitious entries. Rather than being the work of a rogue trader, some 20 global banks have been cited as involved in the scandal. Indeed, it emerged that Libor was an intrabank scandal as well as an interbank affair: traders were colluding with dealers in rival banks to coordinate their distorted submissions. It is also likely that some dealers had always been lax in making their late-morning reports. The rate submitters did not trade on the resultant Libor calculation; they contributed figures for the benefit of others in their own bank and elsewhere. It would not be surprising if busy bankers more interested in their next deal (or lunch) left the task of conveying the figure to an uninterested junior who submitted a vaguely correct number for calculation, knowing it would be discarded if wrong. With so many figures to report each day, some submissions were inevitably erroneous. Equally, that junior may not have spotted a crooked figure. Revelations in the subsequent court cases should dispel any false impression that Libor was being set by the sort of investment bankers seen in corporate finance or research departments: many money-market traders might regard it as a compliment to be called crude or unsophisticated. The banter between desks referred to champagne celebrations or drinks at Greek bars for favours. Even innocent traders called each other Dude, Big Nose, Sarge or Danny the Animal.

And their rate discussions were argued openly and recorded by their employers – so available to compliance departments. Misreporting might have become so common that dealers failed to realise the magnitude of their misdemeanours; maybe they regarded it as a matter merely between them and Libor, or saw it as no more than a chance to make a profit or boost their bank's standing, ignoring the ramifications for the holders of trillions of dollars of instruments around the world. Lying over a basis point or two, even if averaged against some honest submissions, was enormous when multiplied over the affected debt dependent on Libor. A combination of deceit, slackness, lax supervision or bosses turning a blind eye had colossal consequences.

The Culture and the Cost

A world sent into recession by the financial crash wanted someone to blame. And within the whole banking industry, the Libor traders seemed to meet that demand. When distinguished directors were evading censure, never mind trial, the dudes on the dealing desk looked a suitable sacrifice. Heads rolled – some of them into court, charged with criminal behaviour. Because Libor setters were not regulated, the Financial Conduct Authority had no powers to discipline them and their activity was not necessarily market abuse as defined by the Financial Services & Marketing Act. It was left to the Serious Fraud Office to pursue prosecutions, but in the end, few charges turned into convictions and the longest jail sentence of 14 years was reduced on appeal to 11.

The regulators were more successful in reprimanding the banks. Barclays was an early target, when it was fined £59.5m in 2012 by the Financial Services Authority (now the Financial Conduct Authority) and the USA followed with a US$360m penalty. Adding in European regulators, the fines for Libor offences and parallel rigging of currency markets eventually totalled US$9bn. The cost of settling civil claims has been estimated at up to another US$35bn. UK chancellor George Osborne said fines should come from bonus pools and the proceeds diverted to good causes: the memorial to the British troops killed on D-Day, announced in 2019, will be built with £20m from Libor fines.

Even as the punishments were being carried out, the inquests began. The BBA launched its own review of Libor's effectiveness in 2008. The House of Commons Treasury Select Committee looked at the subject, as did the new Parliamentary Committee on Banking Standards. Regulators in Canada, the European Union, Switzerland, the USA, Japan and the UK investigated. In 2013 Iosco, the International Organization of Securities Commissions, published a framework of principles for benchmarks used in financial markets,[7] backed a year later by the Financial Stability Board.

In Britain, Martin Wheatley, a former deputy chief executive of the London Stock Exchange and chairman of FTSE International, was asked to review Libor prior to becoming head of the Financial Conduct Authority. His detailed report concluded that Libor should be reformed rather than replaced but recommended that it be regulated, with key people requiring approval, and the regulator permitted to prosecute manipulation.[8] Market-abuse rules needed tightening too, the report said, and it proposed that submitters be chosen from a wider range of banks, become subject to a code of conduct, keep better records and be externally audited. It also suggested fewer currencies and maturities, and called for a new and more independent Libor administrator. However, the core of the scandal was beyond Wheatley's brief: he was looking at Libor's weaknesses, not the culture that made people want to exploit them. The City's (unofficial) motto is 'My word is my bond', but for this adjunct of the bond market, the banks' word could no longer be trusted. It should not need a regime of regulation, audit, compliance and oversight to ensure fair play. Banks were asked by their trade body to supply accurate rates and they chose to offer false figures instead. The pressure of the financial crisis could not be blamed for a lapse in standards. The transgressions at Barclays dated back to 2005.

As Barclays staggered under the unfolding scandal, it asked Anthony Salz, a respected City lawyer who had moved from Freshfields to Rothschild, to review its failings.[9] His 244-page report blamed 'cultural shortcomings'. The bank had become 'too clever by half' and senior managers did not want to hear bad news. He said Barclays was too focused on short-term financial performance and a culture that put pay and bonuses above the interests of customers and clients. 'Pay contributed significantly to a sense among a few that they were somehow unaffected by the rules. A few investment

---

[7]IOSCO (2013) 'Principles for financial benchmarks: final report'. Available at: https://www.iosco.org/library/pubdocs/pdf/IOSCOPD415.pdf [accessed 20 February 2019].

[8]HM Treasury (2012) 'The Wheatley review of LIBOR: final report'.

[9]Salz A and Collins R (2013) *Salz Review: An independent review of Barclays' business practices*. Available at: https://s3.documentcloud.org/documents/675820/report-faults-culture-at-barclays.pdf [accessed 20 February 2019].

bankers seemed to lose a sense of proportion and humility.' It was an attitude that infected Barclays' other business too, but Salz concluded that the bank was driven by a need to win – in both retail and investment banking. 'Winning at all costs comes at a price: collateral issues of rivalry, arrogance, selfishness and a lack of humility and generosity,' he warned. 'The absence of a common purpose or common set of values has led to conduct problems, reputational damage and a loss of public trust.'

Attempts at Reform

Ethics ought to be seen as an asset rather than a liability, a quality that gives a bank a competitive edge. For some banks submitting Libor rates integrity was regarded as dispensable. The whole finance sector has suffered from this devaluation of trust. Because bankers had shown they could not be trusted, the City rulebooks got longer and the regulators tougher. A committee chaired by Lady Hogg, a former financial journalist who headed the Prime Minister's policy unit, was established to find a successor to the BBA for administering Libor. Wheatley considered a trade body no longer appropriate but did not want a public body either – maybe because so much of the UK banking sector was by then publicly owned. The choice was a subsidiary of Intercontinental Exchange, the US group whose operations include London's Liffe futures market. ICE Benchmark Administration became responsible for Libor from February 2014, completing the changes proposed by Martin Wheatley.

The BBA had already introduced an oversight committee and implemented a code of conduct for panel banks, and Libor was now regulated by the Financial Conduct Authority. Representatives of the US, Swiss and UK central banks sit on the oversight committee, alongside Libor users and non-executives as well as panel-bank members. Another reform is that individual submissions are not now published until 3 months later, in the hope that by then banks will no longer be embarrassed by having had to pay premium rates for money – the problem presumably having by then gone away or become public anyway.

The panels comprise 19 banks but some report on only one or two currencies. The UK's Big Four – Barclays, HSBC, Lloyds and NatWest – together with Deutsche Bank, JP Morgan Chase,

MUFG and UBS submit prices for all five currencies. However, ICE is introducing a 'waterfall' method of collecting data whereby panel banks submit figures based on actual transactions when they are available, but when there are insufficient deals their submission uses past trades, adjusted for market movements. Both steps apply the greatest weight to the most recent trades. Only if there is neither sufficient current nor historic data do the banks resort to using their judgement based on evidence from related instruments, broker pricing or market intelligence.[10]

Goodbye Libor. Hello Sonia, SOFR, Tonar, Ester and Saron

Yet while ICE was being asked to take over Libor, regulators in Britain and abroad were looking for alternatives. The Financial Conduct Authority announced in 2017 that, from the end of 2021, it will no longer persuade or compel banks to make Libor submissions. The Bank of England had established a working group in 2015 to identify a risk-free rate suitable for sterling markets and in April 2017 it announced its backing for the Sterling Overnight Index Average, known as Sonia. Other financial centres have their own preferred alternatives – the USA is backing the Secured Overnight Financing Rate (SOFR), Japan the Tokyo Overnight Average Rate (Tonar), the Eurozone supports Ester, the European Short Term Rate, and Zurich has Saron, the Swiss Average Overnight Rate. Saron is administered by Switzerland's main stock exchange, the other countries' rates by their respective central bank.

It is argued that Sonia tracks the bank rate more closely than Libor has. However, the rates are not directly comparable. Not only do all the proposed alternatives apply only to one currency, but they all measure only the overnight or spot rate. There are no future tenors. The Wheatley Report found in 2012 that responses to a discussion paper on Libor alternatives were generally sceptical and there remain doubts. Libor is forward looking while Sonia looks backward, say users. The London working group is vigorously promoting Sonia, however, arguing that, on average,

---

[10]ICE Benchmark Administration Ltd (2018) 'ICE Libor Evolution'. Available at: https://www.theice.com/publicdocs/ICE_LIBOR_Evolution_Report_25_April_2018.pdf [accessed 20 February 2019].

£45bn of daily transactions underpins it.[11] Certainly longer-tenor sterling-denominated lending has become a small minority of the market: overnight deposits account for about 95% of business. ICE's own test of its waterfall Libor methodology in the final quarter of 2017 found that slightly more than half of submissions for dollar and sterling overnight rates were based on actual transactions, slightly less than half for overnight euros, but almost none for yen or Swiss francs. For longer tenors the proportions fell away sharply. Libor rates are increasingly a matter of opinion rather than fact.

Reach For Your Lawyers

But the arguments against a switch from Libor to Sonia are as much legal as financial. Contracts linking interest rates to Libor cannot be unilaterally altered, and some of these agreements extend into the 2030s. Legal documents often contain a fallback provision for substituting a rate if Libor is unavailable, but these were designed for temporary gaps in data not permanent changes. Because Sonia and Libor are calculated differently, they produce different results. Usually, for the same circumstances, Sonia is lower but adding, say, 30 basis points to existing contractual Libor rates will not automatically compensate – or be well received by retail borrowers. The move will produce winners and some losers, but, while those who benefit are unlikely to complain, those who are disadvantaged are likely to fight – in the law courts if necessary. If agreement cannot be reached, some contracts may be frustrated.

The transition from Libor not only involves renegotiating vast quantities of contracts that have no common standard wording, it also embroils valuations, risk profiles and hedging strategies. The public will be affected through mortgages and other loans. Regulators are becoming increasingly concerned at the upheaval that the move from Libor could bring. Some commentators forecast chaos. The most effective way to avoid Libor-related risk is not to write Libor-referencing business, says Andrew Bailey, chief executive of the Financial Conduct Authority.[12] Trade associations for bond

---

[11]Bank of England (2018) *Preparing for 2022: What you need to know about Libor transition* (from the working group on sterling risk-free reference rates). Available at: www.bankofengland.co.uk/-/media/boe/files/markets/benchmarks/what-you-need-to-know-about-libor-transition.pdf [accessed 20 February 2019].

[12]Bailey A (2018).

markets and other Libor users are busily seeking solutions amid an army of working groups, steering committees, taskforces, technical subgroups and consultations. The warnings from Sonia's supporters of the risks in using Libor are increasingly hectoring, however – the City's own 'Project Fear' being expounded in parallel with Britain's ongoing Brexit debate. Firms face uncertainty while solutions are sought during a transition with a looming deadline: 'fallback' is as contentious as 'backstop'.

Meanwhile ICE, despite investing in Libor technology, is forced to warn that it cannot guarantee to keep publishing average rates beyond 2021. Libor's new administrator claims that users say they still want its rates but it is relying on banks to keep volunteering to make submissions.[13] Keeping Libor, or a synthetic Libor, would satisfy those users who do not or cannot switch contracts; it would also satisfy the appetite for future tenors. But demand is diminishing and will fall further as new contracts incorporate Sonia. Already, all new sterling floating-rate notes reference Sonia.

So, if Libor is facing death, the question is whether the demise will be fast or slow. It could disappear when regulatory support ends in December 2021, but the end could come sooner. Users may be reluctant to be the first to adopt Sonia, but they will not want to be the last to use Libor either. Death could be gradual: rarely traded tenors being dropped and marginal currencies abandoned. But it may be a lack of supply rather than a lack of demand that calls time on Libor: not only might the panel banks have too few deals to produce a robust average, but panels could also have too few members if banks depart, forcing the regulator to intervene. Libor could be killed before it is allowed to die naturally.

What Does the End of Libor Teach Us About Financial Markets?

Perhaps just that the world of slightly cosy, largely domestic markets that Libor assumed is long gone. As Bailey pointed out: 'Banks do not lend to each other much these days on an unsecured basis and the market is not returning, [so] Libor is measuring the rate at which banks are not borrowing from one another.' Most of the activity that now relies on Libor is in interest-rate derivatives, which are not concerned with the bank term credit risk that Libor tracks. Libor was one of the pillars of London's financial might

---

[13]ICE (2018), 12.

for nearly half a century. Now, instead of one family of indices commanding international finance, the benchmarks are being divided over individual national markets, each potentially using different methodologies and standards.

Libor's downfall shows that good intentions are not sufficient in any walk of life: while the theoreticians can write the rules, the practitioners will find and exploit the loopholes. And when derivatives mean the tail becomes bigger than the dog, it takes a skilled handler to control the animal. Across finance, regulation and statistical collation has been taken away from exchanges and trade bodies to impose discipline, demonstrate independence and ensure transparency. Yet regulators often remain loathe to take on this responsibility themselves, preferring to monitor rather than administer.

The story of Libor also shows that markets adapt – at least over time. Bond issues are transitioning to Libor's alternatives – for all their faults – and that will boost their liquidity. For terms other than overnight lending, however, interbank volumes may fall further as liquidity evaporates. In the USA, SOFR has shown worrying volatility this year when volumes have been very low. And the change from one family of indices to a range of different ones is proving more expensive and complicated than regulators assumed. With some difficulty, most existing instruments will be modified but a small remainder may prove extremely troublesome. Derivative traders using Libor will find another target to bet on – or place their wagers elsewhere, on different products in different markets. Borrowers and lenders needing certainty for medium-term contracts can negotiate rates using market intelligence as a benchmark, though some of this activity may cease.

Perhaps, though, the end of Libor is a demonstration of the finance world's enduring creativity. The benchmark was devised to satisfy a demand, but then demand ballooned to exploit the new benchmark. A product designed to facilitate interbank borrowing itself became an instrument for investors to target. There is a lifecycle even for City instruments, and as new ones arrive, some old ones disappear. Look how contracts have come and gone in other markets such as Liffe; look how small-sample stockmarket indices have been replaced by more specialist equity measures. Libor has been through the stages of creation, growth and maturity: now it is on the downswing of the cycle, heading for a self-destruction that, ironically, was a product of its former success.

Boosting UK Bank Competition

Still Many Cliffs to Climb

Martin Stewart

Martin Stewart argues that UK financial regulation should be reformed to support the growth of new banks to help boost choice and lower costs in a market that is still dominated by incumbents.

For 30 years, from the late 1970s to the 2007 financial crisis, business school professors at eminent universities across the globe were united in the strategic thinking that 'big is beautiful' for retail banks. 'Big' brings you economies of scale, the ability to invest in the latest technology, access to capital markets, greater product innovation and so much more. Their students, on graduating, turned the theory into action, whether in the retail banks, in consultancies or at advisors, resulting in consolidation in all the major banking markets.

The risks of such consolidation were not ignored. The systemic importance of larger and larger retail banks in regional and country economies was clearly understood, and the risks these entities gave rise to necessitated effective regulation. So why did this all go so horribly wrong in the 2007 financial crisis? Much has been written as to the root causes of the crisis, but what cannot be ignored is that no jurisdiction, either before or since the financial crisis, has had perfect banking regulation. Whatever regulatory strategy is adopted, and there are many to choose from, they all have strengths and weaknesses and the weaknesses can result in systemic failures. Regulators are smart people and they know they have to address the weaknesses. The response of regulators in every jurisdiction was identical; they introduced more regulation. A very laudable strategy but, when followed year after year, it resulted in greater and greater complexity, producing higher and higher barriers to entry for new banks.

In 2007 the failure of the UK banking market, requiring direct government intervention, prompted a team of consumer champions, marketeers and bankers to conclude that what the UK needed was completely new retail banks to challenge the failed incumbents. The first to come to market was Metro Bank, bringing an approach to retail banking that had been successful in the USA and was very different from that of the UK incumbents. For 3 years it painfully navigated the complexity of regulation and finally opened its doors in 2010. Metro was the first new high street bank in the UK for decades and proved that it was possible to bring a new bank to market – but only if you have very deep pockets. Whether Metro Bank will have long-term success only time will tell, but it was successful in galvanising political thinking behind a theory that – post the financial crisis – the UK needed new 'challenger banks'.

Turning the political idea into public policy landed on my desk in 2012, and for over 12 months a dedicated team worked on this, producing the last ever publication from the Financial Services Authority before it closed its doors on 31 March 2013. In conjunction with the Bank of England, the new custodian of the Prudential Regulation Authority (PRA) in the UK from 1 April 2013, 'A review of the requirements for firms entering into or expanding in the bank sector' would revolutionise thinking on new financial services business models both in the UK and across the globe.

To unpick over 30 years of retail banking business strategy and regulatory strategy was not going to be easy, but the team had access to a new tool no previous regulator had ever had: a recovery and resolution regime. Any new venture, be it in banking or other markets, contains heightened risks that are not present in established ventures. If a banking regulator had no mechanism to deal with failure in an orderly way, then it would be negatively disposed to new banks. This did not mean there were no new banks entering the UK market – 39 had entered the UK between 2006 and 2013 – but we need to look at the origins of all of these. The majority were established overseas banks looking to expand their operations into the UK and, apart from Metro, they were existing financial institutions adding a banking licence to their business operations. In the UK, the negative disposition towards bank start-ups had become so strong that, before Metro, there had been no new retail banks for decades.

Making Failing Safe

The UK Recovery and Resolution Regime, first introduced in the 2009 Banking Act and subsequently enhanced through European legislation, permitted the new banking regulator, the PRA, to make three new and bold statements.

- We expect some new banks to fail.
- If they do so, this should occur in an orderly manner.
- All new banks must have a clear plan to deliver an orderly wind-down. The submission of a recovery and resolution plan was introduced as a requirement for all new banks and this had to demonstrate clear triggers for when a new bank would cease trading and enter into an orderly wind-down process.

With these forming the foundation of the new regulatory approach, radical changes were also introduced.

- In the authorisation process greater clarity of information was made available to all applicants, including introducing dedicated pages on the Bank of England's internet site. This was to facilitate the progress to authorisation as quickly as possible, to provide clear milestones to applicants and to enable them to understand all the regulatory requirements before they committed to major infrastructure investment.
- A critical new step was added to the authorisation process, 'authorisation with restrictions' (AWR), allowing new banks to enter a period of 'mobilisation' before starting to trade. Building IT infrastructure, enabling interfaces into the banking systems and testing these are robust is a complex requirement for any new bank. By granting an AWR, the PRA and the Financial Conduct Authority (FCA) would

recognise that the infrastructure build was not complete when granting a banking licence. The restrictions placed on the new bank would prevent them from growing their balance sheet but would allow them to test their infrastructure in a live environment, without the risk of consumer detriment. The AWR would last for a period of between 3 and 12 months and the new bank would be required to return to the PRA and the FCA with evidence that their infrastructure was complete and fully tested. If satisfied, the regulators would then lift the restrictions.

- Capital requirements for the early years of trading were eased. When setting capital requirements, a regulator would traditionally assess a bank's long-term business plan and ensure that it had sufficient capital for the life of the plan. Under this approach, a new bank would have to hold a disproportionate level of capital on day one of trading. With the existence of an orderly wind-down plan, the PRA now only required a new bank to hold capital to cover its next 12 months of trading. In doing this, the PRA acknowledged that if future capital injections were not forthcoming, the bank would have to cease trading and enter into run-off. The PRA also indicated that it would not add further capital requirements to reflect the increased operational, credit and concentration risks that are inherent in a new bank. The final change of approach was to require the new banks to only hold a capital buffer to cover their wind-down costs, not the traditional formulaic approach based on risk-weighted assets. The combined impact of all three of these changes would typically reduce day one capital required by 80%. The new banks were given a 5 year glide path, at the end of which they would be required to meet the traditional method of capital setting, prohibiting them from having a long-term competitive advantage.

- Liquidity requirements were reduced for the early years of trading. The PRA indicated that it would not add additional liquidity requirements to reflect the increased risks new banks faced, and the Bank of England indicated that new banks would be eligible to apply for access to central bank liquidity facilities during the application process. If the new bank met the Bank of England's requirements for receiving liquidity facilities, these would be made available during their AWR.

From 2013 to 2018, I was the person who signed the PRA's approval for authorisation of every new bank and over these 5 years I saw an incredible diversity in business models. When comparing them, it was clear to me that many were based on fundamentally very different assumptions as to how the UK retail banking market was going to evolve. Therefore, some must fail. It was not my job to try to pick the winners and the losers. I was required to assess whether the business model was plausible and, if it was, whether it met the required regulatory standards.

Over the 5 years, some did fail but a secondary market in new banks was quick to develop and not one of the failures required the Bank of England's Resolution Authority to step in. Prospective new banks realised that their time to launch could be shortened if they identified a bank that had just started trading but had a business model that would not work. Before the failing bank had to enter its orderly wind-down, an offer was made to acquire its operations, including its licence, which could then be redeployed. In developing the new public policy, did we consider this as a likely consequence? No, we didn't, but we were warned by corporate financiers and unfortunately did not listen to their advice. Not being open to this outcome when developing the policy has, to date, not had significant implications for UK retail financial services, but I do wonder whether there are still problems that might emerge.

The problems, if they do emerge, will come from the legacy balance sheets of the fledgling banks, put in place before they were sold in the secondary market. On acquisition there was usually a radical change of strategy to reflect market developments, and assurances were given to the PRA and the FCA regarding adherence to prudential and conduct business standards for the legacy balance sheet. Day one, post-acquisition, part of the previous management team was always retained to manage the legacy balance sheet but, over time, skills, experience and knowledge fade and the challenge of maintaining the regulatory standards will increase. Good governance in these banks will ensure that nothing is missed, but can we be confident that all of them will deliver?

The lesson I took from this personally was the need for the regulator to be open to all the responses it receives when it is holding a public consultation. Too often I saw radical responses being dismissed as implausible, as colleagues were not prepared to step outside their comfort zone. If a regulator is going to be forward-looking, it needs to be prepared to actively consider 'outlying scenarios', not just the 'central scenario'.

Regulators in other jurisdictions watched with interest the policy in the UK of lowering the barriers to entry into some financial services markets – the new approach to banking authorisations at the PRA and the sandbox at the FCA. Most dismissed the UK policy as outside their 'central scenario' and during 2013 and 2014, when I was meeting with other regulators from across the globe, they were keen to highlight the inherent risks in the UK policy. Their reluctance to look at 'outlying scenarios' resulted in them being behind the curve as the pace of technology innovation continued to accelerate. The 'fintech' was born and they didn't have a policy framework within which it could be effectively regulated.

Their responses have been interesting to observe and can be broadly divided into two camps.

The followers. These recognised that the UK had pioneered a new approach and concluded that this is something they should embrace for their jurisdiction. My former team was in huge demand to work with regulators across the globe and to share their thinking, and I was always happy for the Bank of England to make our team available. Banking is a global business and it is fundamental that regulators have a mindset of cooperation, not competition. Some of the team were seduced by the other regulators and decided to start a new life in a very different country.

The defenders. They remained fixed to their strategy – that they already had too many banks in their jurisdiction, many of whom had failing business models, so why should they embrace new entrants. To get to market in these jurisdictions, fintechs had to persuade the incumbents to adopt their technology and many have been successful. Their success comes from the reaction of the incumbents to fintechs and changing consumer behaviour. Rather than resist them, the incumbents recognised that their business model needs to evolve and that fintechs can enable them to do this.

Both the follower strategy and the defender strategy have introduced innovation into financial markets across the globe. Both have strengths and weaknesses, and again the onus on the regulators is to ensure they recognise this and evolve their strategic approach accordingly. To grow, fintechs have adopted agile business strategies. In some countries, they have launched their own banks and in others, they have licensed their technology to the incumbents. Some fintechs have even been prepared to license their technology to the incumbents in the same country where they have launched their own bank. Why are they willing to share their competitive advantage with the incumbents? To answer this, we need to look at how the banking landscape has evolved in the UK from 2013 to 2018.

Making Competition Central

Between 2013 and 2018, 17 new banks came to market but when you review the metrics of competition, the dials have not been moved. They have failed to enhance competition and consumer choice and are only operating at the fringes of the primary banking markets. The incumbents still dominate but are not complacent about their market position. All have either invested in new entrants, or new technologies, and are rapidly changing their business models in response to the emerging threat.

So, can the new banks bring greater competition and consumer choice? Yes, they can, but for this to happen there must be further reform of banking regulation. As a bank gets larger and has greater systemic importance within an economy, it is appropriate that the level of regulation and the regulatory requirements on it increase. This should be a slope up which the bank has to climb, as it gets bigger and has a more diverse business model. Unfortunately, the reality of current banking regulation is not that of a slope but a series of plateaus separated by fearsome cliff faces. To scale the cliff faces requires a bank to invest in complex and expensive climbing equipment, which can take years to assemble, before it can even start to tackle the cliff faces.

What are these cliff faces? There are three that need to be scaled for a bank to grow to a £50bn balance sheet, at which point it will be having a meaningful impact on competition and consumer choice.

- Moving from the standardised capital approach to the internal ratings-based (IRB) capital approach. Bank capital is an incredibly complex subject and for small and new banks the standardised capital approach provides a regulatory framework that is proportionate for their businesses. However, all the major banking groups in the UK operate on the IRB capital approach, which can provide a significant competitive advantage. Gaining regulatory approval for the IRB capital approach remains a very time-consuming and expensive process. A new bank needs to invest in enhanced risk analytics and capabilities and be able to access historic lending data upon which it can build its capital models. New banks typically do not have such historic data built up through many economic cycles. They are looking at potential sources of historic data, but then they also need to convince the regulator that the alternative sources match their business profile. Moving to IRB is a cliff face no new bank has yet climbed.

- Strengthening your balance sheet when you become too big to fail. The UK Recovery and Resolution Regime, while acting as the great facilitator for new-start banks, turns into a cliff face when they approach a balance sheet of £15bn. For small banks, the Bank of England accepts that a failure can occur through a bank insolvency procedure, in which the UK deposit protection scheme will pay out to eligible depositors. However, the failure of a larger bank would have an impact on the UK economy and rather than allowing it to be put into insolvency, the Bank of England requires it to hold debt that can be converted into equity – 'bailed in' – should it be about to fail. The major banks all have established debt-raising programmes. However, to start one from scratch is no small undertaking. A bank needs to build the people capability, risk capability, operational capability and then get a credit rating. Once it has all of this, it can approach the market to raise debt for the first time. How is the market going to price the new issuance? Clearly higher than for the existing players, and it will take years for a new bank to build a strong debt market presence. Another cliff face no new bank has yet climbed.
- Becoming a ring-fenced bank when your balance sheet reaches £25bn. A critical component of the post-financial crisis UK banking regulatory regime was to require the major banking groups to separate their activities into a ring-fenced bank and a non-ring-fenced bank. While a very sound approach for the major banking groups, the critical question when drafting the legislation was the threshold above which ring-fencing would

apply. The initial proposal was for this to apply to all banks, but this would have raised a further barrier to entry, so as part of a good old political compromise, the threshold was set at £25bn. There remains the question: Is a threshold needed at all? For the incumbent major banking groups, ring-fencing was clearly necessary as a future safeguard of the economy but when it comes to a new growing bank, with no intention of creating a highly diverse business model, what economic benefit is there in forcing it to meet the requirements of the ring-fencing legislation? By setting this threshold, the regulator created another cliff face no new bank has yet climbed.

In 2013, the UK regulator successfully lowered the barriers to entry to banking. But for there to be enhanced competition and consumer choice in UK financial services over the medium term, the regulators must now tackle the barriers to growth. A regulatory regime of plateaus separated by fearsome cliff faces is not a good one, and I would encourage my successors at the Bank of England's PRA to address this problem with the ingenuity and tenacity we had when tackling the barriers to entry.

11

Changing the Face of Banking and Finance

Shelley Doorey-Williams

Shelley Doorey-Williams examines why gender diversity in the senior ranks of financial services firms is still limited, why that needs to change and what might be done about it.

Workplace gender diversity and inclusion is a polarising and multi-faceted topic but, seen objectively, it is a compelling business opportunity. This chapter aims to demonstrate the importance and value of gender diversity, with an analysis in four main sections: the business opportunity; where we are today and where we are going; an exploration of potential hurdles; and, finally, an overview of best practices.

In advance, it is important to stress that there are so many dimensions to the topic that it would be impossible to consider everything here. For example, positive discrimination, gender quotas, the emerging culture of speaking up (e.g. #metoo) and how to address pay gaps have not been included. My focus is on the significance of the topic and on providing an overview of some best practices. The hope is to spark thought and action on how we can all participate in driving a positive change.

This is also not a sermon. I must say that for the vast majority of my 28-year career, I have been gender blind. First, this was partly my coping mechanism; by taking an 'observe and ignore' approach I was able to deflect any potential discrimination and get on with my work. Second, as a business leader I had grossly underestimated the economic and business case for gender diversity. My mistake. The birth of my daughter in 2014 changed my life and opened my eyes. Not only did becoming a working parent impact my career, but having a daughter led me to think about what her future workplace would be like. I began to research gender diversity in the workplace and to feel passionately about the importance of a much more level playing field for her and her generation. I am for ever indebted to my daughter for providing the catalyst for my exploration of the issue.

Each industry I have worked in has its own dynamics and traits, which is what makes moving between industries so fascinating. Banking and finance, where I have spent the last 12 years of my career, has very distinct dynamics and cultures that impact gender diversity and inclusion. It is not always as client-centric as other industries and is sometimes slow to change. London is one of the largest exporters of financial services globally, and was ranked second (just two points behind New York) in the most recently published Global Financial Centres Index.[1] Therefore, if we can address gender balance in the UK, we will be going a long way to making a difference on the global stage. It is vitally important that we, in the UK banking and finance industry, take bold action to increase gender diversity and inclusion.

It is a credit to The London Institute of Banking & Finance that they sought to include this important topic in their 140th anniversary book. However, it is also a disappointment that in 2019 it *is* even a topic. It is only by all of us working together that we will create the type of diverse and inclusive industry that many of us believe in. If we can be successful in our mission, there should be no need for a chapter such as this at the next major anniversary publication.

Gender Diversity – A Business Opportunity Too Good to Miss

There is a clear business imperative for improving gender diversity in the workplace and, arguably, the benefits would be particularly marked in banking and finance. McKinsey & Co, the consulting firm, has estimated that, if women were able to participate in economies

---

[1]Yeandle M, Wardle M and Mainelli M (2018) *Global Financial Centres Index 24*. London: Z/Yen and CDI. Available at: https://www.zyen.com/publications/public-reports/global-financial-centres-index-24/ [accessed 7 March 2019].

on an identical footing with men, an additional US$28tn could be added to annual global GDP by 2025, or around 26%.[2] Achieving gender parity may be a tall order over such a short timeframe, but the potentially more realistic scenario, 'best in region', would still add US$12tn to global GDP by 2025. 'Best in region' assumes that all countries in a region match the rate of improvement of the best performer and would bring a boost equivalent to the 2015 GDP of Japan, Germany and the UK combined.

Group and Business Performance

What makes the performance of some groups better than others? It is not raw brainpower. Studies show that the collective intelligence of a group is not strongly correlated with the combined or maximum individual intelligence of individual members. There are, though, three distinct characteristics of higher-performing groups: members show social sensitivity towards each other; they give each other equal amounts of time in discussions ('turn-taking'); and there is a higher proportion of women in the group.[3]

Research conducted across nine countries and in over 159 banks in the period 2004–2010 shows that, in regions with strong regulatory environments and good investor protection, gender diversity improved bank performance.[4] Research published in 2013 in Sweden cites several studies that show a positive correlation between the proportion of women on boards and improvement in a number of business performance indicators such as sales.[5] Catalyst,

---

[2]Woetzel J, Madgavkar A, Ellingrud K, Labaye E, Devillard S, Kutcher E, Manyika J, Dobbs R and Krishnan M (2015) *How Advancing Women's Equality can add $12 Trillion to Global Growth*, McKinsey Global Institute. Available at: https://www.mckinsey.com/featured-insights/employment-and-growth/how-advancing-womens-equality-can-add-12-trillion-to-global-growth [accessed 1 March 2019].

[3]Williams Woolley A, Chabris CF, Pentland A, Hasmi N and Malone TW (2010) 'Evidence for a collective intelligence factor in the performance of human groups', *Science*, 330, 686–688. Available at: https://www.chabris.com/Woolley2010a.pdf [accessed 1 March 2019].

[4]García-Meca E, García-Sánchez I-M and Martínez-Ferrero J (2015) 'Board diversity and its effects on bank performance: an international analysis', *Journal of Banking & Finance*, 53(C), 202–214.

[5]Clarke C (2013) 'Research shows profitable companies have more women on the board', *Financial Times*, 25 July. Available at: https://www.ft.com/content/2d320562-f52d-11e2-94e9-00144feabdc0 [accessed 1 March 2019].

an organisation set up in 1962 as a not-for-profit to help build workplaces that work for women, found strong links between having women on company boards and positive business performance. Companies with more women on their boards, all else being equal, had stronger performance on three key metrics: return on equity, return on sales and return on invested capital.[6]

Furthermore, by being more gender inclusive during selection and promotion processes, businesses can tap into a broader talent pool to improve overall performance. The 2003 Higgs Review of the role and effectiveness of non-executive directors, for example, highlighted that just 6% of non-executive directors of FTSE 350 companies at the time were women. It recommended that boards should 'draw more actively' on the skills and experience that women could bring from areas such as human resources, change management and customer care, because they are relevant and important in the boardroom.[7]

Innovation

Firms not only want to hit certain performance metrics. They also want to innovate, and there is compelling evidence that increased gender diversity goes hand in hand with greater innovation. Further, not only does gender diversity in teams positively impact innovation, it can also increase the *radicalness* of the innovation. The type of radical innovations that come from such teams can lead to paradigm shifts that, in turn, can lead to the creation of new markets.[8] One study by Lorenzo and Reeves quantified the increase in revenues

---

[6]Catalyst (2011) *The Bottom Line: Corporate performance and women's representations on boards (2004–2008)*. Available at: https://www.catalyst.org/research/the-bottom-line-corporate-performance-and-womens-representation-on-boards-2004-2008/ [accessed 1 March 2019].

[7]Higgs D (2003) *Review of the Role and Effectiveness of Non-executive Directors*, Department of Trade and Industry. Available at: https://www.ecgi.org/codes/documents/ higgsreport.pdf   https://webarchive.nationalarchives.gov.uk/20121106105616/ http://www.bis.gov.uk/files/file23012.pdf

[8]Díaz-García C, González-Moreno A and Sáez-Martínez FJ (2013) 'Gender diversity within R&D teams: its impact on radicalness of innovation', *Innovation, Management Policy & Practice*, 15(2), 149–160. Available at: https://www.tandfonline.com/ doi/abs/10.5172/impp.2013.15.2.149 [accessed 1 March 2019].

that comes from the innovation boost of gender diversity at 2.5%.[9] However, it is also clear that innovation does not increase significantly until there are sufficient numbers of women (20% or more) in management roles.[10]

Corporate Governance

There is evidence that increased gender diversity on boards improves corporate governance. Women tend to have fewer attendance issues than men, they are more likely to be appointed to monitoring committees (e.g. audit, nomination and corporate governance committees) and boards with increased gender diversity tend to be more likely to hold CEOs to account for poor stock performance.[11] A conclusion of the European Commission's High-Level Group on Financial Supervision in the EU and the OECD following the financial crisis was that the management boards of credit institutions should be sufficiently diverse to avoid group-think as well as to facilitate critical challenge. Furthermore, the directive stresses the 'particular' importance of gender diversity in order to be more representative of demographic reality.[12]

Culture

Culture has a central role to play in the success (or otherwise) of organisations and improving gender diversity can be part of how cultures are positively transformed. Culture is often seen as a little nebulous. There is, however, a lot of hard data to back up the

[9]Lorenzo R and Reeves M (2018) 'How and where diversity drives financial performance', *Harvard Business Review*, 30 January. Available at: https://hbr.org/2018/01/how-and-where-diversity-drives-financial-performance [accessed 5 March 2019].

[10]Lorenzo R, Voigt N, Schetelig K, Zawadzki A, Welpe I and Brosi P (2017) *The Mix that Matters: Innovation through diversity*, Boston Consulting Group. Available at: https://www.bcg.com/publications/2017/people-organization-leadership-talent-innovation-through-diversity-mix-that-matters.aspx [accessed 1 March 2019].

[11]Adams RB and Ferreira D (2009) 'Women in the boardroom and their impact on governance and performance', *Journal of Financial Economics*, 94, 291–309. Available at: http://personal.lse.ac.uk/ferreird/gender.pdf [accessed 5 March 2019].

[12]European Commission (2011) *Proposal for a Directive of the European Parliament and of the Council*, 453. www.europarl.europa.eu/RegData/docs_autres_institutions/commission_europeenne/com/2011/0453/COM_COM

call for changing male-dominated cultures. An extensive survey involving approximately 600 executive directors, non-executive directors and senior managers in 2013, for example, found that the primary barrier between women and the top of organisations was male-dominated corporate cultures and the fact that 'behaviours are so engrained that gender bias is endemic and largely unconscious'.[13] Research in 2011 into 'neuroeconomics' found some reasons why that may be so. Young men, in particular, can lose perspective and take too many risks because, when they feel they are winning, their testosterone levels rise, which encourages further risktaking.[14] By the same token, women may be the people who have to clear up after a financial crisis. Iceland, for example, was one of the first countries to go into the financial crisis of 2007/2008 and one of the first to come out, and the lead out of crisis was predominantly taken by women. The culture that had led to the crisis, in contrast, was 'overwhelmingly male'.[15] Regulators are taking note. The Financial Conduct Authority (FCA), for example, is encouraging transformation of the culture in the financial services industry, moving beyond the mindset of compliance where rules are enough. As part of this, they want more diversity in the workplace and supervisors from the FCA may therefore ask firms questions about their diversity policies. The emphasis of the FCA is on increasing the (slow) pace of change.

The Regulator's Case

The FCA is outspoken and clear about the vital importance of gender diversity. In a speech made at the Women in Finance Summit in London in March 2018, Megan Butler, director of supervision – investment, wholesale and specialists at the FCA, spoke

---

[13]Bailey A and Rosati C (2013) 'The Balancing Act: A study of how to balance the talent pipeline in business'. Available at: https://www.harveynash.com/inspire/documents/Inspire-TheBalancingAct_LR.pdf.

[14]Adams T (2011) 'Testosterone and high finance do not mix: so bring on the women', *The Guardian*, 19 June. Available at: https://www.theguardian.com/world/2011/jun/19/neuroeconomics-women-city-financial-crash [accessed 5 March 2019].

[15]Sunderland R (2009) 'After the crash, Iceland's women lead the rescue', *The Guardian*, 22 February. Available at: https://www.theguardian.com/world/2009/feb/22/iceland-women [accessed 5 March 2019].

about how diversity is a key supervisory issue.[16] She cited the fact that firms that promote gender diversity have lower conduct risk and gave three central reasons for this. First, research[17] indicates that, when teams include more women, their collective intelligence rises. Second, having a wider range of perspectives can reduce group-think. Third, groups that lack diversity can develop too positive a view of their own skills. The FCA is equally firm in its belief that action is needed to 'stamp out unacceptable discrimination and outdated behavior' within the industry as Christopher Woolard, executive director of strategy and competition (and the executive board member for gender diversity at the FCA) put it. Woolard argues that the industry needs to avoid a 'false consensus' on gender equality, in which people talk about change but no actual action is taken.[18] In the same speech, he cited statistics indicating that whistleblowing complaints to the FCA about sexual misconduct and discrimination had increased by 300% in 2018 to 64 cases. On the one hand, that is a depressingly large number. On the other hand, the fact that more people are coming forward to complain may show that there has been a shift towards greater fairness.

The Moral Case

Men who discriminate against women may not, of course, feel that a drive for greater diversity is fair. However, in his widely viewed *Ted Talk*, Michael Kimmel, an American sociologist and academic, points out that gender diversity is good for everyone, including men.[19] Kimmel discusses research that suggests that gender-neutral countries

---

[16]Butler M (2018) 'Women in finance: keeping up the pressure for progress'. FCA Speech, 22 March. Available at: https://www.fca.org.uk/news/speeches/women-finance-keeping-pressure-progress [accessed 6 March 2019].

[17]Woolley A and Malone TW (2011) 'Defend your research: what makes a team smarter? More women', *Harvard Business Review*, June. Available at: https://hbr.org/2011/06/defend-your-research-what-makes-a-team-smarter-more-women [accessed 6 March 2019].

[18]Angeloni C (2018) 'Gender equality shouldn't be a "false consensus"', *International Adviser*, 21 December. Available at: https://international-adviser.com/gender-equality-shouldnt-be-a-false-consensus-says-fca/ [accessed 6 March 2019].

[19]Kimmel M (2015) 'Why gender equality is good for everyone: men included', *Ted Talk*, 6 October. Available at: https://youtu.be/7n9IOH0NvyY [accessed 6 March 2019].

score higher in happiness stakes, and that companies with more gender balance score better on employee happiness – reducing employee turnover – and on productivity. Further, he discusses how, in households where the parents share more of the domestic and parental responsibilities, families are healthier and happier. He points out that 'privilege is invisible to those who have it' and that gender diversity is not a zero-sum game. The first step to creating more gender diversity is, Kimmel argues, making gender issues more visible to men. Some of Kimmel's co-workers have argued that Kimmel needs to begin with his own gender awareness – and have accused him of sexual discrimination and harassment. However, that does not negate his research findings.

The Client Case

If you are still not convinced there is a case for gender diversity in financial services, then this last perspective will hopefully convert you. Globally, the wealth and income of women is growing faster than ever before. This is due to a number of factors, including: more women in the workplace; narrowing pay gaps; more women entering higher education; and women representing an increasingly important segment for savings and retirement as they typically live longer than men, but retire earlier. In 2014, the CFA Institute estimated that, by 2028, women will control 75% of discretionary spending around the world. More importantly, women are set to become the largest benefactors of the intergenerational wealth transfer of US$30tn due over the next 25 years in the USA alone. This is largely because women tend to outlive their husbands and stand to inherit from baby-boomer parents.

There are some emerging service offerings and firms focused on better serving the specific needs of women. Some are new organisations targeting women, such as Ellevest,[20] others are part of existing wealth management businesses. That is not to say that women want an adviser who is a woman. It is about an industry that has more gender diversity and, hence, more ability collectively to understand and address the needs of women. Carolanne Minashi, global head of diversity at UBS (the firm that employs me), says the aim is to be able

---

[20]Avery H (2019) 'Women in private banking: why we need a new normal', *Euromoney*, 6 February. Available at: https://www.euromoney.com/article/b1cy287 h3qq4vs/women-in-private-banking-why-we-need-a-new-normal [accessed 6 March 2019].

to serve women clients in a more 'gender-intelligent' way.[21] Further, she points out that, across the industry, there is currently a limited pool of talent when it comes to female wealth managers. This means that relying on poaching talent from competitors will not solve the challenge of having a diverse workforce at an industry level.

Such lack of a diverse workforce means that, despite the fact that women are gaining more economic power and financial independence, they are not (yet) well served by the wealth management industry. In the UK, 73% of female wealth management and private banking clients say that their advisers do not understand their goals or have empathy with their lifestyle.[22] This may be partly because there are important differences in approach to wealth management between the genders. EY found, for example, that women are more likely to place value on reaching personal goals rather than on absolute investment performance.[23]

As an industry, we should be adapting and responding to the needs of women more widely. A survey of 1,700 couples conducted by UBS found that 56% of women had no role in their family's long-term investment and financial planning, deferring to their spouse.[24] This has obvious potential consequences for those who become widowed or divorced. Around 56% of those surveyed said that they had discovered financial 'surprises' after the death of their spouse, or on becoming divorced. Such surprises included high debt, outdated wills and hidden accounts. Times are changing, though. For example, an organisation – Wealth for Women – was set up in the UK in 2012 by Mary Waring, a chartered accountant and financial planner, to offer financial advice to women going through a divorce or separation, with the slogan 'a man is not a financial plan'.

---

[21]Avery H (2019).

[22]EY (2017) 'Women and wealth: the case for a customised approach'. Available at: https://www.ey.com/Publication/vwLUAssets/EY-women-investors/$FILE/EY-women-and-wealth.pdf [accessed 6 March 2019].

[23]EY (2017).

[24]UBS (2018) *Own Your Worth: How women can break the cycle of abdication and take control of their wealth.* Available at: https://www.ubs.com/content/dam/Wealth ManagementAmericas/documents/2018-37666-UBS-Own-Your-Worth-report-R32 .pdf [accessed 6 March 2019].

The Level Playing Field

Despite the vast body of research pointing to the business benefits of greater gender diversity and inclusion, it would be remiss not to look at the research that finds either no, or no significant, relationship between increased gender diversity and business benefits. Three analyses stand out. First, some researchers set out to examine whether having more women on boards can, as is often argued, prevent excessive risktaking. They found no evidence that female boardroom representation influences equity risk.[25]

Second, research conducted in the USA set itself the task of investigating 'the relationship between the number of women directors and the number of ethnic minority directors on the board … and financial performance measured as return on assets'. It found no effect, either positive or negative.[26] Third, a study conducted by Morningstar in 2015 sought to explain why women were under-represented in the fund management industry. And the under-representation was vast. Their study revealed that, in the period between 1990 and 2017, the number of US active-equity and fixed-income funds swelled from 1,900 to roughly 8,500. However, of the new roles created over the same period, approximately 85–90% had been taken by men. This led Morningstar to try to understand the gender imbalance. They wanted to see if there could be a variation in fund performance (i.e. whether women are just not as good when it comes to fund management as their male equivalents). What they found was 'no statistically significant difference' … in either equity or fixed-income asset classes.[27] What these three pieces of research point to, I would argue, is that there should be a level playing field when it comes to hiring, which – given where we are today – is still a long way off.

There is one more important point to consider. Levelling the playing field will not be achieved without learning from the research available and adapting our practices and mindsets. This is

---

[25] Sila V, Gonzalez A and Hagendorff J (2016) 'Women on board: does boardroom gender diversity affect firm risk?', *Journal of Corporate Finance*, 36(C), 26–53.

[26] Carter DA, D'Souza F, Simkins BJ and Simpson GA (2010) 'The gender and ethnic diversity of US boards and board committees and firm financial performance', *Corporate Governance: An International Review*, 18(5), 396–414.

[27] Sargis M and Wing K (2015) 'Female fund manager performance: what does gender have to do with it?', *Morningstar Inc.* Available at: https://www.morningstar.com/blog/2018/03/08/female-fund-managers.html [accessed 6 March 2019].

particularly true in relation to how we recruit, develop, promote and retain talent. Iris Bohnet, a behavioural psychologist, points out that 'gender equality is not just a numbers game. Numbers matter, but how those numbers came to be and how they work with each other is quite possibly even more important'.[28] She argues that it is necessary to 'de-bias' organisations and redesign how businesses hire, promote and evaluate people.[29]

Summary

In summary, as an industry we absolutely do need to take more steps at a faster pace to address gender diversity and inclusion. As has been seen, there is a vast and comprehensive body of research from multiple perspectives pointing to the economic, business and client benefits of increasing gender diversity and inclusion. Of all of these, the one that I believe is most likely to lead to radical changes in financial services is the client case for greater gender diversity and inclusion. As the economic power and financial independence of women grow, these will act as catalysts for change – women will demand it.

The UK Banking and Finance Industry

If we accept that there are compelling reasons why gender diversity and inclusion are important, how far have we come within the banking and finance industry in the UK? Overall, according to the FCA, there are c. 137,500 approved persons in UK financial services and of those only 23,000 (17%) are women.[30] In June 2015, the Treasury asked Dame Jayne-Anne Gadhia, then CEO of Virgin Money, to lead a review on women in financial services. The review looked at 200 financial services firms and found that women made up 23% of board members overall, but only 14% of executive committees. The report found that 'the gender balance followed a "pyramid" model, with the number of women diminishing in line with seniority'. It noted a 'permafrost' in mid-tier jobs where women either stay put or leave

---

[28]Bohnet I (2016) *What Works: Gender Equaity by Design*. Harvard University Press.

[29]Dubner SJ (2016) 'What are gender barriers made of?', Freakonomics.com, 20 July. Available at: http://freakonomics.com/podcast/gender-barriers/ [accessed 6 March 2019].

[30]Romeo V (2017) 'FCA data reveals major gender gap in authorised firms'. *Money Marketing*, 20 September. Available at: https://www.moneymarketing.co.uk/diversity-fca-data-reveals-major-gender-gap-in-authorised-firms/ [accessed 6 March 2019].

the sector.[31] That means the area that needs significant attention is in the more senior ranks within banking and finance. Here you might say that, surely, banking and finance is no worse than any other industry. The reality is that the comparisons do not flatter. In banks and building societies the average mean pay gap per hour is 35%. The bonus gap at banks is 52%. In book publishing, the mean pay gap per hour is 17% and in engineering firms it is 24%.[32] Clearly there is a long way to go.

The US Banking and Finance Industry

In the USA, the biggest global hub for financial services, the issue of gender diversity in financial services has been taken up by Congress. Between 2004 and 2010, Congress hearings were held on the topic of inclusion of women and minorities in the industry, with concerns being raised on inclusion levels in key management-level positions.[33] Furthermore, in the USA, diversity and inclusion is a topic addressed by legislation. The Dodd–Frank Wall Street Reform and Consumer Protection Act required certain federal financial agencies and Federal Reserve Banks to establish an Office of Minority and Women Inclusion.[34] Given the significance of the topic in the USA, one might think that progress on increasing diversity might be faster there than in the UK. However, despite the efforts of the industry, progress is very slow. Depressingly, between 2007 and 2011 the percentage of women represented at senior level declined from 30% to 28.4%.[35]

---

[31] Gadhia J-A (2015) *Empowering Productivity: Harnessing the talents of women in financial services*. HM Treasury and Virgin Money. Available at: https://uk.virginmoney.com/virgin/assets/pdf/Virgin-Money-Empowering-Productivity-Report.pdf [accessed 6 March 2019].

[32] House of Commons Treasury Committee (2018) 'Women in finance', HC 477. Available at: https://publications.parliament.uk/pa/cm201719/cmselect/cmtreasy/477/477.pdf [accessed 6 March 2019].

[33] United States Government Accountability Office (2013) 'Diversity management: trends and practices in the financial services industry and agencies after the recent financial crisis'. Available at: https://www.gao.gov/assets/660/653814.pdf [accessed 6 March 2019].

[34] Miller SK and Tucker JJ (2013) 'Diversity trends, practices and challenges in the financial services industry', *Journal of Financial Service Professionals*, 67(6), 46–57.

[35] United States Government Accountability Office (2013), 16.

Looking Ahead

What does the future hold for gender diversity in the banking and finance industry? Well, on current trends financial services globally will not reach 50% female representation at executive committee level until 2107. That is not a typo. Yes, it will be 2107 before we reach parity. According to extensive research by management consultant firm Oliver Wyman, progress is being made, but only at a slow pace.[36] Their study finds that within financial services globally, female representation at board level was 20% in 2016 and at executive committee level 16%. They estimate that at current rates of change, 30% female representation at executive committee level will not be achieved until 2048. When we compare the industry in the UK to that in other countries, the UK is broadly in the middle of the pack. The percentage of executive committee members in UK financial services who are women is 17%, while the global average is 16%. The countries that lead on diversity are Norway (33%), Sweden (32%) and Thailand (31%). Countries with the lowest levels of diversity are Japan (2%), South Korea (4%) and Switzerland (5%).

What is Holding Up Diversity?

Research conducted within the financial services industry in 2016, across 381 companies in 32 countries, highlighted that exit rates for women in the mid-part of their careers were higher than that for men and were significantly higher in financial services compared to other industries. Women in financial services who are managers, senior managers or executives are 20–30% more likely to leave than their peers in other industries. So, why do so many women leave at that stage of their career? The main factors found by this piece of research will probably not surprise most people. There are four:

- A lack of flexible working options, or stigma if they are used.
- Family responsibilities not being sufficiently supported for working parents.
- Promotion process and pay issues (e.g. lack of transparency and equality on promotions).
- Cultures of low inclusion (e.g. invisible, unconscious biases).

---

[36]Oliver Wyman (2016) *Women in financial services.* Available at: https://www .oliverwyman.com/our-expertise/insights/2016/jun/women-in-financial-services-2016.html [accessed 6 March 2019].

Some radical changes will be needed to address these issues, according to the Oliver Wyman report.

Some of the reasons why the changes will have to be radical were examined in a study conducted by McKinsey in 2012.[37] In it they researched 60 corporations in the USA and found four principle reasons for the under-representation of women in more senior roles, which they referred to as stubborn or entrenched barriers.

- Structural obstacles – although the majority of CEOs at the firms said they were committed to gender diversity, only about half of the employees believed the CEOs were committed.
- Lifestyle choices – about half the women interviewed said that they were the primary breadwinner and the primary caregiver, whereas most of the men who were primary breadwinners were not also the primary caregiver.
- Institutional mindsets – leaders may expect women to act like men, and when women don't act that way the leaders see differences that can limit the options for women.
- Individual mindsets – more than half of the successful women who were interviewed said they believed they had held themselves back and that they should have cultivated sponsors earlier than they had and that they had not raised their hands for stretch roles.

Their research also revealed that, despite these challenges, there are some very successful women making it to senior ranks.

As the McKinsey research indicates, there are varied and intertwined barriers to improving gender diversity and inclusion. Barriers identified by the Treasury Committee review included: culture (workplace culture, 'alpha-male' culture, bonus culture and presenteeism) and the impact that unconscious bias can play. Maternity leave was also seen as a potential barrier. This was because some women did not return post-pregnancy to roles that were as senior or remunerative as the roles they held originally, and because some managers might not consider women with families for certain roles believing that they would not want them.

---

[37] Barsh G and Yee L (2012) *Unlocking the Full Potential of Women at Work*, McKinsey & Company. Available at: https://www.mckinsey.com/business-functions/organization/our-insights/unlocking-the-full-potential-of-women-at-work [accessed 6 March 2019].

Addressing all of these interlocking challenges will take a variety of initiatives and approaches, and each organization will be different. However, we can all learn from each other and there are some best practices that every firm can implement.

On the Cusp of Positive Change

The tone thus far has been rather negative, but now I can shed some light and positivity on the topic. We could be on the cusp of making a leap forward. The chance is there for the taking. There seems to be a real momentum and urgency to these activities and initiatives, as if there had been a 'eureka' moment. However, we must remember that the various initiatives will only help towards positive change if there is consistency and tenacity. Only then will we see real improvement. We will also have to be realistic. Oliver Wyman predicted that we will not have 30% representation at executive committee level before 2048. I hope we can do better, but progress will not come overnight.

There are already many firms with well-established, and active, gender diversity programmes. For example, at UBS the comprehensive programme focused on diversity and inclusion includes mentoring and sponsorship, monitoring of gender diversity statistics and networking events with inspirational speakers. And UBS is not only addressing gender diversity within the firm, but also taking significant steps to better serve women clients. It is well into a 5 year plan that includes embedding a gender view into standard processes and procedures, making the products and services it offers better suited to women's needs and training client adviser in gender awareness.[38]

Organisations such as Girls Who Invest, which was established in 2015 by a veteran of the industry to encourage more women into portfolio management and executive leadership in the asset management industry, are encouraging new talent. In 2001, three women in finance joined together to form 100 Women in Finance, an organisation that now has 15,000 members globally and focuses on three main areas: education, peer engagement and philanthropy.

---

[38]Mookerjee I (2017) 'UBS Wealth to target client segment worth $13 trillion', *CityWire Asia*, 27 January. Available at: https://citywireasia.com/news/ubs-wealth-to-target-client-segment-worth-13-trillion/a987542 [accessed 6 March 2019].

At the government level, the UK has made a commitment to supporting isolated and marginalised women, launching a £500,000 fund to help start innovative programmes to help these women return to work. Furthermore, to ensure that the Government Equalities Office is at the heart of government, it joined the Cabinet Office in April 2019. It is clear that the UK is committed to addressing 'burning injustices', as Theresa May put it in her first statement as Prime Minister, and gender discrimination is clearly one of those injustices. As has been mentioned already, the Treasury Committee commissioned a review into women in finance and also launched the Women in Finance Charter. The Charter asks firms to make commitments to four industry actions that include: having a member of the senior executive team responsible and accountable for gender diversity and inclusion; setting internal targets for gender diversity in senior management; publishing on its website, on an annual basis, the progress made; and 'having an intention to ensure' that the pay of the senior executive team is linked to hitting gender diversity targets.[39]

Conclusion

Despite the vast evidence of the benefits of increased gender diversity (only a small selection of which I had space to examine here), the UK banking and finance industry continues to see a very slow pace of change. With a number of initiatives underway in 2019, there are reasons for optimism but, in reality, the pace needs to pick up further. In the UK, we have a unique opportunity to influence the world, as we are one of the most significant global financial centres – but grasping that opportunity needs to be intentional. While this chapter has outlined a number of leading practices at company, industry and government level, I wanted to leave you with a call to action. Coming back to my daughter, I ask you: What world do you want for your children and grandchildren? We've got a real opportunity – but it is one that requires you, me and many around us to make intentional choices to grasp that opportunity, each and every day.

---

[39]House of Commons Treasury Committee (2018), 'Women in finance' HC 477. Available at: https://publications.parliament.uk/pa/cm201719/cmselect/cmtreasy/477/477.pdf [accessed 6 March 2019].

12

Getting the Right Stuff

Mike Thompson

Mike Thompson argues that the way in which banks approach career development needs to undergo a sea change if they are to ensure that the sector continues to thrive by hiring and training diverse talent in partnership with educational providers.

During my career in banking I have often heard the throw-away line: 'banks are just tech companies with a balance sheet'. While this has an element of truth, the reality is that banks are still, at their heart, service organisations, and service organisations fundamentally rely on the calibre and skills of their people. The advent of large-scale fintech will not alter that. What fintech will change, I would argue, is the way in which banks need to address staff education. Further, and somewhat ironically, the demands of cutting-edge technology are going to make banks return to recruitment and training models they used in the past: the support of professional bodies and school-leaver apprenticeships.

That might sound unlikely. After all, it is clear that, across all sectors of the economy, the conveniences of technology are upending consumer behaviours and preferences at a fast clip. That puts pressure on financial services to keep up, and in a number of ways, as does the inexorable growth in regulation. However, none of the innovation has altered what financial services firms actually do for consumers and for society more widely, which is manage financial risk. So, while the skills and capabilities required to be successful within retail banking have altered – banks will employ many more IT professionals, for example – staff will still be central to delivering the high standards of banking on which the economy depends. Having a skilled banking sector that enjoys and deserves public trust has obvious social and economic benefits, but it is also of profound importance for the performance of individual firms. Those that do not invest heavily over the coming decade in developing their workforce risk extinction. New players, better placed to serve consumer needs, will take over.

Truly disruptive competition is a relative novelty in the recent history of UK retail banking. It has long been dominated by a handful of incumbent players. Barriers to entry include the cost of capital, the challenges of complying with regulation and the need to have trained staff. However, the financial crisis and its attendant scandals made regulators keen to shake up the sector with fresh competition. Open Banking, high-capacity mobile networks and smartphones have helped enable that competition. According to the telecom regulator Ofcom's *The Communications Market 2018* report,[1] c. 78% of UK adults 'personally use a smartphone' and 6 in 10 say they 'cannot live' without their mobile phone. Among 25 to 34-year-olds, 71% never turn their mobile phone off. Mobile technology has, for many people, become the portal to a range of fundamental services from all sorts of sectors. Eighty-four percent of adults agree that online banking has made their life easier. That is why, in 2017, the average monthly household spend on mobile voice and data was £45.99, even as the telecom operators cut charges. Still, even if many consumers are emotionally and logistically dependent on mobile services, financial services still command a much greater share of wallet. The average monthly spend on mortgage interest payments and insurance in the UK (in the financial year to March 2018) was £166.80, according to the Office for National Statistics.

The expectation of an always-on and excellent service at an affordable price, which smartphones have fostered, has implications

---

[1]Ofcom (2018) *The Communications Market 2018*. Available at: https://www.ofcom .org.uk/research-and-data/multi-sector-research/cmr/cmr-2018.

for financial services. As fintech challengers come into the market, all banks will be expected to be cheaper and more responsive. That, together with the sheer convenience of mobile banking, will mean fewer bank branches and fewer bank employees. In just the 10 years following the financial crisis and the launch of the iPhone in 2007, UK banks closed around 37% of their branches, according to a House of Commons briefing paper.[2] As generation Y move into the workforce, it is hard to image that they will visit a branch or even call a service centre. Instant transactions on the latest device in their pocket or video/online chat are far more likely to be the norm.

New entrants have recognised this and are increasingly offering slick, simple and fast mobile banking solutions. Not a branch in sight. That is not only more convenient for (most) consumers, and less cost-intensive for the bank, it also provides a much better overview of customer data that can be used to inform better services. Banks are not alone in making this shift. If you look at other parts of financial services, the same themes play out. Insurance is being re-imagined with tailored app-based products set to become the norm. Insurers can, for example, use telematics to know, in real time, how a driver is behaving and price that individual's cover accordingly. Insurance risk need no longer be pooled. In business banking, alternative sources of finance are flourishing and challenging the traditional credit and relationship model – as well as the traditional deposit-funding model. Investment banking too is being democratised and automated. The same applies to wealth management.

To respond to all of this upheaval, financial services need to recognise that the workforce skills required in the future will be vastly different from those on which the sector relied for decades (and arguably centuries). Customer services and relationship skills will still be hugely important, but so too will data analytics, artificial intelligence, digital and technology skills.

The greatest change in the financial services workforce of the future will be in its shape. Large numbers of lower-skilled service roles will be replaced by fewer, but higher-skilled, roles managing technology innovation and process re-engineering. This is inevitable as the major players reconfigure themselves for the future. Rapid

---

[2]Edmonds T (2018) 'Bank branch closures', House of Commons Briefing Paper No. 385, 19 October.

growth in technology, operations and compliance functions will fundamentally reshape organisations.

What does this mean for existing and future workforces within the sector? Existing employees will need to be re-skilled, and at a far higher level, in order to remain relevant. Achieving that will be no mean feat for incumbents when you consider not just the scale of the sector, but also the demographic spread of the workforce, which spans multiple generations. New entrants, in contrast, will not have to wrestle with this huge challenge because they will start with streamlined, modern products, built on technologies developed by people fully conversant with them from day one. Compare this with traditional players who wrestle with grafting new tech onto ancient operating platforms and processes. At the same time, they will have to re-skill staff who were trained and skilled on 'old technology' and outdated processes.

Incumbent banks will have to make multi-million-pound investments in re-skilling and up-skilling existing workforces. The question is how to fund that when learning and development budgets have been cut back year on year for the past decade. Even bringing all employees to a base level of digital knowledge can require significant investment. To take people to a truly expert level requires long-term development programmes at Foundation Degree or Masters level. This has both serious financial implications (the average degree currently costs c. £27k per person in fees) and operational impacts, since staff will require time to undertake the study required.

The problem of how best to support the proper training of staff is, of course, not new. When The London Institute of Banking & Finance was founded in 1879, much of the impetus came from bank workers. However, when banks realised the benefits to their own businesses of having highly trained staff, they began to reward those who entered for the exams with study time, payment of fees and, if things went well, bonuses and promotions. Over time, taking the Institute's exams became the high road to a senior career in banking.

During the past 30 years, the role of professional bodies such as the Institute has been weakened, as banks have focused more on graduate recruitment than on hiring staff whose education, and ethos, would be shaped by professional training and development. Now, though, banks may have come full circle in terms of staff education, with the introduction of degree and degree-level apprenticeship programmes.

Restoring and Future-Proofing a Profession

The reforms of apprenticeships launched by the government in 2013 have been criticised by many as draconian. In particular, the levy on the financial services sector, which came out at around £100m per annum, was not welcome. In reality, the new apprenticeships and the requirement to fund them could not have been better timed. Without the levy it is unlikely that financial services employers would invest the sums required to develop the skills they need for the future. Now they have no choice and are waking up to the opportunity that apprenticeships present. I would argue that being able to fund high-quality degree-level apprenticeship programmes will enable financial services to restore the profession of banking – but in a very modern and innovative way.

Degree-level apprenticeships, such as the Chartered Associateship programme offered by the Institute, which fits the level 6 apprenticeships standards and offers the option of a sector-specific degree, are tailored to delivering the skills needed for the future. (The Institute partners with Barclays to offer a BSc (Hons) in Banking Practice and Management under the Relationship Manager (Banking) apprenticeship.)

The new apprenticeship standards developed by the Financial Services Trailblazer group integrate professional qualifications and deliver far higher levels of skills than traditional learning and development (L&D) programmes ever could. More broadly, the introduction of the degree apprenticeship has given banks and their staff access to higher education in the pivotal areas of leadership and technology. The leadership degree apprenticeship will give far-sighted players in the sector the opportunity to address a long-standing issue, namely, poor workforce productivity. There has been underinvestment in leadership skills by UK plc for decades, with the result that we have a productivity lag against our global competitors. The financial services sector has not been immune to this, with L&D budget cuts biting hardest at the leadership and executive development level. The development of large numbers of 'middle managers' has not been properly funded for over a decade, with inevitable knock-on impacts on leadership capability and overall employee engagement.

The degree apprenticeship programme in leadership and management has been the jewel in the crown of the government's apprenticeship offering for several years – with good reason. By every measure it has been an astonishing success. High progression rates, low attrition rates and strong productivity levels are an L&D managers dream. By serving new and existing staff, it can raise the quality of leadership across an entire organisation.

The more recent arrival of the Masters apprenticeship in leadership and management will also provide a shot in the arm for financial services firms that need to re-skill and up-skill more senior leaders. The next generation of leaders in the sector are often ill prepared to deal with the technology revolution engulfing them. Being able to take a step back from the day-to-day and look at problems and opportunities from a different angle will be invaluable for both staff and their firms. Higher education institutions will give future leaders insight into the sort of external perspectives that quotidian pressures can block out – not least through invaluable research.

Many people who still associate apprenticeships with trades are surprised that they are used to educate senior staff and can be a major boost to productivity. They should not be. There are now sector-specific apprenticeship standards to support the increasingly technical parts of financial services, such as wealth management, investment banking and corporate finance. These degree and Masters level standards offer an alternative to traditional graduate programmes and allow organisations to capture talent earlier (i.e. from school), or to develop internal talent.

Financial services firms that use degree, and degree-level, apprenticeships to educate school leavers find that they can attract excellent candidates – not least because an apprenticeship is cost free to the learner. Given that, the big question for many organisations will be what the optimal mix of talent will look like. Apprenticeships underpinned by levy funding are, simply in terms of expenditure, potentially more attractive than in-house graduate programmes. In functional areas within financial services firms such as tech and operations, it is hard to see graduate programmes surviving.

How will the new training be delivered? The role of professional bodies in supporting this re-skilling across the sector cannot be underestimated. The right training will require modern innovative curricula embedded in an apprenticeship journey. Staying current and relevant will be as big a challenge for professional bodies as it is for their financial services members. What the professional bodies bring is setting the right professional bar. Within the new apprenticeship model, many standards have already integrated professional qualifications. This is reinvigorating the relationship between financial services institutions and the professional bodies that had been eroded by a focus on graduate programmes.

Banks moved away from relying on, and rewarding, professional qualifications to focus on recruiting from the Russell Group of universities for a number of reasons. One was a need to keep up with market developments. New hiring practices meant new workforces. In part, that was deliberate. There were, however, some unintended consequences – such as a decline in diversity. This manifests itself now in a number of ways. Further down the organisation, for example, many banks are struggling to attract black, Asian and minority ethnic employees or employees from less privileged social backgrounds. This is only partly due to an over-reliance on graduate recruitment, but HR teams and business leaders do increasingly recognise that there are sources of future top talent outside universities. Indeed, they know they need to widen the applicant pool if their organisations are to really think innovatively and master the challenges ahead.

Happily, the sizeable sums now available to HR teams through the levy will mean a growth in 'grow your own' talent via apprenticeships. Partnerships will begin to emerge between schools, further education colleges and employers as the new T-levels (post-GCSE qualifications equivalent to three A levels, involving industry input and industry placements) start to land in 2020. Far-sighted employers recognise that attracting talent early will pay dividends in terms of loyalty and skills. Why wait to scrabble for scarce (and expensive) IT skills at the university gate when you can nurture them from age 16 in colleges at almost no cost and ensure the skills are relevant to your business?

Senior managers understand that the continued health and vitality of the financial services sector will rely heavily on how well it can compete for skilled staff. The lure of the fintech and small and medium-sized enterprises for young talent is growing. Those sectors offer, or have the reputation for offering, better conditions; larger financial services firms must recognise this and respond. Banks have the very major advantage of being able to invest heavily in individual skills and qualifications, something a fintech start-up may struggle to do. Banks need to take advantage of that to survive and thrive, and they also need to ensure that they take a longer-term perspective on building a skilled talent pipeline.

What banks did in terms of talent recruitment in the (recent) past was hire very large volumes of graduates, many of whom left after 5 years or less. Moving away from that very short-term fix towards a much more blended talent model will be essential. Talent and early careers managers should be thinking 3 to 5 years ahead, not just to the next round of campus events or school leaver shows. Building long-term partnerships with education and skills partners will be crucial to secure skills and prosper. That will require a sea change in approach and thinking. I'm not sure many firms are yet fully aware of what is needed, but time will tell.

I remain cautiously optimistic that the building blocks for a successful and thriving sector are in place. The money is there through the levy to pay for the skills required; many modern apprenticeship standards are in place, and the diverse talent needed is ready, willing and able to learn. Compare this to 7 years ago when I started out in early careers: money was much harder to come by and there were only out-of-date apprenticeships. Talent was spelt g.r.a.d.u.a.t.e. I think we have come a long way ...

13

CHAPTER

Financial Education

How to Make it Count

Andy Davis

> As people are increasingly required to manage their own pensions and savings, and the young often have to borrow large sums to attend university, financial education is becoming ever more important. Andy Davis examines what is being done, and what needs to be done, to ensure that everyone receives a meaningful financial education and what the financial services industry can do to help.

F inancial education in Britain is not always a matter for national pride. Work to ensure that all schoolchildren gain a basic foundation in financial knowledge, not least by The London Institute of Banking & Finance ('the Institute') through its dedicated qualifications, has been ongoing for years but remains far from complete. This matters. Individuals are increasingly required to manage their own pensions and savings, as defined benefit schemes disappear, and the young often have to borrow large sums to attend university. At the most basic – and fundamentally important – level, financial education is crucial to improving this country's poor levels of adult financial capability. According to the Organisation for Economic Co-operation and Development's 2016 *International Survey of Adult*

Financial Literacy Competencies, the UK scored marginally below the average for financial knowledge, behaviour and attitudes among the 30 countries covered, and slightly further below the average for OECD member states. 'These high-level findings make it possible to draw a first set of policy conclusions', the OECD said. 'The overall low level of financial literacy stresses the importance of starting financial education early and, ideally, in schools.'

As far back as 2006, the then Financial Services Authority (FSA) published its *National Strategy for Financial Capability*, a 'road map' that included 'translating the Government's intention, that the National Curriculum should contain high quality and comprehensive personal financial education, into real change in the classroom'. Well over a decade later, financial education has only a limited and fragmented presence in the curriculum and is entirely absent from some schools. In short, it is still struggling to claim a meaningful place in British classrooms.

This is not for want of attention from policymakers and others. Media-savvy advocates including Martin Lewis, founder of MoneySavingExpert, have been campaigning for schools to teach financial education for years, as did the Institute and other financial education charities. Lewis was one of those closely involved in pushing for the foundation of the All-Party Parliamentary Group on Financial Education in 2011, and in 2018 he personally funded the UK's first 'curriculum-mapped' financial education textbook for 15 to 16-year-olds, *Your Money Matters*, 340,000 copies of which are being distributed free to schools in England.

He is far from alone in being passionate about the need for change. Following trenchant criticism from the Treasury Select Committee in 2013 that it was 'not fit for purpose', the Money Advice Service (MAS) – now part of the newly launched Single Financial Guidance Body (later called the Money and Pensions Service) – redefined its mission and focused on promoting and evaluating financial capability initiatives, including education. MAS launched the 10-year UK Financial Capability Strategy (www.fincap.org.uk) in 2015, which aims among other things 'to ensure that every child and young person gets meaningful financial education by 2025'. As part of that, in 2018 its Young Financial Capability Group (made up of members of different money charities and financial education bodies) developed Financial Education Planning Frameworks for schools to support the planning, teaching and progression of financial education, which were sent to all schools.

In the private sector, meanwhile, banks and other financial institutions have for decades been directly supporting financial education for schoolchildren and young adults, whether by encouraging their staff to go into schools and help run classes, publishing free teaching materials, or funding specialist charities to deliver education programmes. According to research by the MAS published in September 2018, financial services firms are by far the biggest funders of financial education. They contribute to projects that receive £6m overall and within that are the sole funders of projects with budgets totalling £3.7m. This is significantly higher than spending by government agencies, the equivalent figures for which are £4m and £1.5m, respectively.

Undoubtedly there are positives to take from all of this, but there is also strong evidence that the initiatives to date are insufficient. The Institute's *Young Person's Money Index 2018*, which surveyed just over 2,000 pupils aged 15–18, found that 83% wanted to learn more about money in school, up seven percentage points on 2017. Meanwhile, 71% said they worry about money, compared with 62% the year before.

Given the widespread recognition that today's children need a better grounding in everyday finance, the clear desire among pupils to improve their knowledge, the existence of expert, specialist financial education charities and the willingness of private sector actors to provide support, obvious questions arise. Why are we still struggling to put an effective system in place to meet this need? And how best can banks and other financial services firms support the effort to deliver decent financial education for children and young people?

Getting to the Chalk Face

Providing financial education has been a priority in some schools for decades. The UK's largest bank-sponsored financial education initiative, NatWest/RBS's Money Sense, has been running in secondary schools since 1994. The first cohort of sixth-form pupils started studying for The London Institute of Banking & Finance qualification in personal finance in September 2004, well before the FSA published the first *National Strategy for Financial Capability*. In the 2017–2018 academic year, some 54,000 students in 800 schools studied for the Institute's personal finance qualifications and are much more money savvy as a result.

The first appearance of financial education in the mainstream curriculum came in 2007–2008, when 'economic well-being' was added to 'personal, social and health education' to form 'personal, social, health and economic education'. However, PSHE has remained a non-statutory subject, meaning local authority schools are not *obliged* to teach it. A more significant step towards universal access appeared to take place in September 2013, when the coalition government announced that from the following academic year financial education would form part of the National Curriculum for local authority secondary schools in England. For some, at least, it seemed to be 'job done'.

Financial education became part of 'citizenship', a statutory subject for Key Stages 3 and 4. Children in KS3 (aged 11–14) would be taught 'the functions and uses of money, the importance and practice of budgeting, and managing risk', while those in KS4 (aged 14–16) would learn about 'income and expenditure, credit and debt, insurance, savings and pensions, financial products and services, and how public money is raised and spent'. At the same time, elements of financial education were also incorporated into the new maths curriculum, so that 'all young people leave school with an understanding of the mathematics skills needed for personal finance'.

These efforts to make financial education part of the mainstream school curriculum have taken a long time to show evidence of success. Two years after the subject became part of the National Curriculum, The Money Charity surveyed schools and found that a third of teachers did not know this change had happened, and two-thirds classed what their school was delivering as 'somewhat or very ineffective'. While the charity found most schools provided some financial education, 'teachers have little faith in its quality and are held back by insufficient time, negligible resources and school leaderships who do not view it as a high priority'.

By 2018, The London Institute of Banking & Finance's annual survey found that 62% of pupils aged 15–18 said they had received financial education in school, a big improvement on the 44% who reported receiving it in 2017. But only a third of respondents said they had received any teaching in the past month, suggesting that it makes only occasional appearances in most timetables. In addition, the Institute's work shows that pupils are much more likely to receive financial education as part of PSHE, a non-statutory subject (18%), than in their statutory citizenship lessons (6%). Some 16% touched on the subject in maths lessons and 12% did in economics. Only 3% studied dedicated personal finance qualifications.

Jenny Barksfield, deputy chief executive of the PSHE Association, says that making financial education statutory by including it in citizenship, where it had not previously figured, and adding it to maths, was a 'quick fix' that allowed the government to say 'look, we made it statutory. You've got what you wanted'. However, she argues that leaving the subject dispersed between maths, citizenship and PSHE means it is 'everywhere and nowhere'. Maths lessons might show how to calculate compound interest, for example, but will do little to help people make the best decisions about which financial products are suitable for their personal circumstances.

It would be pleasing to suggest that there is light at the end of the tunnel. In 2020, most PSHE topics will become statutory parts of the basic curriculum, which will apply both to local authority schools as well as free schools and academies. This could have removed one of the barriers to wider teaching of financial education: the fact that, as free schools and academies proliferate, a growing proportion of schools are no longer obliged to follow the National Curriculum. However, the economic well-being element of PSHE, which includes financial education, is the only strand of PSHE which will not be made statutory from 2020. Barksfield says this is because financial education already figures in statutory citizenship and maths curricula. 'Those things have conspired to mean that [financial education] really is the Cinderella element of this Cinderella subject.'

The opportunity that risks being missed here was highlighted recently, one observer noted, at a panel discussion during *Talk Money Week* in late 2018. A first-year university student recounted how she had benefitted from the government's drive to educate young people about the dangers of health and social issues such as drugs as part of the PSHE syllabus: 'I can tell you every kind of drug, how you get it, how you take it, where it comes from, and the effect of it on your body and life. I can tell you all that because I learnt that at school. But I don't know how to manage my current account.'

Delivering Financial Education

The uncertain and fragmented presence of financial education in the school curriculum provides few incentives for schools to achieve excellence in this area. As in other aspects of life, what gets measured gets managed. It also compounds the other major challenges that they face in delivering effective financial education: restricted time and a lack of subject expertise. Staff can lack both knowledge and confidence to teach the subject.

'The people teaching PSHE, particularly in secondary schools, might be a geography teacher who has an extra hour on their timetable, or it could be a school where every form tutor has to teach PSHE whether they want to or not', says Barksfield. 'So, there's also a history going alongside that of teachers lacking confidence and training to teach it because it's not their first subject. Nobody does initial teacher training in PSHE.' The Money Charity's report in 2016 echoed this view: 'Teachers we surveyed called for greater resources, and clearer leadership, and a mixed model of provision that includes direct delivery by experts from outside schools.'

To date, one of the commonest ways for schools to supplement their teachers' knowledge and deliver on their obligations under the National Curriculum has been to enlist the help of charities specialising in financial education. These charities generally take one of two approaches. Organisations such as The Money Charity and MyBnk provide schools with ready-made financial education workshops for pupils, while Young Money (formerly the Personal Finance Education Group) concentrates on training teachers to deliver financial education at both primary and secondary levels.

MyBnk, for example, offers secondary schools a programme of three 100-minute sessions that cover the National Curriculum for financial education. In 2017, MyBnk reached almost 33,000 young people, says its chief executive, Guy Ridgen. 'I think in our age group [7 to 25-year-olds] there's something like 14 million', he adds. 'There's no problem with saturation here.' Schools may also choose to develop their in-house expertise by using the free service provided by Young Money and may choose to use the free teaching materials and lesson plans published by banks, including RBS/NatWest (Money Sense), Barclays (LifeSkills) and the Nationwide Building Society to plan their own classes, whether under PSHE or citizenship.

In some cases, classroom sessions are delivered by volunteers from financial services companies. The Money Charity, for example, uses trained volunteers from local firms to deliver classes in areas of England and Wales that it does not cover with its own presenters. However, other charities generally do not use industry volunteers to lead the delivery of financial education, despite their knowledge of the subject. In dealing with the major practical challenge financial education presents – that teachers are not experts and experts are not teachers – they argue that the core professional skill of experienced educators – the ability to engage and inspire children in the classroom – must be the foundation on which successful programmes are built. Knowledge of personal finance is, by comparison, secondary and can be taught to those with the right level of teaching skills and experience.

Russell Winnard, director of programmes and services at the charity Young Money, which trains about 1,500 teachers a year to deliver financial education and provides in-school mentoring for them, points to an evaluation of the charity's work by the University of Edinburgh Business School as evidence of the effectiveness of this approach. The study, the largest UK randomised control trial on financial education, found that teachers who had received finance training from Young Money made a statistically significant difference to the financial capability of their pupils – in this case post-16s – compared with the control group. It also found a bigger impact among those teachers who had also received the charity's in-school mentoring service.

MyBnk, which uses its own educators and has also had several of its programmes formally evaluated, places a similar premium on practical teaching experience, says Ridgen. 'Not that we've got anything against volunteers, it's just they're very unlikely to be as good at engaging with young people as a teacher would be. If you want to deliver our programmes, you've got to have at least two years' teaching experience or two years' experience in youth work.' MyBnk then trains and tests its delivery staff on the core financial subject matter.

However, this is not to suggest that volunteers from financial services companies and banks have no direct role to play in delivering financial education. Their specialist knowledge has undoubted value and, says Winnard, can be put to good use in the classroom. 'I think there's a compromise area, where the volunteer is not necessarily the main deliverer, that remains the teacher, but they are used to support what the teacher is doing. They can contribute their stories and their specialist knowledge, which maybe the teacher isn't so confident with. They can act as mentors to groups of young people who are working on an activity. Then we see a really impactful outcome for the young people.'

How the Industry Shares its Knowledge

As already indicated, banks and financial services companies are major players in financial education, providing significant funding to education programmes and underwriting the cost of producing large quantities of teaching materials (mainly online resources). In addition, their employees volunteer to go into schools to take part in classroom sessions.

However, the fact that corporate support has been such a significant factor in the provision of financial education in Britain has, at times, proved a double-edged sword. Before the financial crisis, the Money Sense programme run by RBS/NatWest, the UK's oldest and largest corporate financial education initiative, had a national network of around 30 coaches who would both deliver sessions in schools and train teachers. When RBS came close to collapse in the financial crisis, those roles disappeared and have never been replaced. As a result, a significant resource that schools had been able to call upon to support their work in financial education fell away, just as efforts among policymakers to improve provision were getting going.

NatWest/RBS returned in earnest to financial education in 2013–2014, when the subject became part of the National Curriculum. It revamped the Money Sense programme, turning it into an online resource with teaching materials matched to the National Curriculum and accredited by Young Money, and extending it to including primary schoolchildren in KS1/2 in 2015.

By the end of 2018, according to Caroline Edwards, senior community programmes manager at RBS Sustainability, 2m young people had been taught using materials downloaded from the Money Sense website after the relaunch. During 2018 it was used in 86% of secondary schools in England and Wales and 98% in Scotland. Some 30% of primary schools also use Money Sense resources. In total, the bank has registered 22,000 teachers across 12,000 schools.

Although it no longer employs coaches, the Money Sense programme offers workshops to its registered schools across KS1–4 and provides local volunteers from its staff to support teachers in delivering them. During 2018, about 65,000 pupils took part in these workshops.

The other major programme of face-to-face financial education provided by a high-street bank is Money for Life, which is owned and funded by Lloyds Banking Group and delivered on the bank's behalf by the charity UK Youth, a national umbrella organisation for local youth organisations. Money for Life started in 2010 and was significantly revamped in 2016, when UK Youth was selected as Lloyds' delivery partner for the 3 years to March 2019. The programme does not target children in schools. Instead, UK Youth trains local youth workers to deliver the programmes to youth clubs and groups, although sessions are open to people as young as 14 and up to 25.

The Money for Life programme incorporates a face-to-face Money Masterclass backed by online resources and aims to help young people at the point when they are starting to live independently and face 'the reality of good and bad financial decisions' as David Rowsell, head of education and employability programmes at Lloyds Banking Group, puts it. The programme places special emphasis on reaching those from deprived areas, aiming to deliver Money Masterclass to 32,000 young people over the initial 3 year period, a target it is on course to meet. During 2018, UK Youth says 1.1m people accessed the Money for Life website and online resources.

Projects such as these represent major direct contributions by leading financial services providers to the goal of ensuring that children and young people develop greater capability and confidence in managing their personal financial lives. As such, they must be regarded as encouraging bright spots. In spite of positives such as these, however, the overall picture of financial education in Britain remains a jigsaw and continues to suffer from the fact that significant pieces are missing, or do not fit together.

Putting Together the Jigsaw

If there is one word that best describes the problem with financial education in the UK today, it is 'disjointed'. Viewed from almost any angle, financial education is beset by problems of fragmentation, blurred lines of accountability and policies that work at cross purposes. Although a lack of resources may be a problem in this field, it is far from clear that this is the main issue, especially in view of the major role that the private sector plays in funding financial education initiatives. Christina Hicks, head of programmes at UK Youth, identifies coordination and collaboration among the many organisations active in this field as central areas of concern. 'There's a lot of talk in the sector about how lots of people are doing great things and how that can all be linked up', she says. 'But there's no consistent messaging going across and that's the tricky bit.'

Equally, a lack of expertise among teachers is widely accepted as a big hurdle to improvement, but this problem is exacerbated by other stumbling blocks that, together, conspire to make effective delivery much harder to achieve. Arguably, even if the UK did possess enough expert teachers, it is perfectly possible that we would still be falling far short of the results we should aspire to.

Why is this? A degree of complacency at the political level is one reason. Far from being 'job done', the decision in 2013 to sprinkle financial education into the National Curriculum – like hundreds and thousands onto a cake – has resulted in an ill-defined subject that crops up here and there across maths, citizenship, PSHE and economics, and therefore can always be regarded as some other department's responsibility. The trouble with sprinkles, after all, is that they look nice but tend to fall through the cracks. Against this background, the government's decision not to include financial well-being alongside the other elements of the PSHE curriculum that will become parts of the statutory Basic Curriculum in 2020 is troubling. However, even if it were included, this would not change the fundamental problem: an important subject is badly fragmented across different areas of the curriculum and lacks any cohesive vision and framework that schools and teachers can follow.

Similarly, the policy of promoting free schools and academies in recent years has meant that a growing number of schools are no longer obliged to follow the National Curriculum and so can choose not to provide financial education. There is evidence, for example in the statistics that banks publish about the proportions of schools that use their materials, that many decide to do so – RBS/NatWest says its materials are used in 86% of secondary schools in England and Wales and 98% in Scotland. But there is very little evidence of consistency in what is provided or in what contexts financial education appears on the syllabus.

As a result, even though financial education is part of the National Curriculum, the practical decisions over how and when it is taught remain almost entirely with individual schools and their leadership teams. As Lloyds' David Rowsell points out, this leads to vastly differing provision from one school to the next. 'Only a few schools have really taken this onboard and properly integrated it. When you get a school that integrates financial education into much of what it's doing, it works brilliantly. It forms part and parcel of many different lessons.' But that is inevitably the exception. According to The London Institute of Banking & Finance's survey, most children report receiving some exposure to financial education: 33% in the month before the survey – according to the *Young Person's Money Index 2018* – and another 14% in the previous term. But the data make clear that many receive almost no teaching in this area, and very few are given the sustained exposure to the subject necessary to build knowledge and confidence. The Institute is calling for a sustained, dedicated, programme in all schools, with more guidance for teachers and a mandatory number of hours for financial education. It also says that schools need to be able to provide evidence of impact.

There are limits to what even the best provision by specialist charities can do to bridge this gap. A limited number of sessions with a skilled, knowledgeable educator can be immensely valuable. It is questionable, however, that it is sufficient to meet the aspirations for a subject deemed important enough for inclusion in the National Curriculum. Are we not in danger simply of providing schools with convenient ways to achieve 'Rolls-Royce box ticking' where financial education is concerned?

Other issues also loom large. Although the MAS has led vital efforts to establish what works in financial education and assemble a national body of knowledge on best practice, this remains a work in progress. It is incomplete not least because academically rigorous evaluations of financial education programmes are large, complex and costly exercises to undertake.

Finally, the financial services companies that become involved in this field often fail to collaborate or to share best practice. While firms such as asset managers club together to fund delivery organisations like MyBnk, major banks almost always run their own, separate programmes and publish their own educational resources (albeit their teaching materials are usually approved by leading financial education charities). The result is that their teaching resources frequently overlap with other banks' output. It is particularly telling that when Lloyds Banking Group was considering how to become involved in financial education, it decided to avoid schools because this sector was already crowded with its competitors.

And because financial services companies are such important funders of financial education charities, their disjointed approach can have unfortunate side-effects. The availability of funding for certain types of activity can influence which projects get off the ground. If decisions are not taken as part of an overarching national strategy, the resulting coverage can be patchy, or uncoordinated. 'It's often the way that funding becomes available, people react to it, and programmes develop in that way', says Hicks. 'But it's not necessarily the right way to go about doing things.'

How to Make it Count: A Mini-manifesto

There is no doubt that the financial services industry is already providing a great deal of vital support for financial education in this country. But it is equally clear that much remains to be done and that not all of it is within the gift of the industry. The most glaring need is for a coherent national approach to providing financial education for schoolchildren and young adults, along with clear national guidance on best practice and which interventions are most likely to work. The MAS is already making important progress in this area and the recent launch of the Single Financial Guidance Body must build on the gains made so far.

How should banks and other financial services companies support these efforts? Here are six brief suggestions.

- They should continue to fund charitable services that provide high-quality training for teachers and build expertise within schools.
- They should commit stable, long-term funding to organisations that provide free face-to-face courses delivered by trained educators in primary and secondary schools, and through youth organisations.
- They should fund the production of accredited teaching materials but collaborate far more effectively to avoid duplication and overlap between the online and printed resources that different companies publish.
- They should commit significantly more funding to support rigorous, controlled evaluations of different financial education interventions, both their own and others'. This could provide a very important boost to the body of best practice.

- They should use their scale and access to government ministers to lobby for a review of financial education's disjointed presence in the statutory school curriculum. The industry must become a much more active, concerted advocate among policymakers for better financial education. Its ability to speak directly to ministers makes it uniquely well placed to argue the case that the current fragmented approach to this vital subject needs to be comprehensively overhauled and rationalised.
- Finally, financial services companies must stop treating financial education simply as part of their corporate social responsibility (CSR) activities. If financial education remains part of a CSR-focused effort intended, at least in part, to strengthen brand recognition and gain some degree of competitive advantage, effective collaboration between financial services companies will remain elusive. The result will be competing standalone programmes and a degree of duplication and waste. However, if the industry migrates towards a sharper focus on creating positive social impacts that are reinforced by effective collaboration, a different dynamic could emerge. In short, the effectiveness of the industry's contribution will depend greatly on how the major companies' policies towards social impact evolve from here.

There is much more to be done before financial education becomes more than an eternal work in progress in this country. The financial services industry cannot solve this problem. But it can do a huge amount to help.

CHAPTER 14

Banking on Identity

David G. W. Birch

This chapter examines the strategic value that banks could find in becoming the guarantors of digital identities.

At the beginning of 2019, the Governor of the Bank of England, Mark Carney, suggested that it was time to introduce digital identity cards because they 'would make it safer for people to access money online'.[1] Mr Carney is absolutely right about this. The friction introduced into not only online financial services, but also online everything else by the lack of an effective digital identity infrastructure is evident. Indeed, only a day after Mr Carney's remarks, the UK's Emerging Payments Association (EPA) released its report on money laundering and payments-related financial crime, calling for UK financial institutions to create a 'national digital identity scheme to tackle these threats'.[2]

Mr Carney was wrong, however, when he went on to say that such a scheme could also prove controversial and could 'only be

---

[1] Wallace T (2019) 'Digital ID cards could keep online finance safe, says Carney', *The Daily Telegraph*, 28 January 2019.

[2] Emerging Payments Association (2019) 'Facing up to financial crime'. Available at: https://www.emergingpayments.org/assets/uploads/2019/01/EPA-Facing-Up-to-Financial-Crime-Whitepaper-Full-Version-v2.0-1.pdf [accessed 6 May 2019].

introduced by the Government rather than the Bank of England'. In my opinion the controversial notion of a British national digital identity card of some kind should not be confused with the uncontroversial notion of some form of financial sector-specific, digital identity for the purposes of interacting with regulated financial institutions.

The British government's approach to digital identity (the 'Verify' scheme) ran into the sand and never delivered what was hoped for.[3] When it comes to online identification, authentication and authorisation, not only is the situation bad but it is getting worse. This is for the obvious reason that life in general is shifting online and money is going with it. As *The Economist* phrased it recently: 'the need for secure online identities will become more urgent as the world digitises further'.[4] In the UK, a useful digital identity card for financial services can only be introduced by the banking sector itself.

Let's bring all of these things together. The need to do something about online identity, Mr Carney's call for a digital identity card and the EPA's call for a digital identity scheme, can be integrated and resolved with a 'financial services passport'. If we are smart about how we set out this identity infrastructure for the twenty-first century, we can do something that delivers value to banks and the banking system, government and customers alike: we can raise the bar on both security and privacy without having to trade them off.

This is not a new idea. In my 2014 book *Identity is the New Money*, I noted that one very specific use of digital identity infrastructure should be to 'greatly reduce the cost and complexity of executing transactions in the UK' and I called for the regulators to 'set in motion plans for a Financial Services Passport'.[5] This was an informed perspective. I served as co-chair of the techUK Financial Services Passport Working Group, set up by the recommendation of an earlier techUK report *Towards a New Financial Services*, developed back in 2013.[6] In section 3 of that report, called 'Identity and

---

[3]National Audit Office (2019) 'Investigation into Verify'. Available at: https://www .nao.org.uk/report/investigation-into-verify [accessed 6 May 2019].

[4]'Making you you', *The Economist*, 18 December 2018.

[5]Birch GW (2014) *Identity is the New Money*, London Publishing Partnership.

[6]TechUK (2014) *Towards a New Financial Services' Report*. Available at: https://www .techuk.org/insights/reports/item/884-towards-a-new-financial-services [accessed 6 May 2019].

authentication: time for a digital financial services passport', there is a call for a standardised approach by the UK's financial services sector both to realise new opportunities for the sector as well as to enable wider societal benefits. It also notes that 'moving from the current fragmented identity infrastructure to a standardised financial services passport would require overcoming several challenges', including corporate coopetition and regulatory reorganisation.

The time has come to face up to those challenges and make some form of financial services passport central to the strategy of Britain's financial services. That would not be another layer of costly and cumbersome compliance. It would be a strategic differentiator helping them thrive by cutting transaction costs, boosting transaction security and revolutionising the user experience in financial services. With the Bank of England providing pressure for collaboration and regulatory reorganisation, a more targeted attempt at identity infrastructure for financial services can succeed where the government's 'Verify' digital identity scheme did not.

Practical Passports

What could a practical financial services passport actually look like? In the techUK discussions, we explored three broad architectures.

1. A centralised solution, some sort of 'know your customer' (KYC) utility funded by the banks. This was seen as being the cheapest solution, but with some problems of governance and control. It could also be a single point of failure for the financial system and therefore unwise given that we are now in a cyberwar without end.
2. A decentralised 'blockchain' (it wouldn't really be a blockchain, of course, it would be some form of shared ledger), where financial institutions (and regulators) would operate the nodes and all of the identity 'crud' ('create, read, update and delete') would be recorded permanently.
3. A federated solution where each bank would be responsible for managing the identities of its own customers and providing relevant information to other banks as and when required.

The technology needed to implement any of these options exists and while I favour a federated solution, any of them would work.

The issues that need to be resolved are those around the business model and the legal framework. Within that framework, issues around transaction liability are manageable because transaction liability can be limited to the transaction value. The regulators, however, will need to allow financial services organisations and others to shift liability by using a passport instead of doing their own KYC.

There is no reason to think that some form of interchange scheme cannot solve both of these problems. Since it would save many organisations (and not only banks or other financial institutions) considerable sums of money if they could rely on a solid bank KYC over creating and managing their own KYC procedures, they will, presumably, be enthusiastic. Compensating the passport issuers in return for accepting transaction liability while, at the same time, reducing industry costs through a federated KYC seems to me to be both feasible and desirable.

Building Checkpoints

Let's agree, then, that a financial services passport is needed and move on to what it might look like. One way to do this could be to use the 'three domain identity' (3DID) model that I developed with colleagues at Consult Hyperion. This model, as shown in Figure 14.1, frames digital identity as the bridge between the mundane and virtual worlds and sets out a clear framework for thinking about the dynamics of the bindings with either of them.

Now, using this model, we can think of the financial services passport as the digital identity and the personas as visas stamped into that passport. In practical terms, I could go to, say, Barclays to open a bank account, at which point Barclays gives me a passport (a digital identity) and stamps it with a visa to visit the land of Barclays (a persona, let's call it dgwbirch#barclays). I can take this same passport to

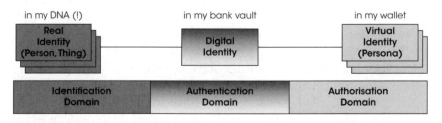

Figure 14.1   Three domain identity.

HSBC and get a stamp to visit the land of HSBC (another persona, dgwbirch#hsbc).

The details of the cryptography that forms the links between the person and the passport, and between the passport and the personas that customers will use in transactions, are not important to this chapter. It is sufficient to know only that these bindings are highly asymmetric: it is time-consuming, complicated and expensive to bind a digital identity to something in the real world, but it is inexpensive and quick to bind the digital identity to something in the virtual world. It's all about encryption and keys and how you manage them.[7]

There are a number of reasons for thinking that while there are a wide variety of organisations that could support these bindings, and indeed a number of different institutional arrangements that could come into existence around these bindings, it should be banks that are in the vanguard.

My view on this was reinforced recently when a friend had some problems with his Facebook account being taken over by fraudsters. He was extremely frustrated by his efforts to contact Facebook and have something done about it. As I pointed out to him, I could not see any reason why he should have expected anything different. Facebook has no statutory obligation to remedy such problems. Banks, in contrast, are regulated financial institutions that (were they to provide identity services) would be required to act. If your bank account is taken over by thieves, then you might reasonably expect the bank to do something about it after notification and to have some procedures in place to establish quite who the rightful owner of the bank account is, to restore control of the bank account to that person and to provide appropriate compensation if the bank had behaved negligently in any way.

One of the key attractions of this architecture is (and I'm sure that I am not the only person who thinks this) that it gives an expectation of redress in the event of inevitable failure. Things always go wrong. What's important is what the structures, mechanisms and processes for dealing with those failures are. If some fraudsters take over my bank account and use my identity to create a fake profile on a

---

[7]Birch GW and McEvoy NA (2007) 'A model for digital identity'. In: Birch GW (ed.), *Digital Identity Management: Technological, Business and Social Implications*, Routledge, 95–104.

dating site, then I'd expect the bank to have mechanisms in place to revoke the tokens and inform both the dating site and me that such revocation has taken place without disclosing any of my personally identifiable information (PII). This is important because PII is in essence a kind of toxic waste that no companies really want to deal with unless they absolutely have to. Under the new provisions of the General Data Protection Regulation (GDPR), the potential fines for disclosing PII without the consent of the data subject are astronomical. Hence the complete cycle needs to be thought through. It would be crazy to have an infrastructure that protects my personal data when the system is operating normally but gives it up when the system fails, or when we attempt recovery from failure.

First Steps

To see how banks are beginning to take advantage of the new opportunities in this space, let us take a short world tour to see what Barclays are doing in the UK, what 'itsme' is doing in Belgium, what the Commonwealth Bank of Australia (CBA) is up to down under, and what Toronto Dominion are doing in Canada. The way in which these first steps into the identity space have been evolving shows how the scope and sophistication of bank-led approaches are growing.

Barclays became one of the 'identity providers' for the British government's Verify service back in 2016. In order to use this service to access a variety of government services online, you have to first create an online identity. To do this, you can choose one of a number of private sector organisations to validate your personal details and bind them to the online identity. Barclays is one of these organisations. To date, this scheme has met with limited success since there are few places to use the government identity.

In Belgium, the 'itsme' service, launched in 2017, takes a very different approach. It's a very interesting collaboration between the Belgian banks and Belgian mobile operators: Belfius Bank, BNP Paribas, KBC/CBC and ING working with the telecom operators Orange, Proximus and Telenet. To use this, you download the itsme app and verify your identity (which is easy in Belgium, since everyone already has an eID card), then use it to log in to participating websites. To begin with these sites are (as usual) for tax filings, but insurance companies and retailers are joining the programme. Soon, users will be able to sign official documents using their mobile phones and have secure remote access to a wide variety of systems. The combination of the identity, the SIM and the app delivers a very secure and reliable environment. To be completely honest, I don't understand why banks and mobile operators were not cooperating in this way a decade ago.

In 2017, the CBA began a pilot service with Airtasker to provide verification services. In the growing 'gig economy' it is a significant step, because providing identity infrastructure to these marketplaces is a way for banks to be involved in the transactions. Airtasker is an Australian online community where people and businesses go to out-source tasks (e.g. 'build my IKEA furniture for me'). If you have an Airtasker profile you can go through the CBA verification process and the system will add a badge to your profile. The badge tells people that the CBA know who you are. It does not give away any personal information, it merely tells prospective users of your skills and time that the bank knows who you are. This simple expression of reputa-tion gives comfort to those prospective users and illustrates a central point about the coming collaborative economy, which is that repu-tation is much more important than identity (and much harder to counterfeit).

The main Canadian banks (including Bank of Montreal, CIBC, Royal Bank of Canada, National Bank, Scotiabank and Toronto Dominion) are part of a nationwide consortium that developed a sophisticated digital identity infrastructure, launched in March 2019, to bring security and convenience to their marketplace. As in the case of itsme, customers will use the service via an app. However, in the Canadian scheme the trusted credentials are stored on a shared ledger built using IBM's blockchain service (implementing hyper-ledger fabric). The scheme uses a 'triple blinding' implementation so that the people relying on the trusted credentials and the people providing the trusted credentials never see each other's identity.

Privacy as Proposition

I like the bank-centric vision of the future emerging from these examples. It's a win/win for the banks and the consumers. And it bakes in privacy, rather than adding it as an afterthought, to the point where it might become part of the banks' fundamental consumer proposition and a fundamental defence against disinter-mediation. I'll use a non-financial use case to show what I mean.

Let's imagine I go to an internet dating site and create an account. As part of this process the dating site asks me to log in using Facebook, Google, Amazon or the financial services passport. I choose to use my passport, at which point my passport (i.e. my mobile phone) displays a list of valid visas (my personae) and asks me to select one.

After I select one of the personae – Dave at work, Dave at home, SuperbiaInProelia or Mr X – the system bounces me to my bank (where the passport came from) to undertake the appropriate two-factor authentication to establish that I am indeed the passport holder. The bank then returns an appropriate cryptographic token to the internet dating site, telling the dating site that I am over 18 and resident in the UK.

Unlike a physical passport, modern cryptography means that the service provider, whether an internet dating service or anything else, does not get to see my passport, only the visas stamped in it. They see the persona, not the person. My real identity is safely locked up back in the bank vault. So my internet dating persona contains no PII, but if I use that persona to get up to no good then the dating site can provide the token to the police, the police can see that the token comes from Barclays and Barclays will tell them that it belongs to Dave Birch. This seems to me a very appropriate distribution of responsibilities. When the internet dating site gets hacked, as they inevitably do, all the criminals will obtain is a meaningless token: they have no idea who it belongs to and Barclays won't tell them.

ID Need

Digital identity is critical infrastructure for the new economy. The management consultants McKinsey – who studied the identity infrastructure in Brazil, China, Ethiopia, India, Nigeria, the UK and the USA – estimate that extending full digital ID coverage could unlock what they call 'economic value' equivalent to 3–13% of GDP in a decade in the countries it focused on.[8] Banks ought to obtain significant advantage as key providers of the new infrastructure, because the collaborative economy stakeholders do not want to have

---

[8]White O, Madgavkar A, et al. (2019) *Digital Identification: A key to inclusive growth*, McKinsey Global Institute. Available at: https://www.mckinsey.com/business-functions/digital-mckinsey/our-insights/digital-identification-a-key-to-inclusive-growth [accessed 6 May 2019].

to create their own identification, authentication and authorisation infrastructures. I might go even further and say that the view that banks will in future become stores of digital identities is a practical and realistic view of what banking will become.[9]

But, and this is a big but… there is no inevitability about this bank-centric vision. There is, as the World Economic Forum made clear in its study of the topic, a role for regulated financial institutions in delivering digital identity and everything that goes with it (privacy, security and the attendant costs and benefits) to the mass market.[10] However, digital identity is not the right of the banks to exploit. If banks do not offer digital identity services that are relevant to the post-industrial revolution, they won't simply miss out on the opportunity to offset some of their costs with some revenue-generating (and generally useful) new services. They will cut themselves off from the sources of data that they need to feed their artificial intelligence engines of the future. They will not be able to do risk analysis or information management of any value without the vast quantities of information, relationship and reputation data needed to feed the voracious appetites of the machine learning behemoths that will be at the heart of banks of the next generation.

Digital identity must be central to bank strategy.

---

[9]Davies S (2014) 'Banks want to keep your digital ID in their vaults', *Financial Times*, 2 September.

[10]World Economic Forum (2016) *A Blueprint for Digital Identity*. Available at: https://www3.weforum.org/docs/WEF_A_Blueprint_for_Digital_Identity.pdf [accessed 6 May 2019].

Going Over the Top

Renier Lemmens

Renier Lemmens examines the challenges that incumbent banks face in avoiding becoming utilities that provide the commoditised, underlying 'plumbing' of the banking industry while higher-margin, 'over the top' financial services that consumers see and love are offered by other players.

The World Wide Web has already upended many industries, among them retailing, music and newspapers. Banking will be next. There are a couple of reasons for this. First, it is a big sector that has a number of profit pools, which makes it an attractive target. Finance and insurance businesses represent around 6.5% of UK GDP. Second, the data associated with finance have value to technology companies that make money by analysing what consumers do online and – increasingly – almost every aspect of society. Third, most consumers in developed markets now have smartphones – high-performance personal computers they carry in their pocket. And consumers like their smartphones. The average UK adult checks their mobile phone every 12 minutes and is online for 24 hours a week, according to Ofcom.[1] That is why, unlike

---

[1] Ofcom (2018) *The Communications Market 2018.* Available at: https://www.ofcom .org.uk/research-and-data/multi-sector-research/cmr/cmr-2018.

early PC-based online banking, mobile banking is not just another product channel. It can support engaged, hyper-personalised services and, by extension, deep product unbundling. Fourth, regulators want to see more competition and are changing the rules to encourage it. Consequently, the regulatory entry barriers for new industry participants are lower than ever. But before we look at some of the nitty-gritty of where banking will go, perhaps we should step back and examine what brought us to where we are.

'The dream behind the web is of a common information space in which we communicate by sharing information. Its universality is essential: the fact that a hypertext link can point to anything, be it personal, local or global,'[2] wrote Tim Berners-Lee, the 'father' of the web, in 1998. Putting information into a common space is not just a tremendous boon, it breaks down business silos. The 'moats' that made many industries both necessary and lucrative – such as the investment in printing presses and fleets of lorries once required to run newspapers – are, in many instances, gone. Now, a newspaper can be published globally with a few clicks. 3D printers can make a single part, to order, where it is needed, without waste or shipping costs. Online distribution of information is cheap, instant and everywhere.

What makes the web, and the internet connectivity that supports it, such a disruptive force is that it is a 'network of networks'. But why does that matter to banking? After all, it has been over 20 years since Google launched, but UK banks still run high street branches and the incumbents still control the market. There are 73m personal current accounts in the UK, according to the FCA (the high number reflects the fact that around 40% of people have more than one account). However, the largest four banks are still the main providers of accounts into which people pay their salary, and the concentration is even higher when it comes to business current accounts. So, one could argue that despite all the bluster and headlines, nothing has really changed.

What makes banking different to the businesses that were quickly hollowed out by the internet, such as music publishing, is that its business is keeping data private. Banking is also not easy

---

[2]Berners-Lee T (1998) *The World Wide Web: A very short personal history.* Available at: https://www.w3.org/People/Berners-Lee/ShortHistory.html.

to do. Entering retail banking means getting a licence to operate, raising sufficient capital, being trusted with people's money and keeping data secure. And, while all of that is necessary, it is not sufficient. Competitors also need to be able to get consumers to switch. Lack of competition with bite meant the incumbent banks in the UK historically did not have to change the way in which they operated, or their underlying systems. That had the advantage that they could continue to operate inefficient, legacy IT systems built up over decades that kept customer data in silos and were not designed to enable creative data analysis. The disadvantage, of course, was that they could continue to operate clunky legacy systems ...

Fintechs, in contrast, are digital natives. They are on the rise now, rather than 5 or 10 years ago, because of steep falls in the cost of computing power, a huge leap in the capability of the phones in our pockets and because regulators are opening up bank data silos. Open Banking in the UK, for example, requires all banks to comply, by 14 September 2019, with the technical standards that will permit customers to give third parties direct access to their bank data. Fintechs are already challenging the incumbents on the basis of one or more of the following: better and more convenient service; a smooth product experience and customer journey; offering service personalisation and solutions to unmet needs; and lower cost. Open Banking, however, will be a step change. Together, these factors enable fintechs to bring very specific products to finely targeted customer segments, attacking hitherto well-hidden profit pools of the incumbent banks, without the need to build expensive mass-market infrastructure.

What Open Banking does is dismantle the data silos that hampered the provision of genuinely new, web-based customer services in retail banking. In the meantime, online-only providers can already make market inroads, and build their brand in readiness for Open Banking, with, for example, lower costs for end consumers, or simply better-designed buying and consumption experiences. Incumbents have to shoulder the costs of running branch networks, of creaking mainframes and of offering a wide range of products to a wide range of customers at the same time as they need to gear up fintech services to compete with much nimbler newcomers. A better product at a lower price is a proposition that is hard to beat.

Lower cost, and often more narrowly focused, fintech operations do mean that, over time, financial margins will fall. Take remittances for example. International payments have been a key focus area for fintechs. Overcharging for slow service by incumbents created the perfect umbrella for fintechs to compete. It is estimated that incumbents will lose up to 85% of the profits from these services. The 'long tail' of the internet, the cost-effective discovery and servicing of very niche markets, means that financial services firms can start to offer products that were not possible before – for example, for the under-banked and unbanked. Even when the sums of money involved in each individual product may be small, the ability to find a lot of people who will pay for a 'niche' offering, which the web makes possible, creates a viable business.

Where the Value Lies

This suggests that what will be decisive in making fintech services attractive to consumers is not only price, but targeted service and quality in equal measure. Consumers will expect instant, highly personalised, seamless and engaging products and services – thanks to fintechs that offer them a very wide range of choice not available in the offline world.

The UK has seen six new digital banks authorised since 2015, the Bank of England said at the end of March 2019. At that point it had another 16 fintech firms going through pre-application or application, including digital banks, account aggregators and firms working with crypto-assets. Globally, there are many thousands of fintechs in the market, but there is a relatively small number of full fintech retail banks. Whether a financial service provider is a bank or not does not, of course, necessarily interest the consumer. The fact that many challenger banks partially wrap themselves around incumbent legacy infrastructure is also unlikely to deter customers. What matters is whether a fintech offers a service they perceive as personalised, trustworthy and value-added.

That, of course, plays to the strengths of the thousands of fintechs globally who are setting out to unbundle financial services without the cost and complexity of managing a retail current account. The current account, a recent PwC report argued, is seen by many as 'an old-fashioned product'. Certainly, if Open Banking becomes popular with consumers, then a customer's current account in the UK could end up being little more than a secure pot maintained by the bank (for free), into which other companies dip to provide the financial services that consumers actually use – such as push payments or 'nudging' on savings or spending. That is because non-bank fintechs focus on specific consumer pain points and use targeting capabilities to offer proactive, intelligent solutions – often to individual problems. In the past, for example, it was difficult for freelancers, who often see their income fluctuate from month to month, to get a mortgage. Now, fintech providers can use data from a wide range of sources, such as profiling based on mobile data, to underwrite mortgage products for freelancers in a much more nuanced and personalised way.

The legacy business at banks relied on selling one-size-fits-all products to a large, and largely captive, base. The data processing was done in batches and did not necessarily draw on non-financial data. Indeed, one of the complaints about the shift to a reliance on computers at banks in the late 1980s – away from a system based on the local knowledge of bank managers – was that credit assessments became much cruder. There was good reason for the relative bluntness of the computers' decisions. As Berners-Lee noted in 1998: 'one of the things computers have not done for an organization is to be able to store random associations between disparate things, although this is something the brain has always done relatively well'. Now, however, the availability of vast quantities of varied data in real time via the web, and of the artificial intelligence that can begin to analyse it creatively, has radically changed what automation can accomplish. Computers are beginning to be able to make the sort of subtle analyses that, until now, only the best human experts could undertake. DeepMind, the London-based AI group owned by Google, for example, recently announced a prototype device that can carry out a retinal scan to diagnose a number of eye diseases. One commentator described its performance as 'jaw dropping'. Already many firms are applying similar deep learning capabilities to design targeted marketing campaigns, credit scoring, investment advice, compliance processes, etc.

What Fintechs Do Well

Challenger banks do have a number of advantages over incumbent banks. These include short decision lines, a strong focus on the user experience and on tailoring products, and quick build–learn cycles supported by deep-pocketed investors who allow them to make mistakes responsibly. That means they can bring creative problem-solving and new ways of doing things to banking. Importantly, this creativity is as much in the back-end of banking – including compliance and risk management – as it is in the 'visible', customer-facing part of the business.

If incumbents are, in contrast, bureaucratic, not particularly customer-centric and hobbled by the need to maintain expensive, but clunky, infrastructure, it would seem that they run the risk of becoming the 'utilities' that run the expensive underlying pipes and see the profitable opportunities in products and segments picked off by others. This is happening already. Apart from the remittance example mentioned above, fintechs have made inroads in wealth management solutions through robo-adviseries, in SME banking, and in payments of all kinds, just to name a few. This phenomenon is akin to what has already happened in the telecom industry, where 'over the top' providers of internet services, such as Google or Facebook, have higher margins than the telecom operators who keep the network running. A utility role for banks is very much a potential outcome – particularly under Open Banking. Young consumers, for example, are likely to associate banking services with their phone, rather than with a bank branch. Around 63% of consumers surveyed by Worldpay for a report in November 2018, for instance, said they expected smartphones to replace physical wallets in the next 5 years.[3] I recently sampled an audience of 400 students, and more respondents had an account with one of the challenger banks than with an incumbent. More than 50% had not visited a branch in more than a year.

The Incumbent Fightback

The incumbent banks do, however, have some advantages. First, they have strong brands and a customer base that rarely switches provider – they are trusted to take care of money. Then, they can act as 'over the top' providers themselves by building their own fintech start-ups. A number are taking this route. RBS, for example, is about to launch a mobile-only bank called Bó. Bó runs on its own infrastructure, unencumbered by the legacy architecture and

---

[3]Worldpay (2018) *Global Payments Report.* Available at: https://www.worldpay.com/global/insight/articles/2018-11/global-payments-report-2018.

(one assumes) the legacy product thinking of the parent bank. The incumbents also still have deep pockets, which enables them to experiment with projects like Bó. Not least, they have institutional knowledge and industry expertise that, if managed properly, can be used to avoid mistakes when setting up a challenger.

Their own challenges are almost always cultural. They need to truly liberate their internal innovators and allow them to 'challenge' the business practices of the mothership. For the success of their initiatives it is very important that they do not import pay structures, compliance processes, IT procedures, risk frameworks, and so on through the back door and thus encumber or smother the new initiatives.

The Incumbent Insurgents

The real challenge to banks in the long run, however, may not be the challenger banks. The existing 'over-the-top' providers of web services that consumers use on a regular basis, including Amazon, Facebook, Google and PayPal, have very deep relationships with tens or hundreds of millions of customers who admire their brands and value their service.

These have long track records of providing 'products' that consumers simply love to use. The web giants' services are also designed to be compelling – some people find that their life becomes a distraction from their mobile phone.[4] A lot of people, for example, spend time scrolling/strolling through eBay without buying anything, just as people used to window shop. This is light years away from the levels of customer engagement and satisfaction that incumbent banks generate.

Just how big and powerful a fintech can be in financial services is demonstrated by Tencent and Alibaba in China. Tencent runs WeChatPay, which, as the name suggests, is more than a payments service. It uses data from the many hundreds of daily interactions with its site that each user might make to become a personal portal on the world. WeChat surpassed over 1bn 'monthly active user accounts' in 2018. Tencent has a similar model, and both Tencent

---

[4]Roberts JA and David ME (2016) 'My life has become a major distraction from my cell phone: partner phubbing and relationship satisfaction among romantic partners', *Computers in Human Behaviour*, 54, 134–141.

and Alibaba have datasets of a scale that others cannot match. They can analyse those datasets, often in real time, to enable them to make their services cheap and compelling – and to dictate terms to the banks that provide the underlying financial services.

Their power is also not just a function of their datasets, or of their technology. When the web began to take off in 1998, a start-up with a service that went viral could expect to raise enough funding to compete with other web services. Now, tech behemoths of the scale of Tencent or Amazon have war chests and resources that far out-strip what fintechs can raise from a typical venture capital investor (unless big tech is that investor), or, indeed, what incumbent banks can muster. Google, for example, had cash, cash equivalents and mar-ketable securities of US\$109bn at the end of 2018, and it could easily raise substantial sums in the capital markets if it wanted to undertake a project that could not be funded out of existing resources.

Hiding in Plain Sight

Because financial data are largely held in banks, and the big tech players excel at analysing 'over-the-top' consumer data, big tech is often perceived as not being active in financial services. That, however, is a mistake. They already have a financial relationship with hundreds of millions of customers. The credit and debit cards in Amazon store accounts, card and bank details with PayPal or Tencent, represent formidable beachheads from which to launch an assault with an ever-growing array of financial services. Moreover, Amazon, for example, already has a very sizeable financial services business, which began with the provision of working capital to sellers on its site. Google acquired a European licence as a payments institution at the end of December 2018 (from the Irish regulator). That allows it, under PSD2 and Open Banking, to be a payment initiation service provider (taking money out of a bank account at a consumer's request to make payments) and an account information service provider (providing information to the consumer on what is in their account). PayPal is a regulated bank in Europe and is offering a plethora of services already. All of them could, in principle, combine data gathered from being a payments institution with data from other, in-house services to develop new consumer payment and account information services that others cannot match.

They certainly have access to types of data, and quantities of data, that banks do not.

Conclusion

The jury is still out on who will provide the most compelling retail financial services: incumbent banks, fintechs or tech giants. The incumbent banks have the steepest hill to climb, and a lot of cultural and technical baggage to carry up the mountain. The cost and complexity of running legacy infrastructure is a drag on their performance and hampers investment in new technology; they need to build out fintech services that cannibalise their existing product lines; and, perhaps most importantly, they have limited access to data outside of their own – and that data will soon have to be shared with formidable competitors. They will face humongous challenges in avoiding relegation to utility status. Fintechs have a lot of advantages, but they will need to continue to grow fast towards profitability if they are to access essential funding and then delight the IPO-market. The big tech players are coming from behind, but with formidable assets and tremendous capabilities. They can pick off profitable segments without ever needing to worry about banking licences.

My money is mainly on the big tech players and a select few fintechs. We will see the more far-sighted incumbents develop compelling challengers in-house. The market will be much more competitive as the bold and the beautiful displace the old and the dutiful.

CHAPTER 16

Banking Technology

Can the Centre Hold?

Anthony Gandy

Anthony Gandy analyses how technological developments over the past 60 years have informed the business model of retail banks and asks whether the disaggregated computing made possible by the cloud and real-time processing could trigger a paradigm shift in retail banking.

Technology is fundamental to the banking sector and has been for many years. While, historically, it would be hard to say that banking is a part of the technology sector, it is an industry that is focused on the ability to transport, store, collate, retrieve, transform and view data. Such a profile makes it closely aligned to change in information technology and destined to be an enormous user of the latest capabilities in information processing.

Technology has fundamentally changed banking. That change is now continuous as it incorporates developments not just in hardware, networks and software, but also increasingly in the business model. Again, this is not new. The introduction of ever more advanced information processing tools, coupled to global networks and decision systems that operate in close to real time, has created a standard model for banks, one that tries to aggregate many services within a single entity. This is only possible in its current form thanks to advances in technology. However, this model is now very much threatened by new, disaggregated strategies that also rely on technology and could undermine the accepted norm.

Here we look at some of the innovations that have changed the core processing of banking information; how the logic of these led to large institutions that use a data-driven model to target every corner of a customer's life throughout their life; and at the models that are now competing with this established, scale-based paradigm.

Banking and the Adoption of Technology

For a bank intermediary, processing transactions, keeping records of the transactions and providing access to those records is at the core of the business. In this context, it is not surprising that banking has long been a prime consumer of information processing technologies. When The London Institute of Banking & Finance was a mere 75 years old, the importance of banking to the future of technology, and indeed the importance of technology to the banking industry, became quite clear. An industry already automated with punched card tabulators and accounting machines began to adopt the computer. There is no single starting point, but there is a good argument for it being on the West Coast of the USA in 1958, when Bank of America began receiving ERMA (Electronic Recording Machine, Accounting) computers. At a time when computers were the domain of military engineers and scientists, modelling nuclear weapons and aerodynamics, Bank of America contracted General Electric to order 32 of these ERMA machines.[1]

ERMA was based on 5 years of research undertaken at the Stanford Research Institute and at GE, including advances in magnetic ink character recognition (MICR) that allowed machines to operate autonomously when collating data. Of course, punched cards allowed this as well, but MICR meant that what was meaningful data to a human was also meaningful data to a computer. ERMA could exploit this in building Bank of America's customer accounts. Bank of America expected accounts clerks to be able to process 250 transactions an hour using their older NCR and Burroughs

---

[1]Edwards R and Gandy A (2014) 'Navigating the M-Form: product scope review and the development of the General Electric Computer Department', *Business History*, 56(8).

punched card system. Each of the ERMA systems, based in regional processing centres rather than in branch back offices, could process 10 'checks' a second.

What was decisive was that the bank structure could exploit these benefits. The use of computers in banks ushered in an era of data centralisation, automated processing and increasing economies of scale. Banks were big batch processors of information, updating accounts, registering transactions and preparing data daily, often overnight. Data collation and transformation were carried out offline. That meant a wait for the information generated – whether you were management or a customer. Both the technology and the way it was used favoured large volumes. Back offices could, and indeed needed to, be centralised and the greater the scale the lower the cost of banking services. It is no surprise that during this time access to bank accounts started to move beyond the upper and middle classes.

Of course, better customer service can be provided, and decisions made in a timelier manner, if batch processing is supplemented by real-time transactions and real-time information. To achieve this, radical enhancements needed to be made to the computers of the 1950s. Throughout the 1960s and 1970s, the reality of turning information into a truly accessible commodity would prove challenging and again it would, initially, favour the large enterprise. Real-time control was something the military was very interested in. Guiding an aircraft or a missile to its target, or processing radar signals and identifying threats, couldn't really wait for an overnight batch process. However, exploitation of the initial advancements in real time, multi-user, computing in the commercial world was not initially led by banks. Transportation was further ahead. Booking airline seats was a big headache. Airlines wanted to sell as many seats on a flight as possible without double-booking. Enabling simultaneous access to booking systems by many agents, and real-time transparency on whether a seat was booked or free, would increase plane utilisation massively. To make this happen, however, required complex operating systems that could allow multiple users, multiple applications and multiple tasks to be undertaken simultaneously and this needed to be supported by equally complex hardware.

Airline booking systems owed a lot to military technology. For example, NORAD's SAGE system-controlled air defences in North America had large numbers of radar inputs, real-time processing and many controllers who had to be active at the same time.

The technologies behind this system influenced directly developments such as SABRE, the American Airlines booking system.[2] The first SABRE system was installed on two IBM 7090 computers, directly developed from SAGE. Development of SABRE cost almost US$40m. But by 1960 it could support 1,500 terminals and could process 84,000 telephone transactions per day.

Banking systems would remain somewhat less ambitious when it came to real-time challenges. Indeed, for UK banks, just automating basic account handling using overnight batch processing was the only aim in the 1960s. UK banks were loyal to UK-produced technologies to begin with. This made sense; the UK was by far the leading computer technology centre outside the USA and central technologies such as virtual memory, essential for real-time computing, were developing in the UK. In 1961, Martins Bank rented a Ferranti Pegasus computer while Barclays opened a data centre and purchased EMI EMIDEC1100 computers (see Figure 16.1).[3] Midland Bank initially adopted early English Electric computers. Both Barclays and Midland would quickly deploy US technology. In the case of Barclays, it was IBM mainframes. Midland Bank, driven by the inability of English Electric to deliver its systems in time for the conversion to decimal currency in 1971, they went with Burroughs.[4] The focus was still on batch processing, even with the US kit being adopted.

In the Here and Now

The complexity of real-time access to information was one of the reasons why a schism in technology – and two separate technological routes at UK banks – developed in the 1970s and 1980s. The routes were as follows.

- Big integrated centralised batch and real-time systems with multi-user access.
- A move to smaller-scale, local processing.

---

[2]Sabre Corporation (2014) 'The Sabre Story'.

[3]Ackrill M and Hannah L (2001) *Barclays: The Business of Banking, 1690–1996*, Cambridge University Press.

[4]Martin I (2012) 'Too far ahead of its time: Barclays, Burroughs and real-time banking', *IEEE Annals of the History of Computing*, 34(2).

Figure 16.1   Barclays inspect their EMIDEC 1100 computer at the opening of the Drummond Street Computer Centre, 1961.

Source: Courtesy of Barclays Group Archives (ref 30/3426).

This second trend was generated directly by frustration with centralised systems and their complexity. Bell Lab scientists and others waited interminably for the successful completion of integrated multi-user systems (in their case the massive Multix system) and this encouraged them and others to create UNIX and other smaller-scale systems that gave access to computing power at laboratory level.[5] This move to smaller-scale systems was not unique to Bell Labs. The logos of minicomputer firms like Digital Equipment Corp (DEC) would become common in bank computer centres in the 1970s and 1980s and UNIX itself, with firms such as Hewlett Packard and IBM, would become dominant in the 1990s, heralding the way to standards-based, open-source systems including the Linux operating system.

---

[5]Campbell-Kelly M, Aspray W, Ensmenger N and Yost JR (2014) *Computer: A History of the Information Machine* (3rd edn), Westview Press.

The schism between large-scale computing and small-scale computing was evident in banks. Large banks would go through 20 years of green screen monitors interacting with mainframe computers. This gave them the scale to exploit batch processing to generate ample, non-real-time data at low cost and then work with these data intra-day to provide good – if not the most up-to-date – customer information. Often these large systems would co-exist alongside minicomputers when immediacy, at least on a smaller scale, was key. The minicomputer became especially important for smaller banks and international bank subsidiaries when a new generation of pre-packaged software emerged that equated to a 'bank in a box'. Some of these packages were based on DEC systems and then UNIX; many other packages sat on IBM's AS400 machines, which integrated a relational database into the operating system, so creating a perfect small-scale banking platform. This meant that, come the end of the 1980s, even small banks could adopt cutting-edge technologies.

For larger banks, the 1980s saw a model in which they operated big mainframe systems as a core banking platform – which handled very large transaction volumes and large overnight tasks – alongside an increasing number of smaller systems that carried out more tactical activities. It was the tactical activities that were most likely to be close to customers and to provide direct services. That made it necessary to link large-scale systems to smaller ones, and this became more formalised with the adoption of client–server computing. Here the concept was to break up the 'system' into different layers and each layer then became, to some degree, independent. By doing this a bank (and others) could create flexible systems that separated data, applications, networks and user interfaces. Then individual elements could be changed without impacting the others, and data could be available to multiple systems simultaneously.

This approach allowed different user interfaces, such as customer service and credit checking, to hang off the same data system and it also allowed easier development of management information. A central example of this was the customer relationship management (CRM) system. Different applications, such as customer enquiries and transactions, could co-exist with CRM and marketing systems. That allowed some real-time decision support, but this was not one coherent system. In order to have real-time information and to integrate the big central transaction engines, a 'middleware' layer of technology, software and networks was required. Middleware provided a set of 'plugs' through which multiple types of software application could tap the same common dataset and it allowed communications and data flows between even quite dissimilar technologies.

Linking disparate technologies demanded standards to ensure interoperability, and here again Stanford Research Institute's name crops up. It was one of the institutions involved in the development of the US computer network ARPANET.[6] This network of interlinked supercomputers started small but would become a vital resource connecting computers across the USA and the UK, and then beyond. Global interoperability was not a given. Critically, on 1 January 1983, ARPANET would switch to the transmission control protocol/internet protocol (TCP/IP) and the foundations of the internet were in place. The internet is, by design, a multi-user environment with (nowadays) real-time processing of data packets. That advance would eventually allow once internally focused bank IT systems to expand from the banks' own properties and take their systems directly into customers' homes.

By the 1990s, using technology to take retail financial services beyond the branch – something already common in capital and wholesale financial markets – began to develop. Initially, some banks devised proprietary technologies for delivering banking services to their corporate and retail customers, still others would look to 'walled-garden' internet services such as CompuServe and AOL, but arguably the biggest step forward was the provision of online banking in the open internet environment. Again, it is hard to say where this began, but Security First Network Bank (SFNB) was a critical launch pad for a whole new way of not just offering banking services, but also of innovating how banks were built. SFNB, set up in 1995, was an early (if not the earliest) internet-only bank.

SFNB existed on the public internet and was delivered using the World Wide Web interface, which meant its servers were using protocols and computer languages matched to the desktop clients of its customers. It was a model that marshalled in dotcom banking v1, because it showed that banks could be small but still have a very

---

[6]Norberg AL and O'Neill JE (1996) *Transforming Computer Technology – Information Processing for the Pentagon 1962–1986*, Johns Hopkins University Press.

long reach, and that customers were happy to self-drive their banking services.

In one respect this turned out to be less of a threat to the major banks than might have been expected. The first-generation internet banking brands – Egg, SFNB, Netbank and many others – would fail to establish a long-term presence. From another standpoint, it was revolutionary because large banks incorporated the model themselves. They used the internet to reach customers in the same way that the start-ups did while exploiting client–server computing to develop their preferred strategy – a strategy of offering customers aggregated financial services within large, monolithic banking organisations.

Keeping it Within the Firm

By the 1990s, a technology-led strategy was well established in retail banks. It used a combination of the new technologies to build a model that targeted customers intelligently and focused on service delivery, but nevertheless exploited economies of scale and scope. Technology allowed banks, especially larger-scale ones, to focus on the supposed lifetime value (LTV) of their customers and try to increase the customers' propensity to cross-buy products. Banks would begin to see such value as a capital asset,[7] and banks actively looked to curate these assets.[8]

It is often assumed that there is a magic 20% of customers who deliver 80% of the profits while the rest do not offer much return, or at least not much yet. If a bank can identify the upcoming 20%, and model their customer lifetime value (CLV), that should be very valuable. Identifying that 20% is one of the dark arts of marketing, but the techniques are reasonably well known.[9] Searching for the 20% is a clear reason why banks have made such large investments in CRM technologies. However, this focus can lead to concerns about

---

[7]Malthouse EC and Blattberg RC (2005) 'Can we predict customer lifetime value?', *Journal of Interactive Marketing*, 19(1).

[8]Persson A (2011) 'The management of customer relationships as assets in the retail banking sector', *Journal of Strategic Marketing*, 19(1).

[9]Ekinci Y, Uray N and Ülengin F (2014) 'A customer lifetime value model for the banking industry: a guide to marketing actions', *European Journal of Marketing*, 48(3/4), 761–784.

the appropriate use of data and the negative reaction bank staff and customers alike can have to incessant targeting.[10]

The CRM-led CLV models are based on the assumption that, as a customer moves through life, they will generate more value for a bank. For this to work, customers have to both adopt the bank as their service provider and then take more services from that bank, especially those services that generate income. It may be worthwhile offering a current/checking account and not making money on this for many years in the hope that the customer then takes out a credit card, gets a car loan, buys a house via a mortgage or purchases financial advice on a pension. A key matrix then becomes how many products a customer buys. One bank that regularly answered this question was Wells Fargo. In 1998, when Norwest merged with Wells Fargo, it was reported that the average number of products per retail customer was 3. By 2004 it was 4.6,[11] and would reach 6.11 products per retail customer in November 2015.[12] For wealth management customers, the number of products held in 2015 was 10.55. Increases had also been seen for wholesale customers, where the number of products per relationship increased from 5.3 in 2004 to 7.3 in 2015.[13]

To provide this number of services to large numbers of people across multiple generations of customers implies a massive investment in technology. Not only does a bank need a CRM system to target sales to the right customers, it also needs transaction engines for potentially many dozens of different products, as well as customer systems that can bring together these different systems and make a consolidated view available to the marketing team, the customer service centres, in branches, on customers' PCs and, more recently, on customers' mobile device. The CRM-led CLV strategy is a technology-intensive option.

Of course, there have been challenges to the model, even without new competitors offering a different strategy. Wells Fargo, for example, stopped producing such eye-popping product sales

---

[10]Durkin M and Kerr R (2016) 'Relationship banking in practice: perspectives from retired and serving retail branch managers', *Strategic Change*, 25(1).

[11]Wells Fargo Annual Report 2004.

[12]Wells Fargo Annual Report 2015.

[13]Wells Fargo Annual Report 2015.

numbers once it became embroiled in a scandal over fraudulent cross-sale claims. Staff, it turned out – incentivised by bonuses and other inducements – had begun to fake sales to meet targets.[14]

Wells Fargo's problems with compliance within the CRM-led CLV targeting strategy are not unique. The scandals in the UK around payment protection insurance and the cross-sale of swaps products to small businesses are further examples of banks trying to exploit every element of a customer relationship, even when some of the cross-sold products are not well designed for the customer and in areas of finance that the bank itself is less familiar with. There is an argument that the CRM-led, CLV targeting, multi-channel economies of scope and scale model has a point where diseconomies of scope are triggered.

There is a further problem with this catch-all strategy: the sheer amount of technology change that large-scale banks must master. While in some sectors of the economy firms can focus on one technological trajectory, banks' strategy of 'being all things to all people' means they have to juggle multiple development paths that do not necessarily replace previous capabilities but often simply build upon them. Innovation is often viewed as an S-curve,[15] where one technology displaces an older technology quite neatly with the old tech of much lesser importance, if not non-existent, over time – a process which continues to happen, as shown in Figure 16.2.

However, banking is not developing a core technology, such as semiconductors or storage systems; instead, it is – effectively – a super-user of technology. For banks, it is not the technology innovations that matter, but the way in which these innovations can be used to improve and/or extend their business model. So, when one innovation comes along, it is not necessarily displacing a previous technology, but introducing a new capability on top of what has been provided before. This new S-curve then starts a new innovation path in its own right. What we are really seeing are stacked S-curves, as shown in Figure 16.3.

---

[14]Armstrong R (2018) 'Wells Fargo to pay $575m more over sales practices', *Financial Times*, 28 December.

[15]Foster R (1986) *Innovation: The Attacker's Advantage*, Summit Books; Christensen CM (1992) 'Exploring the limits of the technology S-curve. Part I: Component technologies', *Production and Operations Management*, 1(4), 334–357.

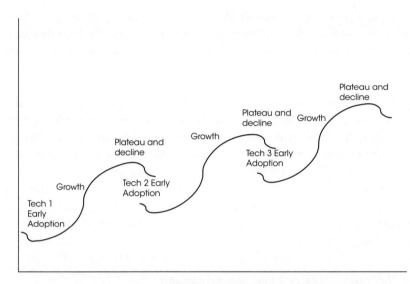

Figure 16.2   Basic innovation S-curve showing the initial slow adoption of a new technology (when resources are being consumed in development), growth and then plateauing of demand and a falling off of the economic advantage of the previous technology.

Source: Based on data from Foster (1986) and Christensen (1992).

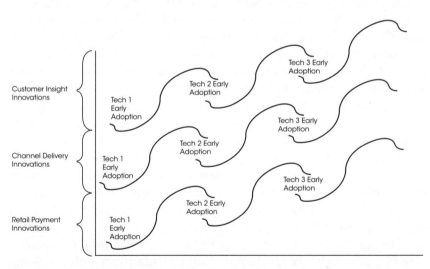

Figure 16.3   Stacked innovation S-curves. In this scenario, banks are not phased with innovation on a single path of S-curves, but have to keep up with innovation across multiple paths simultaneously.

Source: Based on data from *Anthony Gandy*.

In this scenario, established institutions end up having to fight to stay relevant across multiple evolving environments. In payments, for example, when the cheque developed, cash did not end. When the ATM came along, cash and cheques survived. When automated payments and direct debits became possible, cash, cheques and ATMs all continued, as did innovation in the processing of each of them. Card payments, mobile payments and person-to-person payments all add to this mix. Staying on top of all these capabilities while innovating in customer service and customer insight is a massive technological challenge – and an expensive one.

The strategy adopted by banks, which values the cross-selling of all products to as many customers as possible through all available channels, sets them a very complex task. It is a strategy that new rivals are looking to unpick.

The Challenger Model – A New Spin on Spin-off

Not a single new entrant from dotcom banking v1 survived to truly challenge the incumbents. Even the largest, NetBank, would eventually disappear into a 'traditional' bank. Arguably, this is because the dotcom banking v1 firms were trying to emulate traditional banks in a new channel, the internet, but not fundamentally looking to restructure the business model of banking. To a large extent, of course, they had little choice because, at that time, the technology was not particularly supportive of a differentiation strategy based on channel alone. The new generation of client–server computing was as much a boon to established banks as it was to new entrants. They could use client–server technology to isolate their legacy systems from client systems and thus both offer modern front ends (web and mobile access) and build new intelligence systems (such as CRM) without having to change their robust underlying core systems. Major banks could introduce the same capabilities as the dotcom-only banks, but carry on exploiting their greater scope of services, range of channels and the depth of their economies of scale.

The question for the current generation of new entrants is whether there have been changes that provide them with any long-lasting competitive advantage, or which undermine the competitive advantage of established large banking groups in a significant way.

Twenty-five years after the first generation of internet banks, the issues areas follows.

- Software has evolved and become cheaper and development costs are lower – can that impact the minimum economic scale of banking? Could a new generation of challengers exploit this?
- Do new players even need their own IT platforms? With cloud-based applications, can new banks simply sidestep the need to make capital investments in complex IT platforms and software? Does this also undermine the minimum economic scale needed to be in the banking game?
- Most fundamentally, does the 'full service' banking model still make sense when aggregation services can bolt together multiple financial providers through a common interface to create an externally sourced, aggregated financial service?

It is the third question that is the most interesting, as an aggregation approach is less replicable by institutions whose ethos is CRM-led CLV targeting. We are seeing a new generation of technology-enabled challengers experimenting with the banking business model. Three strategies stand out.

1. **Banking-lite and the platform model.** In this model new providers establish themselves to offer only a part of the value proposition larger banks have offered.

   There are many examples of such banking-lite models. Some new banks are focusing on using a stripped-down, mobile-only current account model to establish a new customer base; examples include Monzo. Revolut has taken a more payment-oriented route. ClearBank is predicated on being a bank-enabler offering a 'banking in a box' service to other banks. They are not, as individual institutions, looking to offer the whole spectrum of banking capabilities, nor are they looking to fill out every channel. At least, they are not doing this with their core transactional service.

   That's not to say these banking-lite models do not wish to go toe-to-toe with the major cross-selling banks. They offer a stripped-down version of what an integrated bank offers, but understand this as part of an aggregation of services. Some of these firms aspire to put themselves at the heart of a platform that provides customers with full service through a network of partners. Such models offer a cheap-to-develop core product set enabled by new delivery channels. When the central platform does not offer a particular product itself, it avoids the cost of complying with its regulation, as well as the associated risks. However, through a platform's choice of aggregation partners, it can still offer that product to its customers and take a fee for enabling this. The partnership model means it does not need to build capability to manufacture the full range of financial services products to be able to provide that full range to customers.

Platform-centric services rely on technology and are seen as a part of the fintech world, but their true innovation is the business model. Their strength, and their chance of success, will be in curating the walled garden of services they enable customers to access.

2. **Intermediation-lite and the aggregator model.** The idea that banking could become driven by a platform model has seen notable precedent in recent history in the insurance market and in the comparison services that dominate distribution. Price comparison services don't remove financial intermediation, indeed they reintroduce the concept of the broker, but they do so using low-cost aggregation technologies and by passing the decision making to the customer. They have become an important part of e-commerce, from travel to retail. Comparison websites allow consumers to obtain product and price information at a lower cost and they provide a distribution channel for retailers. They introduce real and virtual competition and can be product vehicles. Though it's an important model for other parts of financial services, it may not yet be right for all core banking products, though it is certainly becoming a key conduit for distributing retail loans. A fundamental element of this model is passing risk assessment back to the customer. This clearly has a cost benefit to the firm, but may not provide the customer with the central strength of the more traditional broking service.

3. **True disintermediation.** Maybe the most fundamental challenge to the traditional banking model is the technologically enabled marketplace – the peer-to-peer network. From Zopa for retail lending and Funding Circle for business loans, to Transferwise for foreign exchange, the use of technology to match one customer who has funds with another who wants funds truly challenges the bank intermediation model. Of course, again, there is a transfer of risk back to the customer. It represents a total break with the banking model.

4. **Invasion of wholesale.** As well as peer-to-peer linking retail borrowers and savers in new ways, we have also seen institutional investors linking to borrowers through market-based solutions. Hedge funds and private equity have used online platforms (and indeed high street outlets) to reach high-risk borrowers and other communities such as business borrowers. This is simply another iteration of the marketplace approach.

Technology enables these challengers to move beyond what was offered by the dotcom v1 banks by more fundamentally challenging the model of banking. Cloud computing, coupled to nascent artificial (and non-artificial) intelligence technologies, begins to offer some new competitors a hope of building virtual CRM–CLV strategies that do not necessarily rely on every system, every channel and every product being owned internally by the platform.

When both customer data and core banking capability are in the cloud (based on widely accepted open standards), there is the prospect of challenging the established institutions in a cost-effective manner. When that happens, the minimum efficient scale needed for the banking (or emulated banking) game can fall. If banks are in part (if not mainly) data processing machines, a shift to a virtual body of customer data accessed and managed by an equally ephemeral core banking engine is a real challenge to existing models. It adds uncertainty to the picture and may bring into question the multi-billion IT budgets deployed by big banks to both perform their function and buy economies of scale. Certainly, the value of these investments is now starting to be questioned. In March 2019, Mizuho Bank took a charge of US$6.1bn covering write-downs on the value of its physical retail network and its legacy IT systems.[16]

---

[16]Obe M and Hirose Y (2019) 'Mizuho to book $6bn charge on pivot from physical banking', *Nikkei Asian Review*, 6 March.

However, the other question is whether there are economies of scale in banking that go beyond IT. If those economies of scale exist, then the disaggregation made possible by the cloud may have little impact bar making established institutions a little bit more efficient as they adopt the model fully. Indeed, if economies of scale in banking are mainly rooted in processing scale, then the real impact could be using new technologies to further improve the effectiveness of the large integrated banks. Banks, and their fundamental ability to transform risk, should also protect the transitional model – but when intelligence is automated, even this cannot be guaranteed.

CHAPTER

17

The Future of Payments

Ruth Wandhöfer

> Ruth Wandhöfer explains why payments are at the centre of financial innovation and transformation, and what this will mean for banks.

The world around us is transforming at a mindboggling rate. Digitisation, automation and artificial intelligence (AI) are expected by some to lead us to 'the singularity' – that is, the development of a computer-based intelligence that will not only be indistinguishable from human intelligence (the Turing test), but will far exceed it and fundamentally change every aspect of society.[1]

For some that may sound too revolutionary to be credible, but many small revolutions are already here, not least in financial services and, in particular, in payments. During the last decade a combination of technological innovation and regulatory realignment has opened up the market for new players, new business models, new products and services and new ways to consume those products and services. In this chapter we examine the developments in payments in Europe and the UK, provide an overview of the state of play and take a look at what the future may hold at the international level.

---

[1]Kurzweil R (2005) *The Singularity is Near: When Humans Transcend Biology*, Viking Press.

Introduction

Payments innovation in Europe arguably started with the arrival of the European Commission's first Payment Services Directive (PSD1) in 2007.[2] The EC's overarching aim was to ensure 'the proper operation of the single market in payment services ... [and] a level playing field for all payment systems, in order to maintain consumer choice, which should mean a considerable step forward in terms of consumer cost, safety and efficiency, as compared with the present national systems'.[3] To do that, the EC opened up the industry to non-banks and, for the first time, allowed them to compete in the payments business alongside credit and e-money institutions.

Making payments might not sound like the most attractive of activities – not least from the perspective of the person paying – but what had been a somewhat stodgy utility function turned out to be the area where consumer convenience and technological innovation would come together to create transformative solutions.

A few architectural changes underpinned that. A major innovation at the system level was, of course, the Single Euro Payments Area (SEPA), which for the first time allowed people to make cashless euro payments across borders with the same convenience and under the same conditions as at home. (SEPA covers credit transfers, direct debits and card payments.) Interestingly, at the same time bitcoin, the world's first ever private cryptocurrency, arrived. That use of distributed ledgers (which were originally conceived as a way to overcome lack of trust across distributed networks) marked the beginning of a parallel world of payments – separate from fiat currencies – which created the opportunity for digital barter. Such barter is now the cornerstone of a digital financial ecosystem that has seen the launch of many crypto coins, initial coin offerings (ICOs), security coins and a general movement towards tokenising any type of asset or data with the aim of enabling a seamless exchange via a distributed ledger.

---

[2]European Commission (2018) 'Information about Directive 2007/64/EC on payment services'. Available at: https://ec.europa.eu/info/law/payment-services-psd-1-directive-2007-64-ec/law-details_en [accessed 14 February 2019].

[3]European Commission (2018) Available at: https://ec.europa.eu/info/law/payment-services-psd-1-directive-2007-64-ec/law-details_en [accessed 14 February 2019].

There are lively debates about the future of digital currencies.[4] However, I would argue that what is much more important is the future of payments as a whole. Will payment innovation be able to deliver improvements not only in domestic markets but also cross-border? Will we see the rise of new payment instruments and the demise of others? Will cryptocurrencies evolve to meet the requirements of an actual currency (a store of value, a unit of exchange and a unit of account), or will central banks consider issuing new forms of digital cash instead? In order to provide some perspectives, let's look at Europe and the journey that European payments have been on so far.

Payments Sans Frontières

The introduction of the euro made it clear rather quickly that efficient euro payments, both within and across borders, would demand a pan-European payment system. The SEPA initiative was conceived in early 2000 and took almost a decade to deliver. European payments legislation, in the form of PSD1, did its part to support regulatory coherence and consistent consumer protection in the single market. However, take-up of the new system and services was initially slow and regulators had to step in again to mandate the switch from 'old' domestic systems to SEPA.

Inspired by the experience of the Faster Payment System (FPS) in the UK, the next step was shaping a faster version of SEPA. The SEPA Instant scheme was eventually launched in 2017 and, since November 2018, transactions can be settled in central bank money via the European Central Bank (ECB) TARGET for Instant Payments Settlement (TIPS) system. (For the uninitiated, TARGET stands for: Trans-European Automated Real-time Gross settlement Express Transfer.) More than 60% of all payments service providers (PSPs) in the eurozone now adhere to the scheme. At the level of the European Payments Council (EPC), which is responsible for maintaining the rulebooks for SEPA, ideas are already being developed to enhance the scheme and enable different use cases, such as paying a merchant online or maybe even in a physical point of sale (POS) environment with a SEPA-compliant card.

[4]Dyson B, Meaning J (2018) 'Would a central bank digital currency disrupt monetary policy', Bank Underground, 30 May. Available at: https://bank underground.co.uk/tag/money/ [accessed 14 February 2019].

That may not sound ground-breaking, but it means that all consumers shopping with a SEPA-enabled card would pay the same payment fees, regardless of where they bank. As of March 2019, SEPA covered 36 jurisdictions (the 28 EU member states together with Iceland, Norway, Liechtenstein, Switzerland, Monaco, San Marino, the Principality of Andorra and the Vatican City State/the Holy See), and those paying in another state or principality with a 'foreign' card could potentially face higher fees than locals.

Reducing the power (and income) of intermediaries in the interests of the consumer has always been one of the primary aims of EC policy on payments. Most recently the EPC has called for the creation of a new working group to consider the functionality of 'request to pay', an alternative to pre-scheduled direct debits that the UK has already decided to implement. Request to pay allows consumers to query bills and to negotiate the timing of payments, rather than being tied to a schedule. That sort of functionality is likely to be popular, as so-called 'gig' working increases and many people have irregular or unpredictable income streams.

The Grip of the Incumbents

Despite the EC's focus on driving competition, the payments market is still controlled by incumbent banks. In its payments statistics for 2017, for example, the ECB reported that retail payment systems in the EU processed 57bn transactions totalling €44tn. The four largest systems – CORE in France, STEP2 (an automated clearing house for banks run by the EBA), BACS in the UK and Retail Payments System in Germany – processed 60% of the volume and 64% of the value.

The EC has long considered that there was more scope to create competition for banks by leveraging the emerging technology and business logic that e-commerce had already brought to Europe. As they drove down transaction costs on the web, merchants were keen to see alternatives to credit card transactions. These were not only expensive, but also tended to suffer from low conversion rates. The largest platforms, such as Amazon, which could both shoulder the transaction costs and securely store card data to enable easy, 'one-click' payment, had an advantage over smaller players. That showed a clear gap in the payments market and some non-bank providers came forward with payment initiation services that let consumers pay online merchants directly from their account.

This was seen as such a benefit to the single market that the EC decided to formally endorse and regulate those types of services. That led to the arrival of PSD2 in January 2018. If PSD2 fulfils its mandate, it could be a highly disruptive piece of legislation. It will mean that consumers can make payments without bank, or credit card, intermediation. That loss of transaction fees could radically alter the business models of some banks and card companies. It could also enable the sort of online micropayments that current processing charges make uneconomic – potentially providing sizeable online revenue streams for sectors such as publishing.

PSD2 is still a work in progress. Final regulatory technical standards (RTS), developed by the European Banking Authority (EBA), come into play from September this year (2019) and they focus on the security of the authentication and authorisation of digital payments. However, a lot more needs to be done when it comes to delivering the data rails that support the core of PSD2 innovation, which, after all, is non-bank access to account data. In principle, consumers are able to authorise payments directly from their account via third-party payment service providers (TPPs). The current requirement is that banks must set up application programming interfaces (APIs) which allow TPPs to 'dock' onto an account. APIs are a technology that has been around for a good three decades, but writing APIs is not easy. Perhaps more importantly, industry standardisation is proving elusive. A plethora of individual bank APIs do meet legal requirements, but if TPPs are really to make inroads there needs to be a small set of harmonised APIs that all of them can use. If API standards were harmonised, it is likely that functionality could also quickly be expanded beyond the initial scope of PSD2. The EPC is already working on this, together with the European Retail Payments Board (ERPB), an entity composed of ECB, EC and market participants that provides support for integration and innovation within the single market for payments in Europe.

What is sometimes overlooked is that, however disruptive the EPC's work may appear from the standpoint of incumbent payment systems, the innovations that it seeks are part of a multitude of developments around the world – some much more radical than anything the EPC is undertaking. Huawei Pay, for example, which digitises a credit card in the same way as ApplePay, launched in Russia at the end of 2018. This was Huawei's second market after its domestic stamping ground of China. Like Apple, Huawei's actual business is the provision of mobile phones and operating systems – the payments are handled by financial services players – but, like Apple, it has a strong brand which could overshadow that of the payment providers. Where that can lead is already clear in China itself. The gorillas in the Chinese payments market are WeChatPay and Alipay, both owned by major online platforms. So dominant are Alipay and WeChatPay, with hundreds of millions of subscribers each, that Chinese banks have effectively been relegated to utility status.

A major part of the appeal of Alipay and WeChatPay is that they allow users to avoid (often very long) service queues by using their mobile to scan QR payment codes. Mobile payment is now part of everyday Chinese life and Chinese tourists expect to be able to use their schemes overseas. That is why Norway and Finland are on track to launch the first ever QR code payment scheme in Europe in 2019, based on Alipay's QR code standard. The direction of travel on payments is towards greater interoperability, lower costs and fewer intermediaries. Alibaba, for example, the owner of Alipay, recently entered into an agreement with the Belgian government to launch an e-commerce trade hub, where payments are bound to play a key role.

A list of all the recent payment initiatives would fill this chapter, but one upshot is crystal clear: the pace of development in payments is becoming more and more challenging for incumbent banks, particularly those that sit on legacy IT. And that, by the way, is before they start to defuse the underlying time bomb of the cyber security threat.

Payment Infrastructure Change in the UK

Though the EC has made many profound changes to payments in the EU, the UK has often been a step or two ahead. The work done by the Payment Strategy Forum (PSF) in 2016 and 2017, for example, provided the foundations for a radical restructuring of retail payments in the UK, which led to the creation of the New Payment System Organisation (NPSO), recently renamed 'Pay.UK'. (At the same time the UK's high-value payment system CHAPS was returned to the control of the Bank of England, which is working on a redesign of its own real-time gross settlement system for banks.) PayUK covers the faster payments system and BACS (the UK's batch processing system) and it is also charged with delivering the new payments architecture that will be enabled by APIs. As is the case with the EPC, Pay.UK aims to make access to the payments system easier, faster and more efficient. That, in turn, should foster more competition and the sort of vibrant payment service innovation that will benefit consumers and commerce in the UK. Challenges with regard to execution remain – not least because of the scale of the endeavour – but once the work has been completed, the UK will have one of the world's most modern and resilient payment infrastructure ecosystems. All in all, it should allow for a more nimble and efficient modus operandi for future innovation and evolution.

Open Banking: New Business Models and Services

One of the things that makes the new payments regulation in the UK potentially radical is the UK's counterpart of PSD2: the so-called Open Banking initiative. The nine biggest banks in the country had to open up their payments to third parties via a standardised API at the start of 2018. Standardisation makes it much easier for small players to come into the market. Further, while PSD2 focuses on payment initiation services and account information services, Open Banking gives the market free rein to innovate in any way that consumers will support. This means that Open Banking has much greater potential than PSD2 to break up the payment oligopoly of the incumbent banks. However, both measures, PSD2 and Open Banking, are only due to truly unfold in 2019 and beyond. They offer the promise of better payment services as well as increased financial inclusion and financial awareness.

For that promise to be met, consumers will need to be educated about what Open Banking can do. Services already range from account information and expenditure analysis to micro savings products, all of which are 'in-app', that is, users do not have to click around to carry out transactions. However, even when products are convenient and useful, there is a clear need for digital and financial education and a change in user habits to realise the potential of Open Banking.

One of the barriers to uptake may be trust. In principle, Open Banking and PSD2 could, for example, make processing mortgages and other types of loans faster and cheaper. However, consumers may be wary of making major financial transactions online. Still, banks already have a great deal of data on customers and once many other parties can access those data a fuller picture of consumers will emerge that enables a wide range of new services. These could include more nuanced credit scoring, helping those in the 'gig' economy get mortgages, as well as more personalised products.

However, the need to win consumer trust and offer 'one-stop' convenience may mean that the real threat to bank business models does not come from new banks, or from nascent financial services firms offering niche products. Platform business models could gain hugely from Open Banking. Players such as Google and Alibaba are already active in the European payments market – both have e-money licences. It will be interesting to see to what extent more services will be built upon their existing payments capability. There are certainly precedents. For example, some Chinese platforms offer investment products alongside payments.

Data in Payments

One of the reasons why large platforms already outperform smaller rivals is the sheer amount of data they can collect and analyse. That is why the next big milestone for payments will be to deliver better data analytics and management. If online data are 'the new oil', payments are the natural place to hit the next big gusher. However, the 'oil' payments produce will only be of real value if analysed at scale and holistically, if companies gather both general and financial data. Until recently, the latter were controlled by banks and card companies. That is no longer the case. There have been calls for financial services companies to be given access to the data held by the big platforms, in a sort of reverse of Open Banking. As things stand, that looks unlikely. However, the advent of non-banks and non-card companies in payments will permit a more rounded and fuller data picture. That should help mitigate the risk of unauthorised, wrongly executed, non-compliant and illegal transactions – as well as opening up a range of new services.

The potential source of heat in all of this is the need for data privacy. The General Data Protection Regulations (GDPR) that came into force in Europe in 2018 underline the role of data as an asset that needs to be protected. That, in turn, requires a radical rethinking of data strategy. Naturally, with data being at the centre of the future of payments, payment systems will need to be equipped to carry and protect these data. SEPA, as it currently stands, does not allow for significant amounts of data to be carried between payer and payee (with the exception of specific country implementations). The same applies to the UK FPS. This means that more could be done to enlarge the standard remittance field, which is the text message that accompanies the payment. That would enable improvements in payment reconciliation and associated efficiencies. The recently launched New Payments Platform (NPP) in Australia shows what can be done. There, users can exchange up to 280 characters of text (rather than 140 and 128 for SEPA and FPS, respectively). While this can pose challenges to compliance with anti-money-laundering (AML) and countering the financing of terrorism (CFT) regulation, a larger structured remittance field is vital for business transactions. There, embedding the legal entity identifier (LEI) will add another layer of compliance efficiency.

And Now, Back to the Future

Let's return to our initial reference to bitcoin. The payments industry has now begun to realise that blockchain technology offers ways to rethink existing business models, services and even the nature of money itself. Once we overcame the initial hype of blockchain, followed by the obligatory blockchain fatigue, banks began gearing up for blockchain delivery. 2019 could be the year in which we see blockchain coming of age.

Trade finance, for example, which suffers from a heavy compliance burden, together with lingering reliance on paper documentation, has been a focus for several blockchain initiatives around the globe. Correspondent banking is another area. Here we have seen the launch of the Interbank Information Network (IIN), which operates on Quorum, a permissioned variant of the Ethereum blockchain. The INN, which is run by JPMorgan and has over 75 bank members, was set up to help correspondent banks resolve compliance and other data queries more quickly. On top of that, SWIFT has recently announced a proof of concept with blockchain consortium R3 to explore connectivity to its global payments innovation (gpi) initiative. Depending on the specifications, blockchain can still have problems around latency and capacity. Work continues on improved consensus algorithms that will allow for immutability and tamper resistance as well as efficiency and speed.

As the use of blockchain develops, and new forms of money are devised, more functionality will be needed – for example the use of smart contracts. To facilitate innovation, we may see the development of so-called sidechains and second-layer chains. One of the advantages they bring is that they are independent of the main ledger. If they fail, or are hacked, the main blockchain can remain unaffected. They also hold out promise in terms of improving liquidity and lowering latency. Despite significant volatility in the price of cryptocurrencies, we are likely to see more innovation in the trading space, with the growth of derivative solutions as well as stable coins. Security tokens are a further development to watch, as the financial industry slowly digitises assets for the purpose of blockchain-based trading.

There are many naysayers when it comes to cryptocurrencies, but 2019 started with an announcement that Mizuho Bank is rolling out a private cryptocurrency – the J-coin – in collaboration with 60 local and regional banks. Other Japanese banks are working on similar projects. What they have in common is an attempt to innovate and drive efficiency in payments and put down a marker against the competitive threat of Chinese giants Alibaba and Tencent. Japan is ahead of Europe when it comes to regulatory support for the use of private cryptocurrencies, but other markets are investigating the option for central bank-issued digital currency as an alternative to physical cash.

China, for example, believes that the role of a central bank in an increasingly digitised world is to provide for a digital form of central bank money. With more than 40 patent applications filed in this space, the digital Currency Research Lab at the People's Bank of China is taking a pragmatic approach to developing an end-to-end solution for central bank digital currency.

There has also been a flurry of activity around what central banks label general purpose central bank digital currencies, ranging from pilots to launches. Uruguay set up its e-peso pilot in November 2017.[5] The e-peso was a legal tender and a peer-to-peer digital money solution (not based on distributed ledger technology), which allowed exchange of e-pesos via mobile text messages and the e-peso app. Unique digital notes were issued to an e-note manager platform for

---

[5]Licandro G (2018) 'Uruguayan e-Peso [in] the context of financial inclusion'. Presentation to the BIS, Basel, 16 November. Available at: https://www.bis.org/events/eopix_1810/licandro_pres.pdf [accessed 15 February 2019].

distribution, which also acted as a central register of ownership. Some of the e-pesos were distributed by a third-party PSP. The Banco Central del Uruguay had a number of aims in view with the pilot, including examining how to increase financial inclusion, lower payment costs and boost security. It deliberately chose an approach that did not require an internet connection, so that rural areas could have easy access. The pilot closed in April 2018.

Dubai took a much bolder step with emcash, a blockchain-based government-issued cryptocurrency launched in October 2018. The solution operates on the basis of a near-field-communication (NFC)-enabled wallet, facilitating faster and lower-cost retail payment transactions.[6]

The Marshall Islands in the Pacific have a population of around 53,000 and a need for economic development. At present the economy depends on fishing, tourism and foreign aid. The sovereign digital currency (SOV), as laid down in the Sovereign Currency Act of 2018, will be legal tender alongside the US dollar. The SOV will be launched via an initial coin offering (which is analogous to a stock listing) and the proceeds are earmarked for various development funds.[7] It is reported that the SOV will come in the form of a physical card that can be used in a 'cash-like' way without the need for an internet connection, but also operates with a blockchain-enabled microprocessor. Internet penetration in the Marshall Islands is low outside tourist resorts, so it may be that the SOV is aimed at generating increased revenue from tourists.

Closer to home, Sweden's e-krona project is slowly taking shape. Commerce in Sweden is already largely cashless. Only around 13% of POS payments in 2018 were in cash, which is why the Riksbank is considering introducing a digital currency.[8] Sweden is focusing

---

[6]Buck J (2017) 'Dubai will issue first ever state crypto currency', *Coin-Telegraph*. Available at: https://cointelegraph.com/news/dubai-will-issue-first-ever-state-cryptocurrency [accessed 16 February 2019].

[7]Republic of the Marshall Islands (2018) 'Declaration and issuance of the sovereign currency act 2018'. Available at: https://rmiparliament.org/cms/images/LEGISLATION/PRINCIPAL/2018/2018-0053/DeclarationandIssuanceoftheSovereignCurrencyAct2018_1.pdf [accessed 15 February 2019].

[8]Sveriges Riksbank (2018) 'The Riksbank's e-krona project'. Available at: https://www.riksbank.se/globalassets/media/rapporter/e-krona/2018/the-riksbanks-e-krona-project-report-2.pdf [accessed 15 February 2019].

on digital retail payments and the e-krona, in its current thinking, would be complementary to physical cash. The Project Plan phase 1 launched in 2017 with the development of a theoretical proposal and a system outline. Phase 2 began in 2018 and focused on regulation and operational considerations, including the choice of technologies. In 2019 a go or no-go decision from the Swedish central bank is to be expected.

Will we see a central bank digital currency (I personally view this as a good space for experimenting with a digital euro)[9] in the developed world any time soon? After all, IMF President Christine Lagarde made it clear that central banks will need to adapt to a digital future and cannot ignore the parallel world of cryptocurrencies forever. It is hard to say what will happen. As Sweden's Riksbank points out,[10] Sweden blazed a trail in digitisation and it has some unique local features, in particular the Swedish Bank-ID app, which ensures secure identification. Even in Sweden, however, officials are concerned about the potential impacts of a cashless society, particularly on social inclusion.[11]

Conclusion

Payments are the cornerstone of a new era of banking. The often overlooked business of moving value is now right at the centre of innovation and transformation. Consumers and businesses increasingly expect payments to offer the level of service and convenience that they are used to online – that is instant, transparent and cheap. Generation X are digital natives and the trust that used to be the privilege of banks has been replaced by a trust in technology and social media. For banks to survive in this whirlwind of change, a focus on customer-centric innovation and agility will be essential.

---

[9] Wandhöfer R (2017) 'The future of digital retail payments in Europe: a role for central bank issued crypto cash?' ECB, Payments Conference 2017 papers. Available at: https://www.ecb.europa.eu/pub/conferences/shared/pdf/20171130_ECB_BdI_conference/payments_conference_2017_academic_paper_wandhoefer.pdf [accessed 16 February 2019].

[10] Sveriges Riksbank (2018) 'The Riksbank's e-krona project', 10.

[11] Sveriges Riskbank (2018) 'All banks should be obliged to handle cash'. Available at: https://www.riksbank.se/en-gb/press-and-published/notices-and-press-releases/notices/2018/all-banks-should-be-obliged-to-handle-cash/ [accessed 15 February 2019].

18

Life Lessons

Alex Fraser

Alex Fraser looks at what changes in banking and the wider finance sector mean for the finance sector professionals of the future and the role the Institute is playing.

Take away my people, but leave my factories and soon grass will grow on the factory floors … Take away my factories, but leave my people and soon we will have a new and better factory.

This quote, attributed to Andrew Carnegie, the US steel magnate, captures an unchanging truth about all businesses: people are central to them. Businesses can, however, undergo significant change, even as the people remain the same. As seen in the introduction to this book, the Institute's examinations were central to the establishment of professional standards in banks, but banking has changed quite dramatically over the last 140 years and so has our role.

First, in the mid-nineteenth century, as banks diversified into broader areas of financial services, changing recruitment patterns resulted in larger numbers of graduate entrants, leading to a diminished role for the Institute's exams.

Second, there was a rapid pace of change in the industry in the 1980s to 1990s, with new roles being created by increased computerisation and a need for a more commercial focus in the face of increased competition, including from foreign banks.

Third, the financial crisis of 2007/2008 resulted in significant changes in attitude towards professional skills within banks. Public opprobrium at the toxic sales-driven culture and increased scrutiny from regulators forced institutions to focus on behaviours and competence. Conduct and professionalism now again featured prominently in banking education and training.

And, finally, today technology is rapidly, and dramatically, changing both how customers interact with the financial sector and also how the sector itself operates.

But conduct and professionalism have never really been at odds with how bankers need to be trained or, indeed, how they work. The 20 years between the Big Bang of 1986 – which opened up UK financial services to much greater competition – and the financial crisis of 2007/2008 saw seismic shifts in financial services and the wider culture. Far greater sums of money began to be at stake in markets. State and employer paternalism gave way to laissez-faire and individualism. Many cultural norms shifted, and the way in which staff were hired and trained shifted with them. However, conduct and professionalism were still central to well-run financial services – even if the amount of money that one individual could seek to gain, and the increasing anonymity of markets, opened the door to abuse. What society saw when it looked at misconduct in banks was, in certain respects, a mirror to wider failings.

The Institute broadened and diversified its approach and educational offerings over time as the sector evolved – launching degree programmes (first in partnership with other universities and then at our own campus after we gained degree-awarding powers in 2010) and a broader range of professional qualifications. The range of specialist and regulatory qualifications provided includes mortgage and financial advice and a suite of trade finance programmes to students in over 120 countries, in partnership with the International Chamber of Commerce. This strategy of providing a much more diverse educational offering was also expanded to include financial capability qualifications for schools and colleges in 2003.

Social and market developments over the past three decades have, we would argue, only increased the need for knowledge of financial services. If the individual is to be able to manage their own financial affairs in a competitive, market-based economy, they will need to understand how to deal with those affairs and how that economy works. And they will need to be able to do that over the course of a lifetime, as markets change.

That is one of the reasons why The London Institute of Banking & Finance aims to be a life-long educational partner, starting with schoolchildren. At the most essential level, we seek to help them learn how to manage their own money and, as things stand, around 50,000 schoolchildren a year take at least one of our courses or qualifications. The courses are also designed to get children genuinely interested in finance – to help them appreciate and understand what banks and other financial services firms do for society and for them, and the role that they might play in that.

Wanting to have a role in financial services is, of course, not the same as being able to take one. Young people have to be able to show potential employers that they have the right knowledge, skills and attitudes – and that they can develop those. For most of its history, the Institute worked very closely with banks on devising courses and examinations that ensured the workforce was well prepared and continued to learn.

Our degree programmes specialise in banking and finance and focus firmly on careers. We have a faculty of academics with experience in the sector, and we work closely with the sector to help our graduates get a foot in the door. We also proactively seek to encourage students from diverse communities to take our degrees – as we do through the broader apprenticeship programmes we've been developing with some of the major sector employers.

The value of The London Institute of Banking & Finance to both students and the finance sector remains in opening up opportunities. We want to develop capabilities and break down barriers to entry. Our aim is that no child should leave school in the UK without the ability to manage their own money. Building on that, anyone who wants to work hard to develop the skills and attitudes that will enable them to play a constructive role in financial services can turn to the Institute for help with finding opportunities. Financial services firms who find it hard to attract staff from the range of backgrounds that represents society as a whole can work with us to fill the gaps.

And our approach is bearing fruit. For example, the Institute has recently witnessed a student who, having studied for the financial capability qualifications while at school, and completed an undergraduate degree with us, is now studying for one of our professional qualifications. This is a unique model of life-long learning within banking.

Increasingly, of course, banks are not run only by staff. Carnegie's recognition of the importance of people, rather than machines, still holds – the difference is that technology can now transform banks' business models. It opens the potential for reductions in operating costs and enhancements to customer service that were not possible before. That is why, in sharp contrast to previous waves of mechanisation and computerisation, which focused on improving administrative tasks and had a direct impact on a relatively small percentage of bank employees, the digital revolution affects everyone who works in banks. Among the key skills needed to thrive within banking today is the ability to engage and interact with digital technology. This applies to someone entering a legacy bank as well as those employed in the many 'challengers'.

The finance sector is adapting to the challenges and opportunities of an increasingly digital world, and responding to changing consumer behaviour. But to take full advantage of this, the sector needs a digitally literate and innovative workforce. We already factor digital literacy into our degree programmes, as well as the soft skills staff need to manage customer relationships over remote channels, and are developing these for our professional qualifications.

We have recently launched our own Centre for Digital Banking & Finance, providing both academic and practical expertise. We're developing qualifications and short courses, as well as undertaking research and thought leadership to assist the UK and international banking and finance sector as it evolves. Our programmes try to look beyond the hype of digital technology and examine the practical current and future implications for banks and their employees, and our work in this area will continue to evolve.

Of course, the universe of education and training providers vying to help the banks manage this major transition is more varied than ever: from small start-ups to established universities and business schools, from professional services firms to professional bodies and industry associations. There is a plethora of choice available to supplement firms' own internal resources.

In this very brief overview of the importance of the Institute's educational offering and how it is evolving, I have focused on exams and qualifications that are the bedrock of supporting long and productive careers. This is, of course, not the complete picture today, nor has it been at any point in the Institute's history. The Institute offers members and students access to a broad range of events – seminars, lectures and other, increasingly virtual, opportunities to hear from leading lights in the industry. It offers members of its community a regular magazine with articles from leading academics and practitioners and access to online learning resources.

All these are important pieces of the educational jigsaw. These additional services have enabled the Institute to create a sense of community and to build long-term relationships with the people and organisations that make up the finance sector today, and in the future.

We hope our unique role in the sector will long continue.

Index